THE LAST PRE-RAPHAELITE

Ford Madox Ford in 1939

THE LAST PRE-RAPHAELITE

A Record of the Life and Writings
of
FORD MADOX FORD

by
DOUGLAS GOLDRING

London
MACDONALD & CO. (Publishers) LTD.

First published 1948

MADE AND PRINTED IN GREAT BRITAIN BY PURNELL AND SONS, LTD.,
PAULTON (SOMERSET) AND LONDON

Preface

SOME words of preliminary explanation are required before offering this biographical sketch to an indulgent public. It is the fourth book which has so far appeared dealing with the career and personality of Ford Madox Ford. The first two were written by women who shared his life over a period of years; the third, *South Lodge*, written by myself, took the form of personal memories, amplified by a mass of material which came into my hands in 1942, on the death of Violet Hunt. The present volume is in no sense a repetition of *South Lodge*, nor does it contain any quotations from its predecessor. The idea of writing Ford's life was indirectly put into my head by a letter I received from his second daughter and my purpose was, with her assistance—which was in the first stages generously forthcoming—to compile a detached and coherent record of her father's career. I was not, at this period, aware who was Ford's literary executor, nor had I any information as to the terms of his will. Rumours had reached England that a biography of Ford, by one of his American admirers, was in course of preparation. While recognising that only some American literary colleague could write with authority about Ford's closing years, I could not imagine how any American could adequately cover the remainder of his life, all the material concerning which was to be found in England. Two points appeared to be established. First, that the literary executor, whoever he or she might prove to be, had no objection in *principle* to a biography being written ; second, that if the American work eventually materialised, there was no reason why it should clash with mine. I accordingly went ahead with my project and succeeded in arranging a contract with my publishers. Later, I discovered that Ford had made Miss Janice Ford Biala his literary executrix and, as soon as I had her address in New York, I wrote to tell her what I had done, in the hope of enlisting her support and approval. In reply, she informed me that Ford had left instructions in his will that no books were to be written about him of a biographical sort and stating that she had, for this reason, dissuaded the American biographer from going on with his project. In my answer I pointed out that three books containing much information about Ford's life had already been written and published in this country. I went on to observe that between twenty and thirty million books had been destroyed in England by enemy action, that even established classics were out of stock and that what could be termed the continuity of tradition had thus been blown up in a way which Ford himself could not possibly have anticipated when he made his will. I added that "precisely the same problem has arisen again and again during the past hundred years in regard to artists and men of letters whose work, by gaining the attention and approval of the public, established them as figures in whose careers the public took a natural and legitimate interest. Had it been possible to comply with their testamentary instructions, there would have been no lives of Thomas Carlyle, Cézanne or George Meredith—to mention the first three names that occur to me. In practice, it was not found possible, and the consensus of opinion has always been that the interest of the community as a whole must override the wishes expressed in his lifetime by a public figure. While no one but the literary executor (in the case of a writer) has the power to 'authorize' a biography, this power only legally covers the use of copyright material. . . ." I also said that I had evidence before me, in Ford's handwriting, that my loyalty to my old editor, over a period of thirty years, had given him considerable satisfaction.

On the question raised by Ford's last wishes, while I fully sympathise with Miss Biala's desire to carry them out, I have to agree with an American correspondent who remarks, without hesitation, that her position is untenable as "the public interest supervenes". It always must, always has, and always will do so. As Havelock Ellis points out in his autobiography, *My Life*, the dead "can feel no modesty and no reserve". " It seems to me," he says, " that the writer who is no longer among the living, and whose sensitiveness can no longer be hurt, is not the fit arbiter of what should or should not be published." Nothing will be found in this book about Ford's "private life" which has not already been given to the world by two of the ladies who shared it with him, and the writer's sole desire has been, by turning a masculine eye upon feminine revelations, to correct errors and restore a certain perspective. In Ford's case, Byron's comment that "man's love is of his life a thing apart" is undeniably true.

By the time Miss Biala's objections reached me I had already done a considerable amount of work in collecting the material for this record, and the reception which had been accorded to *South Lodge* encouraged me to proceed with it. I believe the facts about a great English novelist, hitherto inadequately appreciated in the land of his birth, which will be found in the following chapters, will be of interest to students of contemporary literature and will serve the principal purpose I had in mind in setting them down. This was to call the attention of readers of a younger generation to the work of a remarkable writer whose books, as a result of the war, were in danger of being forgotten. It was a source of great satisfaction to me to discover, after the publication of *South Lodge*, that its appearance had created a demand in the libraries for books by Ford which had been gathering dust on the shelves for many years. I hope that demand will be further stimulated by the present volume.

This book was begun, continued, and has been completed, in face of all sorts of difficulties and set-backs, as what may be termed "a labour of love". I have tried to be as impartial as possible, but the fact remains that I liked and admired Ford when many of my contemporaries didn't. He was exceptionally kind to me when I was a young man and needed kindness, and after an interval of forty years I retain for him a feeling of gratitude and a certain *pietas*. And whatever may be my other qualifications for writing about him, I have, at least, the basic qualification of being both English and a male. I doubt if any woman, however loyal and affectionate, however clearsighted and perspicacious, can ever see a man, especially so elusive and complex an individual as Ford, except in the slightly distorting mirror of her own emotions. It is also in no sense a disparagement of Americans in general, or of Ford's American friends in particular, to point out that there is something about Europeans which eludes the comprehension of the transatlantic mind. Americans cannot get to the bottom of us because, although they talk them, they do not *think* in our languages and have lost—by the breaking of the umbilical cord which once united them to European soil —their understanding of our inherited instincts. The American sub-conscious, and the European, particularly the English, sub-conscious, have become divorced from one another. This fact the events of the past ten years have made increasingly apparent to all except those who, from a variety of motives, insist upon deluding themselves.

In spite of his partially German origin, his French sympathies, his long residence in France, his recognition in the United States, Ford remained an essentially English writer, just as Henry James remained essentially American and Joseph Conrad essentially Polish. There are many passages in Ford's letters which indicate that it would have given him great satisfaction in his lifetime to receive some such tribute, from the land of his birth, as he himself generously accorded to contemporaries whom he admired. The English literary world can take no credit to itself for the fact that even his work in connection with the *English Review* brought him little thanks from his compatriots, no public recognition, and no honours. When his financial and matrimonial affairs got into a muddle, nearly all his older literary associates, particularly those who were strongly entrenched in public esteem, rather ostentatiously dropped him. The Army, in spite of his exceptional ability, his knowledge of languages and his valuable work in explaining the English to the French, and vice versa, could not even find him a Staff job. In 1915, when some malevolent scribbler made a vile personal attack upon him, in what purported to be a review of one of his finest novels, only two of his influential friends, H. G. Wells and Mr. E. S. P. Haynes, sprang openly to his defence. In all the small ways in which English literary circles and the periodicals they support are adepts at slighting men who decline, as school-boys say, to "suck-up", Ford was "disciplined", sent to coventry, blackballed or heavily ignored by the influential, the respectable, the academic. This was quite in the picture, and having regard to our peculiar tradition in such matters, very much what he might have expected. It is only men of genius or, at a lower level, men capable of original or subversive thought, who are subjected to this kind of treatment, and no one realised this better than Ford himself. All the same, he would not have been human, if he had not suffered from it and deeply resented it. Even a rude boy with a catapult and a dried pea can hurt if he hits you in the eye.

It is the treatment which Ford received in his lifetime at the hands of the secure, the popular and the established, which complicates the problem as to who should now set on record the main facts of his career. In a letter printed by the Editor of the *New Statesman and Nation*, on 11th November, 1939, in which I was stung into making a retort to a piece of posthumous denigration which had appeared in that journal, I remarked in conclusion that "I hope a more august and talented pen than mine will one day do him justice". There are several wielders of such pens, still alive to-day, who knew Ford more intimately, if not longer, than myself. But nearly a decade has elapsed since his death, and during that long interval I have not noted so much as a paragraph written by them with the intention of putting Ford where he belongs in the literary history of our times. The obituary notices which appeared in some of the leading newspapers were ill-informed and, for the most part, manifestly unjust. I do not remember that any of our leading literary figures took the trouble to write to protest.

Although, for numerous reasons—among them the fact that Ford never had the son he longed for—anything claiming to be an "official" biography is now out of the question, it has seemed to the writer worth while to make what, in the eighteenth century, was modestly termed "collections for a life of . . ." Accordingly, over a period of three years, the memories of some of those who, in the nature of things, cannot be expected to be long with us, have been put under contribution and a variety of material brought together which may serve as a basis for some future literary monument. It seemed a pity that much of this should be lost, or go by default, merely because no one more eminent than myself had volunteered to do the necessary spade-work. The fact must be faced that there is still a good deal of prejudice, mostly based on ignorance, attaching to Ford's name and few well-known writers, sensitive to matters affecting their own prestige, have so far shown any desire to be, even posthumously, associated with him. Moreover, as Ford's books have never had more than a very limited sale in this country, and his poetry practically none at all, the financial reward for writing his life is too speculative to serve as an inducement to those who have felt no urge to do so out of affection, gratitude, or personal regard.

My cordial thanks to the many people who have helped me in my undertaking are recorded on another page.

Acknowledgments

THE COMPILATION of this volume has necessarily involved a vast amount of correspondence and a bulging file is proof of the generous help which has been accorded me. I wish in the first place to express my gratitude to Mr. Henry James Junior of New York for giving me permission to print the series of letters from his uncle which the owner of them so kindly placed at my disposal. I have also to thank Mr. Leon Edel of New York for supplying me with the list of Ford Madox Ford's copyright publications in the U.S.A., together with the list of his contributions to American periodicals, both of which will be found in an Appendix. Some idea of the magnitude of my indebtedness to Mr. Edel will be gained from the fact that the compilation of these lists, and their transcription, involved a laborious examination of the Library of Congress records at the New York Public Library.

To Mr. Gerard Tetley, of Danville, Va., I am under great obligations, not only for promptly answering numerous queries, but also for obtaining for me back numbers of *The American Mercury* and the *Saturday Review of Literature* and sending me a photograph taken of Ford shortly before his death.

For allowing me to examine letters from Ford in their possession I have to thank Mrs. C. F. G. Masterman, Mr. Percival Hinton, Mr. Oliver Stonor, Miss Ianthe Jerrold, Mr. Charles Bramley and the late Edgar Jepson's literary executor, Mr. John Gawsworth.

The Secretary of the Royal Society for the Protection of Birds has kindly conveyed to me the Society's permission to print several letters by W. H. Hudson of which they own the copyright. Similar permission has been accorded me by the Public Trustee, in regard to a letter by Arnold Bennett. To Mrs. Ada Galsworthy I am indebted for permission to include letters written to Ford by her late husband. The letters from Joseph Conrad which appear *in extenso* are included by arrangement with the joint owners of the copyright.

Among the many who have kindly searched their memories at my request and supplied me with information which might otherwise have been lost I should like to express my thanks to two of Ford's brother officers in the Welch Regiment, Mr. Claude P. Lewis and Mr. Thomas A. Lloyd. Valuable details about Ford's schooldays have been supplied me by Miss Rosalind Praetorius, Mr. Charles Kinross, and Mr. Robert Taylor Skinner, while other interesting letters have been received from Mrs. Peel, Mr. Alec Waugh, Mr. Ralph Cope, Dr. J. R. Glover, Mr. Dan Rider, Dr. John Gibson, Mr. Philip Tilden, Major F. de M. Cunynghame, Mr. F. Seymour Smith, Chief Librarian of the Finchley Public Libraries and the Deputy Secretary of the National Liberal Club.

If, through inadvertence, any names have been omitted from this list which ought to have been included, I hope the persons concerned will accept my assurance that the omission has been accidental and that the help they have accorded me has been fully appreciated.

The portraits of W. M. Rossetti facing page 33 and W. H. Hudson facing page 49 are reproduced by courtesy of the Trustees of the late Sir William Rothenstein.

D. G.

Contents

List of Illustrations

CHAPTER I

Birth and Parentage

I

IN THE late 'seventies of the nineteenth century the "Aesthetic Movement", later satirized by Gilbert and Sullivan in *Patience*, was reaching its climax. The movement owed its first impulses to the pre-Raphaelites, was later developed by William Morris in the direction of arts and crafts and received considerable stimulus from the historical paintings of Ford Madox Brown, who specialized in the glowing colours of medieval pageantry and costume. Like all movements of the kind it quickly became the rage among young women, who were apt to make their innocent children the walking advertisements of their aesthetic predilections, thereby implanting in their minds the seeds of revolt. Boys, even at the tenderest age, possess the herd instinct, dislike being "dressed up", and loathe being made to appear in any way different from "ordinary" little boys.

In the basement kitchen of a large house in Fitzroy Square a child victim of his elders' crazes "might have been seen" on dinner-party nights plaguing the indulgent cook for bits of pie-crust sprinkled with brown sugar. The kitchen was warm, the servants motherly and kind and the little boy, then about five years old, felt momentarily happy because a French smock in blue gabardine concealed his elaborate costume of "the infant pre-Raphaelite genius". Like an actor relaxing in the wings, or a prima donna consuming her bottle of stout in her dressing-room, he was at ease while awaiting his "cue". This came when the dinner-party had reached the dessert stage, and he was due to be exhibited—as quite a little picture—to the well-fed grown-ups. Before being ushered in to the big dining-room, to be

dandled on august knees and regaled with titbits of marrons
glacés and méringues by poets, painters and poet-painters, his
protecting smock was removed and he was revealed, blushing
and stammering, in his aesthetic finery. This consisted of a green
corduroy suit with gold buttons, which showed up his platinum
blond curls. A final picturesque touch, which no doubt increased his discomfort, was the fact that one of his stockings was
scarlet, the other green. His girl-mother, daughter of the great
Ford Madox Brown and herself a promising artist in her own
right, was no doubt justly proud of her first-born, who had
been called Ford, after his grandpapa. The little victim's name
was Fordy Hueffer.

II

Whether it is more fortunate for an artist—writer, poet or
painter—to be born into a conventional middle-class, or prole-
tarian family, or into a dynasty of highly-gifted celebrities, is a
question which has never been decided, and probably never will
be. The advantages of the latter origin—the inherited facilities,
the contacts and connections, the fact of being born inside the
citadel instead of having to storm it—are obviously very great :
the disadvantages, though less obvious, may, in the case of the
over-impressionable and the hyper-sensitive, be even greater.
For better or worse, for good or evil, the subject of this biography found himself, as soon as he was old enough to think,
feel and accumulate impressions, a tiny member of a small,
exclusive, closely-related and, at times, painfully intimate circle.
Not royalties, not even the "cousinship" of the English ruling
class, were more closely bound up with one another than the
pre-Raphaelites and their off-shoots, associates, connections,
friends and enemies. Although the two connected clans of the
Rossettis and the Madox Browns were each remarkable for their
family loyalties and affections, the pre-Raphaelitic group as a
whole was anything but harmonious. Indeed, inside the sacred
enclave, hatreds and jealousies were rampant and the vilest
insinuations were frequently made by one genius about another.
It was only when their position as artists, when the sacredness

of their calling was threatened by the philistine outside the walls of their fortress, that their solidarity was re-established. Again, like royal circles and the "cousinship", the insiders might quarrel among themselves, but they were united against the outsiders. The parents of little Fordy, the child who was destined to be brought-up in a forcing house for geniuses, were an eminent German scholar and musical critic, Dr. Franz Xaver Hüffer, and Catherine Ernely Madox Brown, the daughter of Ford Madox Brown by his second wife, Emma Hill. Dr. Hüffer, who afterwards anglicized his name to Francis Hueffer, was a member of a large and prosperous family of bankers, printers and newspaper proprietors long established at Münster, the capital of Westphalia. His father, who married twice, had (according to Ford) fourteen children, though William Michael Rossetti gives the number as sixteen. The name of the second wife, Dr. Hüffer's mother, is said to have been Kaufman and she is reported to have come from Bavaria. If Jewish by racial origin, as has been suggested, she was undoubtedly Catholic by religion, as the family, with the exception of Ford's father, who was an agnostic, was fanatically devout. Like the Rothschilds, several of the Hüffer brothers, Ford's uncles, left their ancestral home and established themselves in other countries. One went to America and made a fortune, another to Rome and became a baron and dwelt in a palace, a third to Paris, a fourth to Holland. They were an enormous clan. According to Ford there were one hundred and thirty-nine Hüffer relations in Münster alone. In addition there were Tante Laura, and Tante Emma (the latter a countess who lived at Boppard on the Rhine) and Uncle Hermann who was a Professor of History at Bonn University. Ford's French cousin, a Paris banker, was, so Violet Hunt records, "an ardent religionist, and built Catholic churches, and had married his daughter to the Duc de Tancarville, and wrote from the beautiful castle of that name on the Seine". W. M. Rossetti writes "our family connection with Mrs. Hueffer and her husband brought to our knowledge a few members of the numerous Hueffer race, all of them foreign residents. I have however seen them but rarely. One brother was Professor

Hermann Hueffer, a distinguished historical scholar, now deceased. I had a great liking for Hermann, and regretted to learn after some years that he had lost his sight". Ford, who, as will appear, is not a very reliable witness, records that his family name, "in Ruthenian or some Polish dialect", signifies a plover. The legend was that during one of the Crusades one of his ancestors was asleep in the desert and lapwings awakened him just in time to save him from the approaching Paynims. "I should have thought myself," Ford adds, "that plovers, liking marshy places, would have avoided deserts. Be that as it may, three plovers, natural and courant, figured in the first and third quarters of my father's coat of arms and his crest was, equally, a lapwing natural and courant." Ford states that on his arrival in England, Dr. Hueffer "looked in a dictionary and found that Huffer = (a) 'an ass'; (b) 'an idle and boasting fellow'. He therefore incontinently inserted an 'e' into Hüffer, which became Hueffer—a name so suspect and unpronounceable that anyone bearing it might well expect without trial to be shot as a queer enemy spy". A likelier explanation is that Dr. Hüffer inserted the 'e' merely to represent the diaeresis and so to prevent his name from being rhymed with "duffer" or "buffer". That this happened after his first arrival in England in the late 'sixties is indicated by a limerick by his friend Dante Gabriel Rossetti.

> *"There was a young German called Huffer,*
> *A hypochondrial buffer;*
> *To shout Schopenhauer*
> *From the top of a tower*
> *Was the highest enjoyment of Huffer."*

No very clear or detailed character-sketch of Dr. Hueffer has been discovered by the writer, though W. M. Rossetti in his book *Some Reminiscences* (1906) comes nearest to delineating him. "Franz Hüffer, Ph.D., a German of a Roman Catholic family from Münster, a man learned in various ways but principally concerned with matters of music, came over to England towards 1868 and soon showed a disposition to settle here: eventually he naturalized himself as an Englishman and was

known as Francis Hueffer. He made acquaintance with Madox
Brown, and in 1872 married his younger daughter Catharine
(more generally called 'Cathy'). Thus he became a sort of
brother-in-law to myself—husband of my wife's half-sister. Dr.
Hueffer, who acted for several years as musical critic to *The
Times*, was a man of very marked ability: loyal to the standard
of poetical and literary excellence established by monumental
works of the past, but open also to the influences of the present
whenever a fresh and true path seemed to be struck out. As
an intimate of Madox Brown he saw a good deal of Dante
Rossetti, and of myself; after he had become a family connexion
he was less often with my brother, who was shattered in health
in the summer of 1872 and out of London, and who, when he
re-settled here in 1874, had adopted the habits of a confirmed
recluse. Hueffer was a rather bulky but not a tall man, of very
Teutonic physiognomy, brilliant ruddy complexion, brilliant
yellow hair, blue eyes radiant with quickness and penetration.
He was a believer in Schopenhauer, and though not a melancholy person in his ordinary demeanour, had a certain tinge of
hypochondria in his outlook on life. The family to which he
belonged was a very numerous one—not less, I think, than
sixteen brothers or half-brothers and sisters, domiciled in various
parts of Europe. All of them were well-off, more or less—at
least two being strikingly wealthy capitalists : Francis Hueffer,
however, had to depend chiefly upon his own literary exertions
for a maintenance. In January, 1889, aged forty-three, he died
in London very suddenly, of heart-failure coming on in the
course of an attack of erysipelas . . . Madox Brown, though
he was not the trustee appointed under Francis Hueffer's will,
came forward with his unfailing warmth and energy of affection, and was the mainstay of the family for some trying years
following the father's death."

This brief account can be amplified by the obituary notice
which appeared in *The Times*. "Dr. Hueffer's life," it says, "was
uneventful but was busy and industrious and, as is necessarily
the case with journalists, his industry cannot be measured by the
short list of his published works. He was born at Münster in

1845, the son of a banker, and passed most of his youth in Germany, but came to England in 1869. After studying music and philology in London, Paris, Berlin and Leipzig, he published, at the age of twenty-four, a critical edition of the works of Guillem de Cabestanh, a twelfth-century troubadour, for which he received the degree of Ph.D. from Göttingen University. His more ambitious work on *The Troubadours; A History of Provençal Life and Literature in the Middle Ages* was published nine years later, in 1878: and in 1880 he recurred to the subject in his lectures on the Troubadours at the Royal Institution. A great admirer of Richard Wagner, Dr. Hueffer was perhaps the first in England to recognize his merit and to advocate his claims. *Richard Wagner, and the Music of the Future*, appeared in 1874, when Wagner was little appreciated in this country; and a more complete biography followed in 1881. *Musical Studies*, reprinted from our own columns and from the *Fortnightly Review* and other periodicals in 1880, were translated into Italian and were published in Milan in 1883. In the same year, 1883, he published *Italian and other Studies* and wrote for the English Opera at Drury Lane the libretto of a drama, *Colomba*, the music of which was by Mr. A. C. Mackenzie. Two years ago, also in conjunction with Mr. Mackenzie, he produced a second opera, entitled *The Troubadour*, with Guillem de Cabestanh as its hero, and this was favourably received on its performance in Drury Lane. It may be mentioned that he wrote the articles on Beethoven, Handel and other eminent musicians in the *Encyclopædia Britannica*. These are the more enduring works of Dr. Hueffer's too short life, but his learning, his cultivated taste, and his gentle and kindly personality have been not less apparent in the many criticisms and articles from his pen which have appeared in this journal during the last ten years. As a critic he never forgot that criticism consists, not in fault finding, but in right judgment; and when he could not conscientiously praise, he never intentionally inflicted a wound. Undoubtedly he had strong predilections and opinions in musical matters, but they did not in any degree warp the honesty of his criticism. We may add that Dr. Hueffer was by no means an expert in one single art, but that he was able to speak, with less authority, perhaps, but with equal insight, refinement and sympathy, on a fairly wide range of kindred subjects."

Against this background of facts may be set Ford's childhood memories and impressions, as recorded in his various volumes of reminiscences. Ford never knew his father well, as he was sent to a boarding-school at the age of eight and Dr. Hueffer, during the summer holidays, was usually at Bayreuth. The incident which seems to have made the most lasting impression on his youthful mind—since he again and again refers to it—is that Dr. Hueffer once called him "the patient but extremely stupid donkey". Ford says his father was a man of great rectitude and had "strong ideas of discipline", though, after his lights, he was a mild and reasonable man to his children. "He represents for me," says Ford, in *It Was the Nightingale*, " 'the Just Man' . . ." Though W. M. Rossetti mentions that he was bulky but not tall, to the eye of his elder son he loomed up in childhood as a man of enormous stature "with a great red beard and rather a high voice. He comes back to me most frequently as standing back on his heels and visibly growing larger and larger."

Ford does not seem to have been the favourite child of either of his parents, this not always satisfactory position having been filled by his younger brother Oliver. On one occasion, Ford remembers his mother saying to the dread parent: "Frank, isn't it just that Fordie should give his rabbit to his brother?" Oliver, having accidentally stepped on his own rabbit and killed it, his mother considered that Ford as the elder should show an example of magnanimity by giving him his.

"So my father, as large as Rhadamanthus and much more terrible, says: 'No, my dear, it is not *just* that Fordie should give his rabbit to his brother, but if you wish it he must obey your orders as a matter of filial piety. . . .' And then the dread, slow: 'Fordie—give your—rabbit—to your brother—*Et plus vite que ça!*' He was fond of throwing in a French phrase." In spite of similar incidents which might have embittered his relations with Oliver, the two brothers—so dissimilar in temperament and so alike in appearance—remained on fairly good terms throughout their lives. Another memory of his father, which greatly interested Ford in later years, was hearing that, just before his marriage, Dr. Hueffer was offered through the poet Mistral a professional post in Arles. "To this day it thrills me to think that I might have been born in Arles," Ford comments. The project fell through, but some ten years later, when Dr. Hueffer was in Paris, he again met his friend Mistral and expressed his desire to give up his exhausting journalistic activities and settle down for good in the country of the Troubadours. Mistral promised to find him something and in the meantime had him elected a member of the Félibre, the Provence Academy for the promulgation of the Langue d'Oc. Before the project came to anything, Dr. Hueffer died, but he undoubtedly passed on his passion for Provence to his elder son, as Ford himself acknowledges.

In his writings about his father, Ford is never lacking in filial piety or in respect for his remarkable learning and his versatility. Only in one brief reference, which must be read in connection with Ford's complaint that his whole youth was oppressed and overshadowed by the awe-inspiring figures of Eminent Victorians, does he hint a criticism. His father, he says, "had a great respect for the attainments of the distinguished". In this connection he tells us that to him life was simply not worth living because of the existence of Carlyle, of Mr. Ruskin, of Mr. Holman Hunt, of Mr. Browning, or of the gentleman (Sir Joseph Paxton) who built the Crystal Palace. These people were perpetually held up to him as standing upon unattainable heights, and at the same time he was perpetually being told that if he could not attain to these heights he might "just as well not cumber the earth".

Some interesting sidelights on Dr. Hueffer have been kindly supplied me by Mrs. Peel who recalls her mother's impressions of his personality and character. "Dr. Hueffer," she writes, "was very proud of his Rossetti relations and especially of Christina, and talked constantly of Oliver (his 'genius' brother-in-law, who died at the age of seventeen) and of his brilliance. My mother had had some slight acquaintance with the Madox

Browns in Manchester (I believe her relations lived next door) and this was of much interest to Dr. Hueffer. She herself might perhaps have been called a 'Rossetti type' in those days. Her acquaintance with him began during his rehearsals of Mackenzie's opera *Colomba*—for which Dr. Hueffer had written the libretto and in which my mother had a tiny bit of business. She spoke of his great attention to detail. Even the folds of her headdress had to be just so. . . . She told him she was sure the opera would not be a success and she was right. It was very short-lived and I suppose is now forgotten. She said he was a *good* man, kind-hearted and generous. . . . He was also 'proud' (the adjective always used in connection with him) of his naturalization, of his position on *The Times*. He hoped he would be knighted for his services to music when his history of English music was finished, which, alas, he did not live to complete. My impression, somehow, is of a kindly man having with all his learning and literary genius some of the best of the German virtues. Anxious, if not ambitious to do well in his adopted country, conventional at heart, perhaps as a father setting rather too high a standard for nervous and repressed boys. Once asked why he wore his long beard he replied: 'It makes me look venerable!'

"Mrs. Hueffer does not seem to have left much impression on my mother. Though she must have followed the prevailing fashion she does not seem to have taken much part in her husband's public life. I believe her health was not very good at that time." The "prevailing fashion" is, presumably, a reference to the aesthetic movement of which in Ford's childhood, as we have seen, she was an enthusiastic devotee.

Apart from his strain of Teutonic hero-worship, Dr. Hueffer was clearly a man of encyclopaedic knowledge and Ford records that he had a memory that was positively extraordinary and a gift for languages no less great. Whilst his native language was German he was for a long course of years musical critic to the London *Times*, London correspondent to the *Frankfurter Zeitung*, London musical correspondent to *Le Ménestrel* of Paris and the *Tribuna* of Rome. He was thus, we may suppose, a

Good European and a man with an international outlook and cultural sympathies which ignored political frontiers.

In his student days Dr. Hueffer had been a favourite pupil of Schopenhauer, who, as a pronounced anglophile, may have inspired his admiration for the country of his future adoption. Ford once remarked to the writer that his father, and indeed all the Hueffer family, had a deep hatred of Prussia and Prussianism. Dr. Hueffer made his studies at the Prussian University of Berlin, but seems to have got into trouble with the authorities there, perhaps on account of some political indiscretion, and obtained his doctorate at Göttingen, at that time Germany's premier university. Ford says he was "the bad boy of his family", which may have been due to the fact that he was an agnostic, whereas all his family were intensely pious Catholics. The exact reasons why he came to London are not known, though the fact that the Franco-Prussian war broke out the year after his arrival in England may have had a certain bearing on it. A hater of Prussianism (and a lover of Provence) could not have been happy in his native land during that conflict.

Although Dr. Hueffer's father is described by *The Times* as a banker, the Hueffer family had also for many generations been printers, publishers and newspaper proprietors. The principal newspaper of Münster, the *Westphalische Zeitung*, was still in their hands at the outbreak of the second world war.

With such connections, combined with the encouragement of the great Schopenhauer, we may be sure that the twenty-four-year-old German scholar arrived in London with a sheaf of introductions to eminent men of letters. He seems to have settled first in Chelsea, where he lived, according to Ford, half-way between Rossetti and Carlyle, both of whom Ford says were "very much attached to him for various reasons". Although the fact is not recorded, it is fairly safe to guess that one of his first letters of introduction was to Carlyle and that the Carlyles facilitated his *entrée* into the pre-Raphaelite circle, in which he quickly established himself. Once inside that sacred *enclave*, where everyone knew everyone with the greatest intimacy of affection, hatred, jealousy and mutual respect, meeting with

Ford Madox Brown was inevitable. We know, however, very little about his courtship of the painter's seventeen-year-old daughter. Madox Brown could hardly have objected to the marriage on the score of the bride's youth as he had married her mother—the daughter of a Shropshire farmer—at an even earlier age.

The wedding took place in August, 1872, and in a letter to her brother William, dated 3rd September, 1872, Christina Rossetti refers to it. "I am so glad Maria enjoyed Cathy's wedding-feast, and that your shawl shone among the presents. Also I am pleased that the bridal portrait includes my négligée, but not pleased at the inappropriate dismalness of the quotation by Alma-Tadema. I hope Dr. Hüffer is not superstitious." In a note to this letter, William Michael Rossetti says: "For the wedding of Dr. Francis Hueffer and Cathy Brown, Sir Lawrence Alma-Tadema painted portraits of the couple framed jointly: I have now forgotten what the quotation was, but it was something from which an evil omen might have been drawn." Evidently the omens were not evil, except possibly in regard to the bride-groom's too early death, for the marriage appears to have been a happy one. Given the character of their parents, as recorded by their children, it could hardly have been otherwise. Mrs. Juliet Soskice, the youngest of the family, in her book *Chapters from Childhood*, paints a tender and revealing portrait of "Mrs. H", as she came to be known.

"My mother made any room pretty she went into, and my grandfather once said that if a room were to have nothing in it but a few packing-cases and a few rags 'Cathy' would make it look charming in a moment. . . . My mother was very pretty. She had fair hair and an absolutely straight nose, and a nicely-shaped mouth with beautiful even white teeth, and her eyes were a bright clear blue." In temperament she was evidently sensitive, affectionate and extremely sympathetic to anyone in trouble. "She would go off to any distance to help a person, no matter what it might be, even if she did not like them very much. She would sit up night after night to help a friend, or a servant, or anyone who was ill, and never complain and say she was tired next day." She was devoted to her parents, her husband and her children, and sacrificed her own very promising career as a painter, to her family and domestic duties. "If she heard of a strong person ill-treating a weak one her face would grow red and her eyes would shine and she would be nearly as angry as grandfather used to be, and she'd say 'I *hate* injustice'. If she had ever met a tyrant tyrannising she would certainly have attacked him. She was rather timid on her own account . . . but if she was protecting someone weaker than herself she was afraid of nothing."

Of her artistic gifts Mrs. Soskice says: "When she was a girl she had painted some very beautiful pictures which had been admired by famous artists, and placed in exhibitions, and nearly always sold. But she couldn't give much time to painting because there was always someone ill or in trouble, or who wanted taking care of. At first she took care of her father and mother and her brother Oliver, who was said to be a genius. When she was married she took care of my father and her children and her home and servants and a lot of other people besides, and then she gave up painting altogether."

Ford, who remained devotedly attached to his mother all her life, smiles tenderly at her "feminine unreason", which occasionally showed itself in the sort of favouritism towards her younger son of which an example has been given.

The first home of Francis and Cathy Hueffer was at 5 Fairlawn Villas, Merton, Surrey. It was in this house that the future Ford Madox Ford was born on December 17th, 1873. On his birth certificate the names of the child are given as Ford Hermann. The name and surname of the father are given as Franz Xaver Hueffer and of the mother, Catharine Ernely Hueffer, formerly Madox Brown. The rank or profession of the father is that of "gentleman". As Ford, in after life, made numerous rearrangements in his Christian names, it is worth while recording that he had only two to start with.

CHAPTER II

Schooldays

I

Ford's reminiscences of his early days, scattered over half a dozen volumes of quasi-fictional memoirs, are not, he admits, of much evidential value. In the dedicatory letter, addressed to his daughters Christina and Katharine, which prefaces *Ancient Lights and Certain New Reflections*, he acknowledges that the book is "full of inaccuracies as to facts", but claims that its "accuracy as to impressions is absolute". Ford regarded facts as raw material, to be handled by the artist with complete freedom for the purpose of enhancing whatever effect it was his desire to create. Thus he never troubled to verify names or dates and frequently blended invention with his verbal or visual memories. At the same time, where his artistic conscience was concerned, as in impressions of character, his perception was keen and his integrity above suspicion. The artist must indeed always be concerned with essential Truth even if he is only inventing a fairy story to lull a child to sleep, for unless Truth forms the basis of his line and use of colour, if he be a painter, or of his lightest fantasies if he be a poet or novelist, then he must be a bad artist. Such a charge could never be brought against Ford. It is only if we understand what Ford was attempting in his autobiographical writings—and he made no secret of the technique he employed and the licence he permitted himself—that we shall be able to appreciate their value.

In regard to the particular incidents that make up the picture of his childhood and early years which Ford has given us, it would be wasted labour to search newspaper files and a whole library of forgotten books for corroboration or corrections. The main facts are not in dispute. Both in his father's house and even more frequently in the house of his grandfather, the rather nervous and timid child which Ford represents himself as being could not have failed to come in contact with terrifying celebrities. Whether such recorded incidents as his having seen Liszt descend the steps of the St. James's Hall "under a rain of the applauding top-hats of four-wheel cabmen", having invited Turgenev and his translator Ralston to "take a chair" at the age of two and having sat on the great Russian novelist's knee, having seen Swinburne arrive very drunk in a four-wheel cab at Madox Brown's house in Fitzroy Square, and hearing the servants gossip about this and other eminent guests—whether these things actually happened, or happened in the way described, is immaterial. Together, all these scenes and incidents make up a very clear and authentic picture of what it was like to be a rather self-conscious child among the "minatorily bearded, and alarmingly Moral Great" of the mid-Victorian epoch. Luckily for Ford, his grandfather Ford Madox Brown, and Brown's servants—notably Charlotte—did not share Dr. Hueffer's Teutonic reverence for them. Ford observes that the members of the pre-Raphaelite circle, and certainly their society, would have been insupportable if he hadn't been able, when they weren't looking at him, to squint sideways into their faces and say to himself: "Oh yes, you're Mr. Ruskin. . . . My grandfather says you look like a cross between a fiend and a tallow-chandler and Charlotte says . . ." Charlotte, in particular, was no respecter of persons, or rather she had her own standards of value and her own favourites among the frequenters of the house in which she served. Her prime favourite, drunk or sober, was Mr. Swinburne, who, in her eyes, could do no wrong. Swinburne used to give Fordie jujubes, "slipping them out of his waistcoat pocket in his beautiful, long, white fingers". The poet once came on little Fordie on Wimbledon Common, immensely distressed because his dog Dido had gone into one of the ponds and would not come out. So the poet wrote him "a series of little jingles about the adventures of that faithful hound and used to deliver them furtively as if he were slipping me little packets of candy . . . He was like that to children and I daresay to grown-ups".

Apart from Swinburne, of whom he gives us a charming and, as we may believe, authentic portrait as he appeared to one of the children of whom he was always so fond, Ford says in his book *Mightier than the Sword* (1938) of the eminent Victorians— the Ruskins and Carlyles and Wilberforces and Holman Hunts and Wagners who loomed so large throughout his early years— that "they ringed in my young horizon, miching and mowing and telling each other disagreeable stories, each one about all the others who were out of earshot. Yes, that bitter, enormous, greybeard assembly of the Great ringed in my child's horizon. And yet I don't know that it was merely a matter of childhood, it was perhaps an abiding claustrophobia so that, as my eyes take their last glance of the world, I may seem to see myself surrounded by barriers of the Victorian Academic Great".

Their presence, the reverence with which their names were mentioned by his parents, their supposedly high standards of morality, their too often-referred-to "genius", combined with Dr. Hueffer's reference to him as a "donkey", and constant envy of the precocious learning of his Rossetti cousins, to imbue in Ford "a profound sense of original sin" and a torturing lack of confidence in his own talents and abilities.

At the age of eight Ford was sent to a boarding school run on advanced lines by a German couple, Mr. and Mrs. Alfred Praetorius. The school was originally for girls and was established in the West End of London, not far from the Harley Street area. Several eminent specialists entrusted their daughters to the care of Mrs. Praetorius, among them the famous analytical chemist, Dr. William Martindale, compiler of the *Extra Pharmacopeia*, whose daughter Elsie suffered from a tubercular affection of the knee and required special attention. The London girls' school was eventually discontinued and a new boarding school for boys opened by Mr. and Mrs. Praetorius in Folkestone, under the name of Praetoria House. Although it was not intended to be co-educational, a few girl pupils accompanied their headmistress to Praetoria House, among them Vera Beringer, Marie Löhr and Elsie Martindale.

For details concerning Praetoria House I am indebted to Miss

Rosalind Praetorius and to Mr. Robert Taylor Skinner, who, after graduating at Aberdeen University, became a master there in 1888. Mr. Skinner writes :

"Transported from Aberdeen to Folkestone, I felt myself in a new world. True that every grammar school and University had young men able and attractive but somehow or other things were different in the South-East corner of England, the establishment being run by a German from Frankfurt-on-the-Main and his talented wife, the conversation at table being German and French on alternate days. The pupils had interests unlike ours—they were omnivorous readers, they were delightful conversationalists, they had fine manners, they were enthusiastic sportsmen. It was on the boundary of our cricket ground which adjoined the Leas that I had three chats in one week with a gentleman apparently on the verge of seventy —the creator of a new interest in the beauty of nature and art —my acquaintance being none other than John Ruskin, on holiday at the sea-bathing resort of Sandgate. The appearance of Ford Madox Hueffer at fifteen can be recalled—the face oval, the hair sandy and long, the eyes blue, the voice husky. . . . With pardonable pride the brothers, Ford and Oliver, sometimes mentioned the name of William Michael Rossetti —'Uncle William', they used to call him. . . . Ford and Oliver spoke with bated breath of their maternal grandfather, Ford Madox Brown, and of his connection with Scotland. I heard from them of such pictures as his 'Christ Washing Peter's Feet', 'The Entombment', 'Romeo and Juliet'. In his work 'The Last of England' the artist paints his own portrait and that of his second wife (the grandmother of Ford and Oliver Hueffer). . . . Those Hueffer boys impressed me, a raw Aberdonian, and they often talked of the Browns of Haddington. Ford travelled from Hammersmith to Limehouse to see me leave for my Christmas vacation in Aberdeen. I possess even to-day the card which he sent after me: 'The Season's greeting! May the times be propitious to you! May your revels last as long as the Parnell Commission though the

Ford Madox Brown
From a sketch by D. G. Rossetti now in the National Portrait Gallery

William Michael Rossetti
From a painting by Sir William Rothenstein now in the
National Portrait Gallery

cost be not so heavy!' Next month, that is in January 1889, Ford and Oliver mourned the loss of their father and, so far as my memory goes, the friends who thereafter acted as Trustees were Tennyson, Swinburne and Henry Irving."

I can find no confirmation for the concluding statement. Ford himself assured me that his Trustee was Mr. Theodore Watts-Dunton, for whom he cherished a cordial dislike.

Many of Ford and Oliver's contemporaries at Praetoria House were the sons of distinguished parents and an unusually large number of the pupils distinguished themselves in after life. The high-spirited Hueffer boys appear to have been not only popular with their school-mates, but much attached to the Praetorius family. Ford achieved the dignity of being captain of the cricket team. By that time he had struck up a warm boy-and-girl friendship with Elsie Martindale, who was, in consequence, nicknamed "the captain's wife". They used regularly to play chess together in the evenings.

The early death of Dr. Francis Hueffer left his widow in very straitened circumstances. Their home, 90 Brook Green, was temporarily abandoned—it may have been let furnished as they returned to it a few years later—and Mrs. Hueffer went with her two sons to live with her father at his house in St. Edmund's Terrace, Regent's Park. This was almost next door to the home of Mr. and Mrs. William Michael Rossetti, with whose family circle the young Hueffers were already intimate.

Ford left Praetoria House after his father's death and, being then sixteen, became for a year or more a day-boy at University College School. This was the only education of the conventional public-school pattern he ever received. After the wide cultural interests encouraged at Praetoria House, it seems probable that he found both the curriculum and the methods of teaching then in vogue at London day schools equally flat and uninspiring. In any case Ford's energies at this stage in his career were chiefly devoted to the study of music and he evidently had ambitions to become a composer. As he was constantly

c

asking for leave of absence, in order to attend concerts, it is
unlikely that he was looked upon with much favour by his
headmaster.

Mr. Charles Kinross, a contemporary of Ford at University
College School, has kindly supplied me with the following
glimpses of him in the days when they first met.

"I was at school with him," he writes, "in 1889–1890 at
University College School, at that time situated in Gower
Street next to the College itself. His brother Oliver was also
there and as he was my own age I saw more of him out of
school (where he was known as 'the Baron') than of Ford.

"Ford was good at modern languages—French and German
—and we shared the French class together, the school system
at that time ordering a change of class according to one's
presumed abilities. One incident particularly remains in my
memory concerning this class. M. Baudouin, the French
master, a brisk little man, was questioning the class and suddenly
turned to Ford to receive a reply. Ford, a tall, golden-haired
lad (both brothers had this attractive 'chevelure'), rose to answer,
and began in his rather Max Beerbohmish accent to discourse
when, without warning, he fell full length over his desk in
a dead faint. Water was brought whilst the other boys for
once went silent before 'Froggy'. Ford, with the help of the
master, soon came round and merely explained that he didn't
frequently do that kind of thing.

"Perhaps he was a little overgrown at that time—I never
heard of any active interest of his in sport either in or out of
school. He left soon afterwards, and must, I fancy, have gone
abroad, for though I used to see a good deal of Oliver Hueffer
at his grandfather's (Ford Madox Brown) I did not meet
Ford again until I stayed a week-end with him at Winchelsea
after his marriage."

Ford Madox Brown was, like the future Ford Madox Ford,
extremely hospitable and accessible. His grandsons had the run
of the house and were, no doubt, encouraged to bring their

friends to tea there whenever they liked. Referring to No. 1
St. Edmund's Terrace, Mr. Kinross describes in a postscript the
effect this experience had on one of them.

"Did you ever happen to go to Ford Madox Brown's house
at Primrose Hill where the Hueffer brothers lived in their
schooldays? If so, you will remember what a gorgeous introduction it was to the pre-Raphaelite period, with pictures of
the whole brotherhood clamouring for more room on the
walls, and first signed editions of Swinburne, Tennyson, and
Christina Rossetti resplendent on the table. It was certainly
an eye-opener to me at the age of fifteen or so; and as for
grandfather Brown, I feel none of us will see his like again."

All schoolboys tend to be rather snobbish about their "people",
and ultra-sensitive to the effect which their relatives, and their
home (and its furniture and fittings) make on those of their friends
whom they introduce to the family circle. If their parents are
obviously worse off, or slightly lower in the social scale than the
parents of other boys they know, the fact may breed an inferiority
complex which lasts a lifetime. With the Hueffer boys nothing
of this kind was possible. In fact their exceptional good fortune,
as regards their family background, might have been more likely
to have bred in them a sort of *folie de grandeur*. This makes all
the more singular the extraordinary fairy stories about his school
and university career which Ford was at pains to elaborate in
after life. The bluff Anglo-Saxon approach to this psychological
problem—"pooh, the man's just a liar, a snob and a cad"—
merely expresses the congenital dislike felt by the average Englishman for the creative artist and his works. It would be fairer to
describe Ford's weakness as an occupational neurosis or as an
eccentricity of genius of a kind with which the French have
long been familiar. If Ford was never at Westminster, as he
used airily to claim in 1908, still less at Eton, to which school
he promoted himself twenty years later, neither was Stendhal
at Napoleon's side throughout the Hundred Days. George IV,
a man of fine aesthetic appreciations and the nearest approach

to an artist which our Royal Family has so far produced, was
certainly not at the head of his troops at the battle of Waterloo.
The titles, or "particles", used by such famous French writers
as Rivarol, Balzac and Musset were all self-conferred and had
no more validity than the coats-of-arms which the Victorian
nouveaux-riches used to have engraved upon their massive silver.
The French attitude towards the childish oddities, vanities, and
peculiarities of personal conduct of their most illustrious men of
letters is one of benevolent tolerance and complete understanding
of the fact that the man of genius is in a class apart and should
be judged solely on the merit of what he has accomplished.
No Frenchman ever disparaged the poetry of Gerard de Nerval
because of his legendary affection for a tame lobster. As Ford
spent many of the best years of his life in Paris and Provence,
was steeped in French culture and, by origin, only half English,
we have additional reasons for regarding his fantasies with the
same genial amusement as Brousson regarded the eccentricities
of Anatole France.

What sub-conscious urge gave rise to Ford's desire to provide
himself with an old school tie is a question which only a psycho-
analyst could answer with authority. As a layman, the writer
suggests that the origin of this "complex" may be found in
Ford's dislike of being dressed up as a pre-Raphaelite child, and
shown off to grown-ups in red and green stockings. The hunger
to be like everyone else, common to all children and school-
boys and suppressed in Ford's youth, found some outlet on the
cricket field at Praetoria House and might have been satisfied
had he gone on to an ordinary public school, followed by Oxford
or Cambridge. Instead of this he married young and, as will
appear later, buried himself in the country. It was probably
not until he met Marwood, his partner in *The English Review*—
an offshoot of the English squirearchy, who had received the
conventional public school and university education of his class
—that he developed a retrospective dislike of the pre-Raphaelites
and a feeling that he had been somehow cheated. He admired
Marwood enormously and the Tietjens of his four most
famous novels was admittedly a projection of him. It may be

presumed therefore that it was under Marwood's influence that he gradually came to substitute Westminster and Eton—schools at either of which Marwood-Tietjens might have been educated— for Praetoria House and University College School.

This matter has been discussed in the chapter on Ford's school-days, instead of being left till later, because the reader will notice various incidents in the chapters which follow which will either confirm or invalidate the theory here tentatively put forward. Sensitivity to "impressions" was perhaps Ford's greatest gift as a writer and probably the cause of most of his weaknesses and peculiarities as a man.

CHAPTER III

Home Life

AFTER leaving 5 Fairlawn Villas, Merton, Dr. Hueffer moved into London, lived for a time in Bloomfield Terrace, Maida Vale,[1]—separated by the canal from a house then occupied by Robert Browning—and finally settled at 90 Brook Green, Hammersmith.

Brook Green, like Campden Hill, Chelsea and Hampstead, was a favourite place of residence for people connected with the arts. It had the suburban advantages of trees and gardens, combined with accessibility to the City and West End. Dr. Hueffer's friend, William Morris, lived within easy walking distance, at Kelmscott House on Hammersmith Mall, and no doubt the Hueffers had many other friends and acquaintances in their immediate neighbourhood. The house had three storeys, and was of a size which enabled it to be easily run with the aid of two servants. One of these, an Irish girl named Maggie Mullins, had been with Madox Brown. She stayed on with Mrs. Hueffer after her widowhood and later went to The Pent when Ford's elder daughter Christina was born.

With her excellent taste in furniture and interior decoration, her aptitude for "making any room pretty she went into", and the works of art, books and collector's pieces which had accumulated, Mrs. Hueffer made her home an attractive setting for the hospitality which she and her husband dispensed. Mrs. Hueffer, who, as W. M. Rossetti concedes, "had herself some aptitude for music and singing", shared her husband's interests and made an admirable hostess to the numerous composers, pianists and opera singers who were eager to cultivate a figure so influential in their world as the musical critic of *The Times*. Ford had an acute child's-eye view of these figures and disliked "the epic

---

[1] Information supplied to the author verbally by Violet Hunt

jealousies of musicians" with which his father's house re-echoed. It was "dread of these acridities", he tells us, which eventually drove from his mind all idea of making a career as a composer.

Far more important from the children's standpoint than their father's professional acquaintances were their mother's relations— William Michael and Lucy Rossetti and their four children and, above all, their adored grandfather. In Ford's childhood Madox Brown lived at 37 Fitzroy Square, a stone-faced mansion with a doorway surmounted by a carved stone urn with ramshorn handles. This was the house which Thackeray chose as the appropriate setting for his Colonel Newcome. In 1881 Brown left London for Manchester where he spent seven years painting the series of murals which adorn the Manchester Town Hall. In 1888, the year of his wife's death, he returned to London and took 1 St. Edmund's Terrace, Regent's Park, next door but one to the house of William Michael Rossetti.

From what has been disclosed of Ford's schooldays, it will be apparent that he did not acquire either his all-round erudition, or his particular knowledge of Latin, which included a facility for writing Latin verse which remained with him through life, from his official instructors. Not only was classical learning in the blood on both sides of his family—his father and many of his German forebears were classical scholars and his great-great-grandfather, the famous Dr. John Brown, was described as "a man of transcendent classical abilities"—but the tradition was carried on in the person of his aunt, Lucy Rossetti. There is little doubt that, like his Rossetti cousins, he was caught by the full blast of her "educational fury". Many years later, in his first book of reminiscences, he records with what malignity he viewed his cousins' "proficiency in Latin and Greek at ages incredibly small". A searing memory was of being forced to play a part in his cousin Olive's "infernal" Greek play, when, "draped in robes of the most flimsy butter muslin", he was drilled, a lanky boy of twelve or so, to wander round the back drawing-room of the Rossetti home, then in Endsleigh Gardens, imbecilely flapping his naked arms before an audience "singularly distinguished" who were seated in the front room. However secretly exasperated he may have been by his aunt's methods of tuition, the spirit of emulation must have made it impossible for him not to take advantage of it. No boy, thrown constantly into the society of cousins, would willingly allow himself to be outclassed by them.

From his father, who, as we have seen, had a passion for Provence and was in his day the leading authority on the poetry of the Troubadours, Ford seems to have picked up a working knowledge of Provençal, sufficient, at least, to enable him to read—and to translate—Provençal verse. "Somehow it got through to me," he says, in his book on Provence, published a year before his death, "the impression that one of the poems of Guillem de Cabestanh, who was my father's favourite hero and poet . . . was the most beautiful poem in the world." He made a translation of it, at the age, he says, of eleven or twelve, which in the version which he printed—touched up, perhaps, in the course of half a century—has an almost flawless beauty. A year or two later, thanks to a hint given in Gosse's *Northern Studies* and to a poem by Longfellow, the Minnesinger Walther von der Vogelweide took the place of Guillem de Cabestanh in his affections, and his schoolboy translation of *Tandaradei* is no less remarkable.

Ford, in his numerous autobiographical works, though he dwells over and over again on his nervous discomfort in the presence of the Victorian Great, and his distaste "for the hot-house atmosphere of pre-Raphaelism" where he was "being trained for a genius", does not wholly obscure the fact that in his childhood and boyhood he had his full share of normal fun. He records a number of pets—various rabbits, a tame duck, a remarkable dove (given him by his grandmother Brown, who bred them), a dog called Dido—all of which must have made a pleasant escape from too much high art. There seems little doubt that he was extremely happy at Praetoria House, became an enthusiastic player of cricket and tennis, enjoyed his evening games of chess with Elsie Martindale, and explored, with delight, on foot or perhaps on a bicycle, the corner of Kent in which he was, later, to spend so much of his early manhood. We hear of Dr. Hueffer taking rooms at Hythe for the summer holidays and this no doubt gave Ford his first view of Romney Marsh which he afterwards came to know so well. During the holidays at Hythe it is probable that the Rossetti relations sometimes accompanied them, for W. M. Rossetti records that Dr. Hueffer had a severe fall there in 1883, fortunately without breaking a limb.

If some of the older generation of the Great were overpowering, there were numerous young people of Ford's age who, like himself, had to endure the process of being groomed for "genius". With the four Rossetti cousins, the three children of the great Doctor Richard Garnett of the British Museum and, later, the Martindale girls, Elsie and Mary, Ford enjoyed all the advantages of belonging to a large family. No doubt they had their jealousies and rivalries among themselves, as happens in all family groups, but they remained singularly united, loyal and intimate until long after they grew up. They were constantly in and out of each other's homes, helped each other when help was needed, as a matter of course, and took the liveliest interest in each other's concerns. In this they were faithful to the tradition of their elders. Indeed, the Victorian age was pre-eminently an age of warm friendships, sociability and intimacies between large and boisterous families.

If Ford never achieved the startling precocity in classical learning displayed by his cousin Olive he was early determined to "show what he could do". Apart from his verse translations from Guillem de Cabestanh and Walther von der Vogelweide already mentioned, he also tried his hand at original verse and began to write fairy stories in early adolescence. In such a musical household, moreover, it was natural that he should spend much of his time at the piano and begin to make attempts at musical composition. If all these facilities in the arts, all this atmosphere of scholarship and artistic creation which pervaded the home life of Dr. Hueffer seems to the philistine reader almost asphyxiating in its "unhealthiness", we must not forget the correctives supplied by Ford's younger brother. Oliver, who was the apple of his mother's eye and his grandfather Brown's spoiled favourite, comes through to us as an engaging, high-spirited boy with a thirst for normal enjoyment which led him constantly into mischief. Throughout his life he seems to have had all those qualities of humour and gaiety which enable a man to steal a horse and get away with it. Ford, on the other hand, could never so much as look over a hedge without provoking an outburst of denunciation. In spite of their difference of temperament, the two brothers got along reasonably well, and no trace of jealousy, at least on Ford's part, seems ever to have affected their relations.

Up till the time of the Boer War England was singularly free from xenophobia. Germans, out of loyalty to the Royal Family, were perhaps the most highly-esteemed foreigners, especially among the middle-classes, but Frenchmen and Italians were equally welcomed and respected. So much so that, especially in the musical world, English singers complained that it was difficult for them to get recognition unless they adopted a foreign name. The young Hueffers had no more uneasiness about their German origin than had the young Rossettis about their Italian ancestry. If Oliver was nicknamed "the Baron" it was possibly due to an unguarded reference on his part to the fact that some branch of his family had been ennobled. Although the family circumstances were comfortable enough by middle-class standards, the boys were brought up with the belief that sooner or later their rich German relatives would leave them each a fortune. Consequently they never bothered about money or seriously contemplated the necessity of either having to make it or starve. When their father died it became evident that the legacies were still in the future. Mrs. Hueffer found herself very badly off but, although he was not one of the trustees, Madox Brown at once stepped into the breech. "Cathy" and her two sons went to live with him at No. 1 St. Edmund's Terrace while Juliet, the daughter, joined the Rossetti household at No. 3.

CHAPTER IV

The Good Grandfather

I<small>T IS GIVEN</small> to some men, and to some women, after a lively and at times irascible youth and middle-age, to mellow in the autumn of life and be at their best in their closing years. Such a man was Ford Madox Brown, who, Ford tells us, in his old age exactly resembled in appearance the King of Hearts in a pack of cards. The descriptions which Ford gives of his grandfather, in his various revisitations of his youth, are among the most vivid as well as the most reliable passages to be found in them. Less known to the public but no less charming is the account of Madox Brown written by Ford's sister, Mrs. Juliet M. Soskice, in her delightful book *Chapters from Childhood: Reminiscences of an Artist's Granddaughter*. Madox Brown, she tells us,

"was one of the kindest, gentlest, handsomest old gentlemen that ever lived. Everybody loved him. He wore a blue cloth tam-o'-shanter when he was at work, and in the winter sat with his legs in a big bag made of fur inside, like those worn at the North Pole. His cheeks were pink, and he had blue eyes, and his hair fell straight down on both sides of his face nearly to the bottom of his ears, and my grandmother cut it straight and even all the way round. It was wonderfully thick and pure snow white, and so was his beard. He wasn't very tall but his shoulders were broad, and he looked somehow grand and important. . . . He usually wore a shiny top-hat and a black cape, and he used to take my grandmother's little dog out for a walk on Primrose Hill. He couldn't walk very fast, because he had the gout, but the little dog was very old and couldn't go fast either, so it didn't mind. He would stop from time to time to look behind to see if it was coming, and then it used to stop too, and sit down and look up at him, and hang its tongue out and wag its tail, and then they went on again."

No less vivid is Mrs. Soskice's visual memory of the old painter at work on his last picture.

"He used to paint on top of a kind of square barrel. It had a big, thick screw coming up out of the middle of it, and on the top of the screw there was a chair, and when you turned it round it went up and up till it seemed to be going right through the ceiling. My grandfather used to put his tam-o'-shanter on and climb on to the barrel off a small step-ladder and ask someone to wind him up on the chair. That was when he was painting a very big and high picture. It stretched right across the longest wall of the studio and reached nearly to the ceiling."

Ford's appreciation of and devotion to his grandfather were among the static verities in a life that was punctuated with re-valuations of artists and their works. Madox Brown remained for Ford "the finest man I ever knew", and nothing ever dimmed his recollection of the happy days spent in the studio at St. Edmund's Terrace.

"He had his irascibilities," Ford says, "his fits of passion when, tossing his white head, his mane of hair would fly all over his face, and when he would blaspheme impressively after the manner of our great-grandfathers. And in those fits of temper he would frequently say the most unjust things. But I think that he was never unjust or ungenerous in cold blood, and I am quite sure that envy had no part in his nature."

The studio in which Ford spent so many enchanted evenings in his boyhood and adolescence was very long, and one end of it was nearly filled by the great picture that was never to be finished. The walls were covered with gilded leather and the doors were painted dark green.

"The lights would be lit, the fire would glow between the red tiles; my grandfather would sit with his glass of weak whisky-and-water in his hand, and would talk for hours. He had anecdotes more lavish and more picturesque than any man I ever knew. . . . Well, I would sit there on the other side of the rustling fire, listening, and he would revive the splendid ghosts of the pre-Raphaelites, going back to Cornelius and Overbeck and to Baron Leys and Baron Wappers who taught him first to paint in the romantic grand manner. He would talk on. Then Mr. William Rossetti would come in from next door but one, and they would begin to talk of Shelley or Browning and Mazzini and Napoleon III, and Mr. Rossetti, sitting in front of the fire, would sink his head nearer and nearer to the flames."

To the understanding of a character whose complexity was to baffle and bewilder not only his innumerable acquaintances but even his most intimate friends almost to the end of his life, it is essential to lay stress on the Brown side of Ford's ancestry, which in some ways proved predominant. The other strains, the solid Westphalian bankers and newspaper proprietors, possibly mixed with Jewish blood, the Kentish yeoman Madox family and the Herefordshire Hills no doubt made their various influences felt in a descendant so imaginative and so abnormally sensitive to every sort of impression as was Ford, but none left on his character and outlook so lasting an influence as his maternal grandfather.

The earliest known ancestor of Madox Brown was a Berwickshire day-labourer, probably illiterate, who was determined that his son should have the educational advantages denied to himself. Thanks to his father's self-sacrifice, his own remarkable abilities and a measure of good fortune, the future Dr. John Brown, born at Bunkle in 1735, was able to proceed to Edinburgh, where he distinguished himself first as a classical scholar and subsequently as a physician and surgeon. He was the first "anti-lancet" doctor, and as the inventor of the "Brunonian system" achieved European fame. He was a man of lively good temper, something of a *bon viveur*, extremely fond of society and lavish as regards his personal expenditure. A careful and affectionate father, it is recorded that he rose at five in the morning to teach his daughters Greek and Latin. After an illustrious career in the North, he proceeded to London, where he fell into financial difficulties and died on 7th October, 1788. A portrait of him was etched by William Blake in 1787. Of his two sons, the elder, William Cullen Brown, became President of the Edinburgh College of Surgeons and the younger, Ford Brown, a purser in the Royal Navy. Ford Brown, after serving through the Napoleonic wars, married Miss Caroline Madox, "representative of an ancient Kentish family claiming descent from Prince Madoc of Wales", and retired on half pay to Calais, where his son, Ford Madox Brown, was born in 1821. Madox Brown's first wife, the mother of Mrs. Lucy Rossetti, was a Miss Bromley, also of a Kentish family. His second wife, Emma Hill, daughter of a Herefordshire farmer who died leaving his widow "little more than a chancery suit", was a girl of fifteen when he met and fell in love with her. The couple were married in 1848, after a romantic elopement, spent their honeymoon at Pegwell Bay and afterwards settled in a tiny house in Hampstead. Madox Brown kept on his studio in Newman Street, where he worked with renewed energy, frequently using his wife as a model. Her features are recorded for posterity in many of his best-known pictures, including "The Last of England". Ford, in his biography of his grandfather, speaks of her patience as a sitter, her sweetness of temper and her celebrity, in later years, as a hostess. She died in 1888, after a protracted illness through which she was nursed by her daughter Cathy Hueffer. She was given an unsectarian burial and the funeral oration over her grave was made by a then well-known figure, Moncure Conway. Madox Brown was thus, for the second time, a widower when the recently widowed Mrs. Hueffer went to live with him with her two sons, in 1889.

Ford was at his most impressionable age when he came under the formative influence of his grandfather, and there is no doubt that this influence coloured his whole outlook on life and gave him his disinterested passion for the art he practised. Many of Ford's best qualities were, we may suppose, inherited from Madox Brown. At least, in his full-length portrait of his grandfather it is impossible not to trace some of the characteristics which made him so sympathetic a figure to younger contemporaries.

Like his sister Mrs. Soskice, Ford agrees that in the autumn of his life Madox Brown was "the most lovable, the sweetest of all men. . . . To anyone in an inferior position, anyone humble or needy, he was elaborately polite; to anyone whom he suspected of patronising him he was capable of being hastily and singularly disagreeable". This sympathy with the humble was one of the most marked points in his character, as it was in his grandson's. "His sympathies once engaged," Ford says in his biography of Ford Madox Brown (1896), "led him to extravagant lengths, and he would not infrequently declare that the works of any young painter or poet with whom he had lately been in contact were equal to those of Raphael or Milton. To that extent his judgment was continually distorted and his utterances must be listened to with caution." Brown was a man of instinctive and almost limitless generosity. "No one, I think," says Ford, "ever came to him for help of any kind without his rendering all that lay in his power. Of his open-handed, unconsidered charity I have already spoken; in no case could any terms exaggerate this side of his character. . . . Good hater as he was, once an 'enemy' had fallen upon evil days he would go out of his way to do him good by stealth." At the same time Ford does not disguise his grandfather's "preposterous prejudices" and his distrust of official persons, particularly of Royal Academicians.

In his early days, Madox Brown was a conventional member of the Church of England but in his later years he became an "absolute agnostic, with a great dislike of anything in the nature of priestcraft". His political opinions underwent similar modifications. His father was what we should now call a Liberal, at a time when such opinions were a bar to promotion in the Navy, and in his young days Madox Brown shared them. In later life, Ford says, "he was by temperament a good deal of a Tory of the old school, but his intellect made him a Socialist of an extreme type. To this of course, his desire to better the lot of the poor contributed largely".

He was a man of considerable all-round culture, unlike many painters, and widely-read in contemporary French literature. Of his art in general, Ford says he was "a dramatist expressing himself plastically".

Between the two sets of grandchildren it would have been remarkable if twinges of jealousy had not occasionally manifested themselves. Ford and Oliver had the advantage over the Rossetti cousins of actually living under their grandfather's roof. Before this irruption the young Rossettis had had the grandfather more or less to themselves over long periods and now had the mortification of seeing Fordie and Oliver becoming or seeming to become the old painter's favourites. For Oliver Hueffer Madox Brown seems to have had a special affection, partly on account of his wild escapades but perhaps, also, because he was named after his own adored son, the boy genius who died at the age of seventeen.

As a faint undercurrent of impatience, or lack of sympathy, can be discerned in Ford's references to the young Rossettis, it may be fairer to look at them through the eyes of his sister Juliet. Juliet lived in their home, became one of themselves and shared more closely than Ford in their numerous activities.

"I had four cousins," Mrs. Soskice writes, "who, though they were young, were social reformers. Mary was seven; Helen was nine; Arthur was about fourteen; and Olive was fifteen at least. I was eight and I became a social reformer too. . . .

"We were anarchists. We believed that all people should be equal, and that nobody should possess more than anybody else; and we hoped for the social revolution. We had one big red banner in common, and we three little ones had a smaller one of the same colour for our special use."

Even the page-boy, the son of her aunt Lucy's French cook, professed the anarchist creed, but through a natural inertia could be described as "non-practising".

Joseph Conrad

W. H. Hudson

From a painting by Sir William Rothenstein now in the
National Portrait Gallery

"We had an anarchist printing-press down in the front-room of the basement. We printed an anarchist newspaper on it. Olive and Arthur wrote most of the articles themselves. The page always promised to write something for it, but he never did, because he couldn't find the time. Sometimes they got an article from a real outside social reformer. The paper was called *The Torch*, and we used to sell it in Hyde Park on Sunday, and on the platforms of the biggest railway stations . . . I can't remember the headings of any of the articles, but I think there was an incitement to revolution in every copy."

It was in *The Torch* that Ford published his first poem, a wistful little piece which, as he says, "was not very anarchist in coloration". The first two lines ran:

" *'Oh, where shall I find rest?'*
   Wailed the wind from the West . . ."

To the three youngest anarchists, on one occasion, was assigned as a special mission the reformation of policemen. "We came down from Primrose Hill in a row, with the banner flying," writes Mrs. Soskice, in recording this delicious incident. The first subject for reformation was the police officer who stood at the corner of Avenue Road, but it does not appear that he was an easy convert to revolutionary principles. Indeed, we hear that some time later detectives started keeping watch on the home of the eminently respectable Secretary to the Inland Revenue. As the house belonged to his wife, William Michael Rossetti raised no objections to the children's anarchist activities, since she permitted them. After her death, however, when it became his own, *The Torch* and its printing press, according to Ford, were banished to an office in Goodge Street. Mrs. Soskice has given us a vivid description of her Uncle William as seen through the eyes of a child.

"He had a head and face that, joined together, were an exact oval. His head was perfectly bald and shiny on the top, but

D

he had a little white tufty fringe at the back that reached right down to his collar. He was tall and rather bent, and he wore a black frock-coat with a turn-down collar ; and rather wide trousers. He had thick white eyebrows and dark eyes. We loved him almost better than anyone, because he was so gentle and stuck to us through thick and thin about everything, not only about the printing press."

If Madox Brown was the perfect grandfather, William Michael Rossetti was a scarcely less perfect uncle to the Hueffer children who were only his connections by marriage. In after years, he showed endless kindness to Ford and never spared himself in his efforts to be of service to him and advance his interests. On Ford's side, as is the way with young people to their elders, this unfailing avuncular benevolence seems rather to have been taken for granted. Of the Rossetti clan, the only one who evoked his unswerving admiration was his courtesy "aunt", the poetess Christina. Towards Dante Gabriel Rossetti, who died when he was a child, and his fellow members of the pre-Raphaelite brotherhood, Ford gradually came to have the sort of instinctive antipathy which a boy is apt to feel for great figures of his parents' generation. He heard so much about them in his youth that they became a bore to him in later life, though it is questionable whether he ever quite threw off their influence. His father was a great friend of William Morris and we hear of frequent visits to Kelmscott House in Ford's impressionable boyhood. In a letter inviting his contemporary Walter Jerrold to supper at 90 Brook Green, he says, "we meditate moving off in a body after supper to Kelmscott House where there is to be a lecture on 'Socialism Inevitable'—I tell you this in order not to let you in for an unexpected bore". In one of his last books, *Great Trade Route*, the influence of William Morris on Ford's vision of Utopia can be traced unmistakably. Much, therefore, as he objected to the nickname, "the last pre-Raphaelite", it was in fact more apposite than he cared to admit.

CHAPTER V

The Romantic Marriage

BETWEEN the time when Ford left University College School and the date when, after his elopement and romantic marriage to Elsie Martindale, he settled down in the village of Bonnington, on the edge of Romney Marsh, little more than three years elapsed. They were years of rapid mental development, travel, change, excitement, the principal events in which cannot, at this distance of time, be disentangled and arranged in chronological order. One of the most important was his reception into the Roman Catholic Church, which took place in Paris when he was eighteen. The legend of the vast wealth of the Hueffer family, branches of which were established in Rome, Paris and Holland as well as in their native Münster, had no doubt impressed "Cathy" Hueffer, and made her determined, after her husband's death, that her elder son should not lose contact with these fabulously rich Continental relatives. Although both she herself, her parents and her late husband were all agnostics and rationalists, like most of the Rossettis, the Hueffers, as a clan, were fanatically devout Roman Catholics. At some family conclave it must have been decided that Ford, with an eye to the future, should be received into the Church of his ancestors. He was accordingly despatched to Paris, to stay with one of his most opulent relatives and to receive instruction in the Faith. At first Ford appears to have been recalcitrant, but his objections were eventually overruled. In *It was the Nightingale* Ford observes (incorrectly) that when he was a boy he "had an orthodox Roman Catholic training", and quotes an imaginary dialogue between himself and his father confessor. " 'Father,' I said, 'I find it very difficult to believe, to conceive of—the Third Person of the Trinity.' He was an old Passionist, attached to the American Church in the Avenue Hoche. He said: 'Calm yourself, my son;

that is a matter for theologians. Believe as much as you can and be a good boy.'" If it is true that "once a Catholic always a Catholic" it is also true that "once a free-thinker always a free-thinker". Ford throughout his life remained both. The romantic, aesthetic, magical, superstitious and poetic aspects of Catholicism caught and held his imagination but never exercised any influence over his intellectual processes. One interesting result of his Catholic baptism was that he was provided with two new Christian names, Joseph and Leopold, which was presumably to flatter rich uncles from whom legacies were expected. He also added Madox to his other names. While at Paris he appears to have attended some lectures at the Sorbonne on market-gardening —*"une fois biner vaut deux fois engraisser"* is sage advice from a Professor which he used subsequently to recall—but no facts have been established to show how long he spent there. As a young "Catholic" it is believed that he paid visits to his aunt at Boppard and to his uncle Hermann, presumably the friend of William Michael Rossetti, who was a Professor at the University of Bonn. These Continental holidays, which cannot have been of long duration, were later made the basis of one of Ford's most fantastic fairy stories, in which he claimed to have been an officer in the Bonn Hussaren! Even at the time, they must have added to the glamour of the young pre-Raphaelite genius in the eyes of his London contemporaries and particularly in those of Elsie Martindale. Ford, at this period, was evidently full of youthful absurdities and affectations. His appearance seems to have been remarkable. In addition to a thirty-three-year old overcoat, inherited from Dante Gabriel Rossetti, he describes himself as wearing "a watertight German forester's pilot jacket, which I had bought in the Bavarian Spessart for four-and-sixpence, some trousers which I imagine cost eighteen shillings, a leather belt, an old blue shirt which, being made of excellent linen, had already served my grandfather for fifteen years, and a red satin tie which probably cost one shilling". A vivid impression of Ford as a very young man is recorded by Mrs. Juliet Soskice in her *Chapters from Childhood*. "Then one day," she says, "my eldest brother came to stay with us. He was a fair, clever young man, rather scornful, with smooth, pink cheeks and a medium-sized hooked nose like my grandfather's, a high intellectual forehead and quiet, absent-looking blue eyes that seemed as if they were always pondering over something. I was nervous with him, because he was very critical and thought that nearly everyone was stupid and not worth disagreeing with. But he was very kind and liked to take me out to tea. He wore a black coat with a cape over the shoulders, and when we took hands and walked along it floated out a little way behind.

"Once he took me a long way to see a famous gentleman (Prince Peter Kropotkin) who lived outside London. His house was quite a plain-looking little house, and when we went in there were a lot of people sitting round the table in a tiny dining-room, having tea."

Ford had already done something to justify Madox Brown's belief that all his grandchildren were "geniuses". At a preciously early age he had written a fairy story called *The Brown Owl* which was published by T. Fisher Unwin in September, 1892, when Ford was nineteen, as the first of a series called *The Children's Library*.

In *Mightier than the Sword*, Ford gives an amusing description of how the story, which had been written to amuse his sister Juliet, came to be published. Ford at that time had, he tells us, no literary ambitions. He had considered the idea, much to his grandfather's horror, of trying to get into the Indian Civil Service; he also had ambitions to become an Army officer. Any-thing, in short, to escape from the hot-house atmosphere of pre-Raphaelite art into the social "normalcy" for which he always, throughout his life, secretly hankered. "I hadn't wanted to have a book published," he protests, "I hadn't tried to get it published. My grandfather had, as it were, ordered Mr. [Edward] Garnett to get it published . . . I can to this day hear my grandfather's voice saying to Mr. Garnett, who was sitting to him on a model's throne: 'Fordie has written a book, too. . . . Go and get your book, Fordie!' . . . and the manuscript at the end of Mr. Garnett's very thin wrist disappearing into his capacious pocket." Edward Garnett, who must have been very young to have achieved such a position, was literary adviser to that remarkably able but close-fisted publisher, T. Fisher Unwin. Unwin paid £10 for the copyright of *The Brown Owl*, and as Ford bitterly records, "it sold many thousands more copies than any other book I ever wrote . . . and keeps on selling to this day". Madox Brown, besides securing its publication, did two illustrations for it which no doubt helped to gain for it the attention of reviewers. Two other fairy stories, *The Feather* and *The Queen who Flew*, followed in quick succession, but neither achieved the popularity of the first.

From the £10 received from *The Brown Owl* Ford records that his mother let him have ten shillings, out of which sum he purchased his first pipe! The picture we have of him at this period is that of an outwardly "scornful" and perhaps self-assertive youth who was at the same time tortured with self-distrust, diffident, shy, self-conscious, and rather purposeless. Such young men are apt to be lonely and thrust in upon themselves. Quite the opposite was, however, the case with Ford. Except for periods of hermit-like retirement in the wilds of Kent, Sussex or Provence, Ford seems always to have lived surrounded by crowds of friends and acquaintances. Like his grandfather Madox Brown he was instinctively hospitable and to the end of his life he remained incorrigibly sociable and easy of access, especially to the undistinguished. And yet, in spite of all the inherited intimacies, for example those with the Garnetts and Rossettis, and the extraordinary number and variety of his social contacts, his really close friends of either sex were curiously few and not many of these associations proved durable. To say that Ford was only really in love with his "Muse" is perhaps over-simplification, but it remains true that his art and his standard of values were, throughout his career, his only basic fidelities. He needed people, women especially, and was in many superficial ways dependent on them, but he shared his inner life with no one except, possibly, his more discerning readers. In this he was not, of course, exceptional.

This quality of detachment, which became more developed as he grew older, had not prevented him, as a boy, from falling in love with Elsie Martindale. The boy and girl friendship, begun over the chess-board at Praetoria House, became warmer and deeper during the period of adolescence. If left undisturbed by outside influences, it would undoubtedly have resulted in marriage, but only when both parties had reached the normal age for matrimony. There is no evidence that Ford and Elsie were not perfectly contented with their games of chess, their attendance at "Monday Pops", visits to the theatre to see Henry Irving and Ellen Terry, holidays at Hythe and Winchelsea, where the Martindales had a country home called Glebe Cottage, and similar mutual interests. Unfortunately their budding romance attracted, prematurely, the attention of their elders. The families concerned, the Martindales and the Madox Brown clan, being very much unlike one another in their general outlook on life, naturally reacted quite differently to what they assumed to be the "situation". Actually, although Elsie was allowed to wear an engagement ring at the age of sixteen, if the youngsters had been left alone, there would have been no "situation" until they themselves, in their own good time, had been ready to meet it. Elsie's father, Dr. William Martindale, was a figure of considerable distinction in medical circles. He was the foremost analytical chemist of his day, the friend and fellow-worker of Lord Lister and famous as the author of the *Extra Pharmacopeia*, a reference book which every doctor consulted. By origin he was a Westmorland farmer's son and in character a typical dalesman, staunch, upright, rather puritanical in outlook, very good-looking, a man of the greatest rectitude and most humane principles. He had three children, two daughters, Elsie and Mary, and a son, Harri, who also became an analytical chemist and helped to conduct the family establishment in Cavendish Street. Mrs. Martindale, a Yorkshire woman, had been matron at Sir Patrick Dunne's hospital in Dublin and was renowned both for her abilities as a nurse and for her qualities as "an amazingly good housekeeper". The Martindales had a large house, 19 Devonshire Street, in the heart of the medical quarter, lived in considerable style and no doubt had most of their social contacts with the highly respectable members of the medical profession who practised in Harley Street and its immediate neighbourhood. It is thus probable that Dr. Martindale's attitude towards poets and other "Bohemians" did not differ in essentials from that of the now legendary "Barretts of Wimpole Street". As a pillar of the professional *bourgeoisie*, he could hardly be blamed if he regarded his future son-in-law, who was not only a "poet" but dressed the part and also proclaimed outrageous "socialist" views, with some reserve. His feelings as a father were further disturbed by the fact that both his daughters appeared to have "fallen" for the blond-haired young author and he may therefore have foreseen emotional complications. In Ford's favour, we may assume, was his German origin—in Victorian days Germans were highly esteemed on account of their "thoroughness", their "seriousness" and all the other good qualities associated in the public mind with the revered Prince Consort—his father's long association with *The Times*, the eminence of his grandfather, and the latter's friendship with Dr. Richard Garnett of the British Museum and his connection with W. M. Rossetti, the highly-respected Secretary of the Inland Revenue. Dr. Martindale's objections to his daughter's "engagement", if such it could be called, were, however, based less on any personal prejudice against Ford or his relations, than on the belief that these mere children, as no doubt he regarded them, were much too young to "know their own minds". He therefore, in regard to Elsie, brought into play all the traditional machinery of the Victorian "heavy father" as exemplified in an earlier generation by the unfortunate Mr. Barrett. She was forbidden to see Ford, even confined, for a time, to her own room; threatened with being exiled, with her sister, to Germany and, as a last resort, made a ward in Chancery.

All these proceedings had the effect on Ford Madox Brown, that incorrigible old sentimentalist, that anyone who knew him as well as his grandson did could easily have foreseen. As he himself had run off with Ford's grandmother when she was a girl of sixteen, he was hardly the man to discourage early marriages. Why shouldn't the young things be happy together, in the spring-time of their lives? Accordingly, he played the part of "fairy godfather" and Elsie was always sure of a welcome at 1 St. Edmund's Terrace whenever she could escape from her prison. He did more than this. When the decree came that the Martindale girls were to be packed off to Germany, where they would be out of harm's way, he called in person on Dr. Martindale and persuaded him to send them down to his house at Winchelsea instead. By this action he rendered himself morally responsible for Elsie's subsequent elopement. When the girls reached Ashford Elsie saw a train on the opposite platform about to start for London. Without a word of explanation to her sister, she jumped out of the carriage and made for it. From London, taking with her a basket bought at a greengrocer's in lieu of luggage, she proceeded to Bath, took a room there and, by previous arrangement with Ford, advertised her whereabouts in a newspaper. Ford, accompanied by the faithful Robert Garnett, rushed to the rescue. Elsie was transferred to the home of some accommodating friends of the Garnetts, who lived in Bath, and, shortly afterwards, braving superstition, the young couple were married in Gloucester on 17th May, 1894. Ford was then twenty and his bride, born on 3rd October, 1876, was seventeen and a half. Their honeymoon was spent on Exmoor, near the Doone Valley.

While the elopement was taking place, the Martindale family, including Mary, who was almost out of her mind with anxiety, were thrown into a turmoil. Terror of a "fate worse than death" was always present to the Victorian mind when young girls got lost. The police were informed, canals were dragged and, no doubt, a strict watch was kept on No. 1 St. Edmund's Terrace. (There is a legend to the effect that No. 3, the Rossetti home, was simultaneously being watched for "anarchists".)

Ford's fairy story, *The Queen who Flew*, with a frontispiece by Burne-Jones, appeared about this time and, to give the book publicity, details of the elopement were written up by Ford's friend G. H. Perris in *The Star* and other newspapers. This occasioned an action for contempt of court against Ford and Perris for "publishing an account of proceedings relating to a ward" which the judge very properly dismissed as "trivial".

Ford and Elsie had always decided that when they married they would live near Romney Marsh. This part of Kent was familiar to both of them from early childhood. The Hueffer and Rossetti families had frequently stayed at Hythe, Dr. Martindale had a house at Winchelsea and they had first met at Praetoria House, in Folkestone. They knew and loved the Marsh and the surrounding country and accordingly made Hythe the centre of their first house-hunting expedition. While walking to Aldington, a village which afterwards became their home, they heard of a house to be let at the nearby village of Bonnington, and promptly took it. As all the couple had to live on was £1 a week allowed them by Ford's mother, Bloomfield Villa, as the house was called, must have possessed at least the attraction of a low rent. Apart from this, it was an extremely ugly semi-detached stucco villa, built over a stream and with no view from its windows. This must have been very upsetting for Ford, who had a passion for living on hill-tops, overlooking wide, sweeping vistas.

In spite of their lack of ready money, their first home was not uncomfortable, nor was their life too hard. Mrs. Hueffer and the Rossettis helped them with furniture, more came to them after the death of Madox Brown, and the remainder was picked up by Ford, whose taste in such things was unerring, at local sales. In spite of their remoteness, they had constant visitors. The Garnetts and Rossettis, Ford's brother Oliver and sister Juliet, and "Cathy", who became known as "Mrs. H", kept in touch with the young lovers and shared in their long tramps across the Marsh. Ford plunged eagerly into country pursuits, inspired by the arty-crafty doctrines of William Morris, became intimately acquainted with the peasant population, wrote many poems and composed music to accompany them, with the aid of a small "William Morris" piano lent him by William Michael Rossetti. There was, at this time, not a cloud in their sky. Within a year, Dr. Martindale, who at heart was genuinely kind and affectionate, became reconciled to Ford, who, with his inborn capacity for helping others more eagerly than he helped himself, quickly found ways of making himself useful to his father-in-law. Perfect harmony between the two families was thus restored. Although Ford showed no sign at this, or indeed any other period of his life, of "settling down and earning a regular living", in the way that Dr. Martindale, no less than his uncle William Michael Rossetti, may have desired, we can be certain that he was never idle. Many lovely poems of the marshland, among them "Aldington Knoll (the Old Smuggler Speaks)", "The Pedlar leaves the Bar Parlour at Dymchurch", "Gray (for a picture)", "The Song of the Women", and "Auctioneer's Song", subsequently collected in a volume called *Poems for Pictures*, published by John MacQueen in 1900, date from this happy period.

CHAPTER VI

Enter Joseph Conrad

THE DEATH of Ford Madox Brown, following closely upon Ford's marriage, though it removed a relative for whom he had the deepest love and the most profound admiration, had consequences which proved of considerable advantage to his career. The old painter's kindly influence made itself felt beyond the grave and provided Ford with his first foothold on the ladder of fame. The fact that his mother, with Lucy Rossetti, was a joint legatee of Madox Brown's much diminished estate, also made matters financially easier for the family.

Mr. Longman, of the famous publishing firm, who was an admirer of Madox Brown, was anxious to commission a biography and first approached William Morris with the suggestion that he should write it. Morris declined the offer and referred him to William Michael Rossetti. Rossetti also felt unable to undertake the task but recommended Longman to write to his wife, who was staying at Pallanza. Although she was then already an invalid, she started work and had done a not inconsiderable amount at the time of her death. "I mentioned Mr. Ford Madox Hueffer," says William Michael Rossetti, in *Some Reminiscences*, "as being then the most obvious person to consult. He undertook the work and did it well, composing the book, very handsomely got up and illustrated", entitled *Ford Madox Brown: A Record of his Life*, which appeared in 1896, and for which the author received the, in those days, handsome advance of £150. Although Ford was only just of age when he began it, this biography is an accurate and painstaking work, in places almost comically mature in style, but already illuminated by the critical insight and profound appreciation of character which were to distinguish his later writings. The publication of *Ford Madox Brown*, which brought its precociously youthful author considerable

kudos, more or less coincided with his removal from
Bonnington to an old farmhouse, the Pent Farm, near the village
of Postling and a couple of miles or so from Sandling Junction.
By good fortune Mrs. Elsie Hueffer has preserved a letter, dated
12th December, 1896, which she wrote to Olive Garnett at this
time, and has permitted me to quote. In this she mentions that
"Ford has gone up to Manchester, Liverpool, etc., to see if he
can get the loan of most of Madox B(rown)'s pictures out of the
public galleries for an exhibition that is to be at the Grafton
early next spring. Ford and the editor of *The Artist* have had
most to do with it so far and of course it is a splendid opportunity for F in many ways." *The Artist*, a long-forgotten periodical, was started as a rival to *The Studio*, and Ford succeeded in
placing with it articles on various topics, one of them being an
appreciation of his friend William Hyde who was later to illustrate his history of the Cinque Ports. Elsie Hueffer continues,
"We are always miserable when we are separated", and confides
the fact that she is "expecting" in the following June. "We are
both tremendously pleased, of course, in fact F has got almost
well since he has had this to look forward to". There follows a
detailed description of Pent Farm, as it was when they took over.
"In the first place it is a regular Kentish farm and as Mattie said,
going through the yard along by the buildings, it smells like a
real farm." (Mattie, it may be interpolated, was an Irish servant
who had been with Madox Brown and was both a "character"
and a family friend.) "It stands at the foot of those bleak high
downs that we used to see from Aldington Corner. They are
overgrown with a coarse dry grass that gives them a very wind-
swept and russet appearance. The house, tho' standing in a
colder atmosphere than Bonnington, is very well sheltered from
the wind on nearly all sides. We have none of the damp cold
that used to hang about us so persistently at B. The water is
also a great acquisition, a beautiful running spring with a dip
as clear as a crystal." (This stream, which has now disappeared
to make way for company's water, used to run just outside the
kitchen door.) "In the front we have the farm stockyard and
across that half in front of us a most beautiful enormous old barn

where the sparrows are busy all day picking among the chaff and quarrelling on the moss-grown thatch. The house and garden by the way stand up from this stockyard on a sort of terrace.

"And now to come to the house. Outside it is built of red brick and tiled, with four long and rather low windows, two on each side of the front door. . . . Inside, there is a room on each side of the door, dining-room and drawing-room. Both good-sized rooms, seventeen feet long. At the back a huge kitchen, quite twenty feet I should think and a large pantry. Five good-sized bedrooms.

"Our furniture and everything show to so much more advantage than they did at B. and we have just room for it all, not any too much. In fact, we certainly could not have done better." (The old barn referred to above was destroyed by fire, some years later, and not rebuilt.)

At about this time, Ford wrote to his friend, Walter Jerrold, inviting him and his wife and their infant son to stay at the Pent. "You were our first guests in Bonnington—so why not be our first in the paradise to which we have just moved? . . . We are just under the most magnificent sheep-downs near Canterbury, Hythe, etc. The house is a real old farm—very jolly and all the rest of it with oak beams and a number of other advantages on ceiling and floor. . . ." He adds, "we've got room for a small army and welcomes for a large one (this is the old country gentleman style up to wh. we are trying to live.—It is rather difficult. We have only just moved in—last Thursday—and have managed to keep it up so far however)." He adjures Jerrold to bring his cycle as it is "glorious country for that sport. You push up a hill—jump on, ride down—push up and so on for miles and miles."

Jerrold was already well-established as a London literary journalist and had, on several occasions, been useful to Ford—there is a reference to "a well-written log-roller in the *Observer* about arts and crafts"—and Ford accompanied this letter with four songs which he asked Jerrold to place for him. It is not known whether this invitation to stay at the Pent was accepted but in a later letter, written after the birth of Ford's elder daughter, Christina, and the death of Jerrold's infant son, he says, "I am afraid we shall have to put you off again. Elsie's not yet out of her room and to make matters worse our small servant has knocked up and so my sister-in-law (Mary Martindale) and I have the whole house on our hands."

The reference in Mrs. Elsie Hueffer's letter to Olive Garnett, quoted above, to the fact that Ford has "almost got well since he had this", the birth of his first child, "to look forward to" is the first intimation we have both of Ford's persistent ill-health and of the real cause of it. His malady was of a mysterious character and baffled all the attempts of specialists to cure it. Sometimes, it took the form of nervous dyspepsia, when, in spite of his wife's culinary accomplishments, nothing he ate agreed with him; sometimes it was diagnosed as neurasthenia. In either case, it was accompanied by long periods of self-distrust and intense depression. In so far as it had a physical origin it was probably due, as in later years Ford came to believe, to some form of cardiac weakness which he may have inherited from his father. But his wife's reference to the effect on his *health* of having "something to look forward to" probably gives us the real clue to the enigma. Ford's health, throughout his life, largely depended on his "state of mind". The restlessness, frequent trips abroad and numerous changes of habitation, which characterized his attempt, as a young married man, to bury himself in the depths of the country, were, like his frequent illnesses, indications that his subconscious mind was almost constantly in revolt against the pattern of living which, under the influence of William Morris, he had marked out for himself. To reach this conclusion one does not need to be a psycho-analyst: it is inescapable. A contributory cause to his neurosis was, as we shall see later, his close association with Joseph Conrad. Elsie Hueffer, being far more a country woman both by temperament and family origin than Ford ever was, did not suffer to anything like the same degree from those disturbances of the subconscious which had such an unsettling effect on the health and nerves of her "creative artist" husband. On the other hand, since the age of four when, as the result of a fall, she contracted tuberculosis in the bone of the injured leg and had to have her knee straightened by a surgical operation, she was herself a more or less permanent invalid and was only able to lead an outwardly normal life by the exercise of remarkable courage and strength of character. It is advisable to mention these facts at once as, during the next ten years, ill-health was to play a leading part both in their own lives and in those of their intimate circle.

After Christina's birth, in July 1897, Ford's love of games, craving for sociability and improved financial position—one of the rich Hueffer uncles had died in 1895 and left to each of his nephews and nieces a sum of rather more than £3,000—led to his becoming an ardent golf-player. While he was disporting himself on the links at Hythe, his wife had perforce to stay at home and mind the baby. She found the Pent lonely and depressing and in July 1898 they let it furnished to Walter Crane and his wife and migrated to Limpsfield in Surrey, to be near Edward Garnett who had a house there called The Cearne. This move, though they made only a short stay at Grace's Cottage, as their new home was called, was destined to have a profound influence on Ford's subsequent career.

Edward Garnett and Ford, as has already been remarked, were bound together by much the same close intimacy as unites the members of a large family. At the same time, as often happens in families, they had little real sympathy or even liking for each other. The writer has been told that Garnett felt for Ford a sort of instinctive *physical* antipathy. Why this should be so, if it was so, is difficult to understand unless some obscure kind of jealousy was at the bottom of it, for Garnett, though doubtless his brow was furrowed only by the noblest thought, was quite remarkably ugly while Ford, with his fresh complexion, tall lean figure, and blond hair and moustache was, if not good-looking, at all events in appearance reasonably attractive, especially to women. Garnett, however, was already a leading light in what would now be termed highbrow society. Not only was he surrounded by Fabians, whom Ford found extremely disagreeable, but he also knew most of the leading authors of the day. In his capacity as reader to an enterprising publisher and as a result of his own remarkable critical gifts, he was also on terms of friendship with several men who were to make their mark in the future. Among these was Joseph Conrad. As we do not hear of Ford having many contacts with contemporary literary figures before he went to live at Grace's Cottage, whereas afterwards he became intimate not only with Conrad but with Stephen Crane, John Galsworthy, W. H. Hudson, Stephen Reynolds and others who were Garnett's friends and acquaintances, the conclusion is that Garnett to some extent "launched" him into the circle in which he subsequently moved. That he should do so would be taken by Ford as a matter of course. It was in the pre-Raphaelite tradition that, however much the members of the clan might disagree among themselves, they should co-operate, almost automatically, in advancing each other's interests.

In his first book of reminiscences, *Ancient Lights*, Ford gives a romantic "impression" of how he first came to hear of Conrad, while staying at Limpsfield. "We were all dressed more or less mediaevally," he says, "after the manner of the disciples of socialism of the William Morris school. We were drinking, I think, mead out of cups made of bullock's horn. Mr. Garnett was reading his MSS. Suddenly he threw one across to me.

" 'Look at that,' he said.

"I think that then I had the rarest literary pleasure of my existence. It was to come into contact with a spirit of romance, of adventure, of distant lands, and with an English that was new, magic, and unsurpassed. It sang like music; it overwhelmed me like a great warm wave of the sea, and it was as clear as tropical sunlight falling into deep and scented forests of the East. For this MS. was that of *Almayer's Folly*, the first book of Mr. Joseph Conrad, which he had sent up for judgment, sailing away himself, as I believe, for the last time, upon a ship going towards the East. So was Joseph Conrad 'discovered'."

The actual physical meeting between Ford and Conrad took place, almost certainly through Garnett, some years after the publication of *Almayer's Folly*. From the first Ford had a passion

E

for Conrad's *talent*. His feeling for the man, though warm and genuine, came always second to appreciation of his gift. As Conrad had an equally devouring passion for his talent—for his "genius" as he may with some justification have regarded it— it was only natural that he should look on Ford as a useful aid to its development and recognition. In most human relationships there is one who kisses and one who submits, from whatever secret motive, to the proffered embrace. Conrad, in spite of the very warm affection he felt for Ford before they quarrelled, was always the one who "submitted". There were a great many reasons, apart from Ford's literary hero-worship, why he should do so with alacrity. Although he had decided to express himself in English rather than French, owing to his boyish admiration for the novels of Captain Marryat, he was steeped in French literature, wholly French in his attitude towards the art of writing, and, in particular, an avowed disciple of Flaubert and Maupassant. In the cosmopolitan Ford he found, more so than in any other English man of letters of his acquaintance, a kindred spirit. Their views regarding the art they practised were almost identical and their knowledge and appreciation of the masters of contemporary French literature equally profound. To Conrad, who was very much a stranger in a strange island, Ford's German origin must have seemed comfortingly continental. At the same time, as an Englishman born and bred, Ford's idiomatic knowledge of his native language, combined with his already admired prose style, supplied just the element which Conrad lacked. The young Hueffers, moreover, had, or appeared to have, a solid social "background", based upon a whole phalanx of literary and artistic celebrities, which might have seemed useful to Conrad while he was finding his feet in a world he was determined to conquer. The first suggestion that he and Ford should write a book in collaboration came from Conrad, and the agreement between them was made in the autumn of 1898.

As it happened, Ford had just written a romantic novel called *Seraphina*, the MS. of which was already completed. With his usual disregard for his own interests, Ford put this book aside, for the time being, and sketched out the plot for their first joint effort, which appeared in 1901 through Heinemann in England and McClure in America, under the title *The Inheritors*. This was the most laborious and least successful of their two major collaborations. Conrad was a mass of nerves, irascible, exhausting. He did not, as yet, know Ford very well or feel for him the close sympathy which was to develop later. Although, on his side, Ford was a miracle of patience, there were several occasions when the partnership nearly broke up. Even Ford's fidelity and endurance had limits, as the correspondence between them makes clear. Conrad, when they squabbled, unburdened himself to Edward Garnett. In a letter to Garnett, after saying that he considers the acceptance of the book by Heinemann a distinct bit of luck, "Jove, what a lark!", he remarks that he set himself to look upon the thing as a sort of skit on the sort of political (?!) novel, written by a certain sort of fools. "This in my heart of hearts. And poor H was dead in earnest! Oh Lord. How he worked! There is not a chapter I haven't made him write twice —most of them three times over." After referring to Ford's more than angelic patience, he confesses "I've been fiendish. I've been rude to him; if I've not called him names I've *implied* in my remarks and the course of our discussions the most oppro- brious epithets. Pon my word, it was touching. And there's no doubt that in the course of this agony I have been ready to weep more than once. Yet not for him. Not for him." As if rather ashamed of writing in this strain about the man whose collabor- ation he had himself invited, he adds: "You'll have to burn this letter—but I shall say no more. Some day we shall meet and then!" Instead of burning it, Garnett printed it. On 4th August, 1901, Conrad writes, having just pocketed a welcome loan from Ford, "tell good old Ford that he is not utterly undone as yet by the Fatal Partnership, but there is gathering a pretty lot of material for a sombre drama of the literary-domestic order— which he may have an opportunity to write and make his fortune thereby."

When the future collaborators first met Conrad was living at Stanford-le-Hope, in Essex, in a house called Ivy Walls, which he was anxious to give up. The Hueffers were equally tired of the isolation of the Pent which the Walter Cranes had now vacated. They invited the Conrads to look at it, and Conrad, who found isolation and privacy a necessity of his existence, was immediately charmed by the house which was to be his home during ten productive years. In a letter dated 29th September, 1898, written from Stanford-le-Hope and addressed "Dear Mr. Hueffer", he begs Ford to conclude the arrangements with the landlord and remarks that "this opportunity is a perfect godsend to me. It preserves what is left of my piety and belief in a benevolent Providence, and probably also my sanity."

In a letter sent to the faithful Edward Garnett on the previous day, stating that he was writing to Ford to clinch the matter, he mentions that he feels "less hopeless" about work in progress and adds that "when I feel sure of Pent Farm I shall be comparatively happy". On 7th November, 1898, he wrote to Garnett from the Pent telling him that "we are here—over a week now and the place is a success. I reckon Ford told you. I reckon you disapprove." The Hueffers had left behind them a good deal of their furniture, including a writing desk which had belonged to Christina Rossetti. In an undated letter, evidently written shortly before he took up residence, he addresses Ford as "Honoured and dear Landlord" and says that the time approaches "for me to step in amongst your relics. That you do feel the impending desecration I do not doubt. Let me exhort you to be a man and bear up—they are not lost only left behind". He concludes "I hope you are better—you are well in mind and body—same thing though."

After taking a great deal of trouble to see the Conrads safely settled in and provided with a servant, the Hueffers went off on a cycling tour through Normandy to the South of France. On their return they had to look for a new home and were lucky enough to discover a smallholder's cottage at Aldington called Stocks Hill, which commanded a superb view of Romney Marsh and from which, on clear days, Napoleon's Column at Boulogne was plainly visible.

In November 1898, in a letter beginning "my dear Hueffer," Conrad, after remarking that he is very happy at the Pent,

makes a reference to "our joint work", *The Inheritors*, the acceptance of which he says "is assured as far as Pawling" (a partner
in the firm of William Heinemann) "is concerned. McClure I
guess is alright. We must serialize next year on both sides of the
pond". The rest of the letter is taken up with comments on
Ford's early novel, *The Shifting of the Fire*, which had been
published by T. Fisher Unwin in 1892, before Ford was twenty.
Conrad says it is "delightfully" young, not "drearily or morally
or sadly or frightfully or any of these things which politeness
would have induced me to paraphrase". He says he has read it
several times "looking for your 'inside' in that book—the first
impression being that there is a considerable 'inside' in you".
As he asks if Ford has written "for *Serafina* (or *Seraphina?*)",
it seems clear that at this time they were already thinking of
their next "joint work". On 17th November Conrad wrote
saying that "I hear from Pawling G. wrote him a letter com-
mending our partnership on grounds that evidently appeal to P.
G. is not so bad as he pretends to me". ("G" is possibly, but not
certainly, Edward Garnett.)

Conrad goes on to say that he would be "very very pleased to
hear *Serafina* read. I would *afterwards* read it myself."

In a letter dated 30th January, 1899, there is a reference to Ford's
proposal for a book on the Cinque Ports which he says Meldrum,
of the firm of Blackwood, who subsequently published it, had
sent to Edinburgh "with very warm recommendation".

By November 1899 the two collaborators were evidently at it
hammer and tongs. Conrad, by now, addresses Ford by his
Christian name and writes that his letter, to which this is a reply,
distressed him a little by the "sign of nervous irritation and its
exasperated tone. I can quite enter into your feelings. I am sorry
your wife seems to think I've induced you to waste your time".
(No doubt the book on The Cinque Ports had been commissioned
and its completion would have resulted in a substantial cheque).

Conrad says that he had no idea that Ford had any profitable
work to do. "For otherwise effort after expression is not wasted
even it is not paid for". He goes on to tell Ford that what he
has written now "is infinitely nearer to actuality, to life, to reality

than anything (in prose) you have written before. It is nearer 'creation' than *The Shifting of the Fire*. That much for the substance. I do not want to repeat here how highly I think of the purely literary side of your work. You know my opinion". He then remarks that "out of discussion there may come conception" and says that "for discussion I am ready, willing and even anxious". Anyone who, like the writer in his youth, saw the two men together, can easily believe that "discussion"—in a mixture of French and English, of high drawl and low growl—went on endlessly, endlessly, endlessly, day in, day out, week after week, month after month, year after year. Conrad, in this letter, makes the illuminating remark that if he had influence enough with the publishers he would make them publish the book in Ford's name alone, "because the *work* is all yours—I have shared only a little of your worry. Well—you worry very much and so do I—over my own stuff. I sweat and worry and I have no illusions about it. I stick to it with wealth for the brightest prospect—for there may be even a sordid end to my endeavours—some abject ruin material or physical for me—and almost inevitably some ghastly form of poverty for those I love. Voilà—am I on a bed of roses?"

Conrad then says that whether he is worth anything to Ford or not is for Ford to determine. "The proposal" (for collaboration) "certainly came from me under a false impression of my power of work." He says that he is much weaker than he thought he was but that this does not affect Ford fundamentally. "Heinemann (and McClure too, I fancy) are waiting for our joint book and I am not going to draw back if you will truly consent to sweat long enough." He assures Ford that he is not going to make "any sort of difficulty about it" and says "I shall take the money if you make a point of that, I am not going to stick at that trifle. Do come when you like. Bring only one (or at most two) chapters at a time and we shall have it out over each separately." He ends this most revealing letter with his kindest regards.

By 26th March, 1900, *The Inheritors* was sufficiently near completion to be submitted to the publishers and Conrad wires ecstatically to Ford that he has had "splendid reports of novel original popular great hopes society hit McClure takes serializing in both countries as he has good connection wire-pullers . . ." He ends by sending Ford his heartiest congratulations, thereby showing that he regarded Ford as the principal collaborator—which, indeed, he was.

In all his letters written about this time Conrad harps on his favourite theme of misery, depression, ill-health, distaste for any form of literary exertion, agonizing struggles to discover the *mot juste*, titanic wrestling with an implacable fate, and his general "morbid condition". As Ford was extremely impressionable these incessant caterwaulings from Conrad must have had a thoroughly bad effect on his own "state of mind". Such of Ford's letters as I have read suggest that he was determined not to be outdone in misery, ill-health, and domestic worries even by such a specialist in woe as Conrad. Indeed, a certain air of competition in agony can be detected in his correspondence, though it is true that his own and his wife's ill-health was certainly no less genuine than that of Conrad and Mrs. Conrad. The latter, like Elsie Hueffer, had an affection of the knee which necessitated constant (and expensive) medical care and several operations. All the same, had Conrad been more of a stoic, had he set an example of silent suffering, it is fairly certain that no upper lip in Kent would have remained stiffer than Ford's. Occasionally, owing to Conrad's irascibility, or to Ford's irritating manner, the two friends would quarrel and have "words". The "words" we may be sure came mostly from Conrad as Ford suffered acutely from anything in the nature of a scene. Even the mildest tiff seems to have prostrated him for days.

Cheerfulness, as rare as welcome, breaks into Conrad's letters recording McClure's reception of *The Inheritors* which even Conrad regards as "most satisfactory". Stephen Gwynn read the MS. for the American editor and was "distracted with admiration", and "consumed with a desire to make our acquaintance. McC. also wishes to see us. They propose to come down here and beg me to let you know what day I fix for the visit".

He adds that Gwynn says in his report "'it is a work no publisher anxious to produce literature should think of refusing'. The literary quality (and most other things) is all *your own* in that book. I've written thus *ipsissima verba* to McClure". He ends this letter "with love ever yours" and in the next of the series, dated 28th April, 1901, begins "Dearest Ford," which indicates that the friendship between the two men had now reached the closest intimacy. It was therefore quite natural that Conrad should ask Ford to do him a service. English writers, though not exempt from the envy, malice, childish vanity and careerism which are generally regarded as their occupational defects—particularly by self-satisfied businessmen—have a long and fine tradition of generosity to professional comrades in distress. Leigh Hunt was neither a knave nor a Skimpole because he borrowed when he had to, nor was Shelley a fool because, when called upon, he gave or lent. To Ford, who had inherited a full share of his grandfather's liberality, willingness to oblige a fellow-artist to the extreme limit of his capacity was inborn, an essential part of his character. Conrad, owing to his slowness of production, high literary standards and artistic integrity, was in almost continuous financial difficulties before the combined efforts of his influential admirers, in England and America, made him the success which he eventually became. No doubt his friend John Galsworthy, who had what are called "private means", now and then helped the family through tight corners. This, of course, is merely a deduction from what is known of Galsworthy's general nobility of character as he was, naturally, not the man to talk about such things. Ford's helpfulness to Conrad would similarly have remained merely a "deduction" were it not for the chance preservation of some revealing correspondence.

In a letter written on 11th July, 1901, shortly after the publication of *The Inheritors*, Conrad thanks Ford for offering to help him out. The money he requires, "anything between £50 and £60 will do", is, he says, intended to "pay off the first instalment of the loan (from the Insurance Co.) £25 and the premium for the next six months, £22-10-0. The extra pounds I intended to send my grocer". As to raise this sum meant selling out securities, Ford had to refer the matter to Robert Garnett, who had acted, since his marriage, as his *homme d'affaires*.

Robert Garnett, though not without a share of the literary ability of his famous family, was a highly respected and competent solicitor. He was also not only a loyal friend to both Ford and Elsie Hueffer but, through his brother Edward, a friend and admirer of Conrad. He therefore conceived it his duty to try to put the proposed financial transaction between Conrad and Ford on a business footing. Conrad wished to borrow £80 from Ford, £20 of this being rent for Pent Farm which had not been paid for about a year. On 13th July, 1901, Garnett wrote to Conrad to suggest that as he had a £600 Life Policy lodged with his bankers, with a surrender value of something like £400, he should assign this to Ford by way of security. "I quite agree," he says, "that it is wisdom not to go to Heinemann and there can be no harm in making use of Ford's money in a businesslike way. Indeed, I am quite prepared to advise Ford to lend up to the mortgage value of the Policy, either now or hereafter, but whatever he lends, in his position (I allude to his responsibility as paterfamilias) should be *secured*. And you will understand that you cannot give him any legal interest either in this Policy or in the U.S.A. rights of *Inheritors* without a document." He concludes by pointing out that only too often Messrs. Isaac and Co. get their money with high interest while the best friend is left out in the cold just because he *is* a friend and a document therefore thought unnecessary. "In short," he concludes, "my advice to you both is to be businesslike."

Conrad saw no reason why he should give Ford more than his I.O.U. by way of security and Ford instructed Garnett to send him the money. This was provided by the sale of some shares at a loss to Ford of about £4. In his reply to Ford acknowledging receipt of these instructions, Garnett says that for the reason already given he does not look favourably on the present transaction, but none the less hopes that the money will give Conrad an easier time and that in this way Ford will feel rewarded. "If, as I believe, he (Conrad) is made of the right metal he will not allow the fact that you will hold his I.O.U. to sap the good relationship between you. Rather curiously this is often the direct result of pecuniary obligations when not established on a business footing—but I do not like harping on this where you and Conrad are concerned . . ."

Garnett seems to have had his way, eventually, for Conrad writes to Ford on 19th July referring to a new proposal. "Briefly, for the policy, I ask you to advance me £100 in actual cash. You are safe and I am pleased."

Long before the completion of *The Inheritors*, the theme of which, as he disclosed in the letter to Garnett quoted above, never really satisfied Conrad, Ford had read to him the first draft of *Seraphina*. Here was a plot for a romantic novel which fired Conrad's creative imagination, and with complete unselfishness Ford allowed it to form the basis of their next "joint effort". It proved to be a far more successful collaboration, as a work of art, than its predecessor. Following on many months of pre-liminary discussion, work began seriously on the writing of the new book in December 1900, and was continued almost un-interruptedly until July 1902. After numerous vicissitudes and nerve-racking delays, the novel was published in 1903, by the firm of Smith Elder, under the title *Romance*. Ford was anxious to tell the public that Conrad and himself had been at work on the book for six years, but Conrad objected to this on grounds very cogently expressed in the following letter.

My dear Ford,

I am sending the revise on to Beccles[1] by this same post. You are right. The awful *IT* (which I never saw) *vous donne froid aux os!*

The text goes. Your last alterations are all first rate and per-fectly satisfying to my sense of the fitness of things. But there are the dates!

Here my dear Boy you've not to deal with my denseness. I understand perfectly the feeling which induced you to put them there. But you have to deal with the stupidity which will never understand that a mere work of fiction may remain six years in

---

[1] *i.e* To the printers, whose works were established at Beccles.

the making. Anybody disliking the book would jump at such an unguarded confession. Make no mistake; no one will understand the *feeling*; they will only see the fact and far from taking it as imposing they will seize on it for a sneer. It opens a wide door to disparagement to anybody minded for that game. I don't care for the best criticaster of them all—but I don't want to see their ugly paws sprawling over the book (for which I care) more than is absolutely unavoidable.

In figures it is the obvious that strikes; and I imagine them— some of them—saying—but you can imagine yourself what a reviewer could say.

The apparent want of proportion will be jumped upon. Sneers at collaboration—sneers at those two men who took six years to write this "very ordinary tale"—whereas R. L. S., singlehanded, produced his masterpieces etc. etc. and Mr. So and So can write in a year a romance which is more *this* less *that* more *t'other* thing. Moreover we didn't collaborate six years at that. We began in December 1900 and finished in July 1902 really. The rest is delay —horrid delay—because we couldn't get ourselves printed sooner. Why intrude our private affairs for the grin of innumerable swine? And don't forget what they also may say; surely those men have not worked six years on that book. Six years of actual time!

Then why this parade of dates? and if they did, well frankly there's nothing to be proud of; it is well enough but it is not an epoch-making volume. Even Flaubert was not six years writing *Mme. Bovary* which was an epoch-making volume.

Mettez vous au point un peu. You can't express a *feeling* in two dates. I understand them in the light of your note which truly is not meant for reviewers. [It has] brought much doubt and some remorse to me; and it has touched me.

What do you know *"mon très cher"* that I also don't regret that *Seraphina* of the year 1896 which has become the *Romance* of the year 1903?

Il faut garder une certaine mesure. Let it be a twentieth-century book. December 1900 *to September* 1903 is imposing enough— too much! December 1900 to July 1902 is much better for it is long enough for an artistic conscience.

And as it is no one will believe that we worked together all of three years at this tale.

Besides it is pretty well known that the book had been ready for some time. Proof correcting is not *writing* in the sense a critic would look at it.

I would not object to an explanatory note—this novel written from another point of view by F. M. H. in 1896 under the title of *Seraphina*, became the subject of collaboration with J. Conrad at the end of 1900 after much preliminary discussion and was finished in its present shape in July 1902. In italics on the fly leaf at end.

That's one way. But of course it does away with our theory of *welded* collaboration. The dates 1896 *to* 1903 also do away with that. That's a trifle. But to put six years to it is meaningless by its very magnitude.

Consider the discretion of the *note* or accept my proposal Dec. 1900–July (or Aug.) 1902—or nothing at all *peut-être*.

A quoi bon? I have done it once—and nobody cared because nobody's native stupidity was provoked—*ceci est une autre affaire*.

Let us be even absurdly careful,

Yours affectionately,

J. CONRAD.

PS.—I return the revise after all to you.

In later years when Conrad had become world-famous and Ford was still comparatively unknown, efforts were made by Conrad's admirers to suggest that Ford's part in their collaboration was little more than that of an "amanuensis". In spite of their estrangement it is pleasant to find Conrad himself debunking this nonsense in a note, quoted by G. Jean-Aubry in his official two volume biography, which he wrote in T. J. Wise's copy of *Romance* in 1923. In this he states that "the tale as it stands here is based on Ford Madox Hueffer's MS. of *Seraphina*, a much shorter work and quite different in tone. On this we went to work together, developing the action and adding some new characters. We collaborated right through, but it may be said that the middle part of the book is mainly mine with bits of

F. M. H.—while the first part is wholly out of *Seraphina*; the
second part is almost wholly so. The last part is certainly three
quarters ms. F. M. H. with here and there a par by me." Conrad
retained throughout his life a warm feeling for this novel. As
early as June 1902, before the finishing touches had been put to
it, he wrote to Edward Garnett that "strangely enough it is yet
my share of *Romance* (collab-n stuff with Ford) that fills me with
the least dismay". Although the work was exhausting, owing
both to the amount of effort the two writers put into it, and the
nerve strains caused by ill-health and domestic difficulties, the
second collaboration greatly strengthened the friendship which
the first seems to have endangered. When the MS. was completed,
after expressing his gratitude for a visit to Ford at Winchelsea,
Conrad says, "it is a fact I work better in your home in touch
with your sympathy".

Conrad, as has already been observed, can hardly be regarded
as a cheering influence. Had he spent his childhood in England
he would have gained much from the nursery commandment
always to "look on the bright side". In a characteristic note to
Ford, sent with a chapter of *Romance*, he mentions that he is at
work and "beastly seedy with cold, cough and piles and a de-
rangement of the bowels. No doubt paralysis isn't far off". In
another he says his wife is very bad with gastric neuralgia and
that he has had a Hell of a time. "Sometimes I feel as if my
brain were on the point of boiling over the top of my miserable
skull." The reviews of *The Inheritors* were appearing when this
letter was written, and the notices in the *Daily Telegraph* and the
Daily News were sufficiently satisfactory to cause Conrad to tell
Ford that he feels "more and more like a thief of your cleverness.
Upon the whole (apart from cash) this thing must do us good—
at any rate as far as our next book is concerned".

In the spring of 1902 Conrad appears to have been again in
difficulties over the rent of Pent Farm and was uneasy at not
having heard from Ford for several weeks. "I miss collaboration," he writes, "in a most ridiculous manner. I hope you don't
intend dropping me altogether. I see you have not given notice
to old Hog. *Mon cher*, I appreciate your regard for my wretched

affairs." The "old Hog" referred to was presumably the land-lord of Pent Farm to whom, as Conrad was only his sub-tenant, Ford was responsible for the rent.

In the summer of 1902, one of Ford's daughters contracted some infantile infectious complaint and Conrad writes to express his sorrow for the "horrors" accumulating on his friend's devoted head and suggests that the family should come to the Pent for "rest and recovery after the infectious part of the convalescence is over". The invitation was not purely unselfish for Conrad was in urgent need of Ford's help. "Last night," he says, "the lamp exploded here and before I could run back into the room the whole round table was in a blaze—books, cigarettes, MS. Alas! the whole second part of *End of the Tether*, ready to go to Edinburgh. The whole!" No books of Ford's had been burnt, but the round table and brown carpet, which probably belonged to him, had been charred and otherwise damaged. "The fire ran in streams and Jess and I threw blankets and danced around on them; the blaze in the window was remarked in Postling." Within a week, four thousand words of the destroyed MS. had to be re-written and posted to Blackwood's Magazine. There can be little doubt that on this, as on other occasions when Conrad was unable to fulfil obligations to deliver instalments of books undergoing serialization, Ford did indeed act as Conrad's "amanuensis". By this time he understood Conrad's mind and style so completely that he could add twenty or thirty pages to any of Conrad's novels without any ordinary reader detecting the difference. Conrad, in another letter written on the same date, says he "must have another dying effort. Oh, but the heart-break!" Ford could never resist such an appeal. His loyalty and devotion had practically no limits.

The following undated letters, printed here *in extenso* by per-mission of the owners of the copyright, will give the reader an idea of the close intimacy existing between the two families during the period in which *Romance* was being hammered out by its afflicted authors. The first of the series, which refers to the tragic death of Ford's father-in-law, Dr. William Martindale, and the domestic upsets occasioned by it, shows Conrad's genuine warmth of feeling and sincere sympathy. They were the sort of troubles—unlike the literary ones—which, as Conrad remarks in a revealing phrase, "Jessie can understand and feel for".

Monday evening.

MY DEAR FORD,

I have been greatly moved by your letter. And I am still under the painful impression after a day in London, a day of worries during which the idea of your wife and yourself had not left me for a moment, you must have had a most awful time.

I hope she stood this cruel shock with the firmness I imagine to be the foundation of her character. I can't say much to her. Indeed, unless one is perfectly heartless Death is no time for words. The touch of it gives a vision of the world in which words have no place; it unlocks feelings—it sets free thoughts unsuspected in form and substance and nothing outside matters much; but pray, not obtruding my sympathy, tell her that as one who has known Death and its work upon the living I take my part in her affliction in virtue of my great regard for her, no small admiration, and that very sincere sentiment of friendship in which it had been my privilege to include you both.

The effect of your letter quite staggered me; to think of you hung up in that hotel, waiting under the burden of that God-forsaken errand was too awful. I am glad you found it in your heart to write to me. I had not much taste for my journey to London, but had to go having arranged interviews—and so on. I left Jessie greatly affected. I hope you did not think our wire misplaced. She begged me to ask whether she could be useful in that or any other way; and I had just five minutes in Sandling. We thought you could not very well take the children to London and *faute de mieux* it may have eased her mind to know them with a woman who is fairly sensible, with children anyhow and very certainly likes them very much—not to mention myself. Command us in that way at any rate. If you would prefer we could come to Winchelsea for the days you are going to be away, and staying in the Hotel she could keep on them an unobtrusive eye.

I mention this because when I asked Elsie to come here with you she said she did not like leaving the girls with the servants for any time. No more.

With our love,
Always yours,
J. CONRAD.

Thursday.

DEAREST FORD,

Don't think evil of me. I am doing my damnedest. I have been interrupted; I have been upset too; and generally I am not allowed to forget how impossible my position is daily becoming.

Anyhow I have worked as hard as I know how. I think I'll finish my *Castaway* tomorrow; at any rate I intend, if at all possible and you will have me, to come up to you for a couple of days on Monday and work there at *Serafina*. Then Jess would come up for a night and take me home again. I think this the best scheme for getting forward. Only pray beg Elsie not to make preparations and not to treat me as a guest—if I am permitted to come. Or are you going to London just then? Do not let me *interfere* with your *plans*. I can work here too; and I shall work—never fear. Ah, for three days' peace of mind! If I had that I would move mountains. Three days only!

Write me frankly what you think of my intentions.

As to *married*. I say—go on by all means. I shall bring the paper with me (if I can come) and then offer certain minor remarks. The value of creative work of any kind is in the *whole* of it. Till that is seen no judgment is possible. Questions of phrasing and such like—*technique*—may be discussed upon a fragmentary examination. . . . But phrasing, expression—*technique* in short—has importance only when the conception of the whole has a significance of its own apart from the details that go to make it up—If it (the conception) is imaginative, distinct and has an independent life of its own—as apart from the life of the style.

My love to you all,
Yours ever,
JPH. CONRAD.

Pent Farm.

DEAREST FORD,

How are you? Have you slept? I send you the proofs with my suggestions.

Pray note and consider this; on page 32 Kemp *overhears* Carlos and Castro talking. I have corrected the conversation which *per se* is perfectly good and proper for our purpose; but in what language are they talking? Surely not in English—and how comes Kemp to understand Spanish at this stage of his adventures. *Mira Vd?*

My opinion is that the thing may pass and will pass with the general reader, but what about some private reader?

Love from us to you all,
Ever yours,
CONRAD.

Pent Farm,
Sunday.

MY DEAR FORD,

I took the last of *Romance* to London on Friday. I had to engineer an affair with Pinker besides—and I wanted to (besides) hear him talk.

I am confirmed in my judgment as to the great excellence of R.'s last part—for though I appreciate it on other grounds than P., the fact is that he is greatly impressed by it. Now if he isn't an average reader I want to know who is?

My cleverness however lies in the fact that I did perceive the side that would impress a mind of that sort. You mustn't think of suppressing that part for serial publication; no Editor would wish us to do that either I firmly believe.

But that a demand for shortening the thing may be made is very probable; because (don't faint) the book as it stands contains 166,000 words.

I confess this piece of information didn't take me so much aback as you may suppose.

(Says Pinker; But it *reads* short. So it does and that emphatically since his dull senses received that impression.)

F

This being so, I observed, is it worth while operating on it? By the severest pruning we could not hope to eliminate more than 6,000 words, not one tenth, not one twentieth of it I said.

He of course does not complain of the size. On the contrary he says there could not be too much such admirable stuff for the book form.

Only he didn't want to be a year placing it serially. Thereupon he confessed that the MS. was already in Fisher Unwin's (! ! ! !) hands with a proposal to make it a serial for the *New English Magazine* which is going to be enlarged and generally worked up. The point is that F. U. would begin publication at once.

The *N. E. M.* is not choked up with contracts. As to the money Pinker's opinion is that F. U. can find money when he likes.

I made no objection—after all the man must be allowed to do the business, or there would be no point of employing him at all.

For America McClure has an MS. to look over but unless he accepts the terms stated he shall not have it.

He would syndicate the story of course. Otherwise P., who is off to the States in a week or so shall take it with him—to Putnams perhaps—*Voila!*

Upon the whole I have good hopes. I feel slightly fagged out —And I must begin at once something for Blackwood! I haven't a single notion in my head. The "Wonderfulness" you have suggested is nowhere for the moment.

Blackness is the impression of life—past and future; and though it is no doubt true and correct one can hardly fabricate "Maga" stuff out of it. 'Tis too subtle. 'Tain't raw enough. By the bye Blackwood (George) has refused *Falk*.

What's wrong with that damn thing? They seem to treat it as though it has a PEST.

How are you good people getting on? We were glad to hear that Xtina is getting better.

Elsie may say that "*l'air tranquil de ce bonhomme est odieux*" (Flaubert Ed: Sent.) but generally I may say that children are

seldom constitutionally touched. They grow out of early pre-
dispositions.

I had inflammation of the lungs twice (at five and seven) but
whatever else is wrong there is nothing the matter with my
lungs now.

Had she been fifteen I would share Elsie's apprehensions—
which now have my heartfelt sympathy. After all Xtina is a
much better *animal* (not to speak of her vivacious mind) than
Borys who nearly went down before half a dozen grapes. But
life is full of these terrors and on that general ground I take part
in your feelings. We have been smothered in fogs.

Jessie has an awful cough and it makes me wretched no end.
I have nothing to read and nothing to think about. The bleating
of sheep is the only sound. There is a pause in the Drama.

Our love to you all,
Ever yours,
JPH. CONRAD.

The reception of *Romance* by the critics is said by his daughter
Katharine to have caused Ford acute disappointment, which contributed to the nervous breakdown which followed soon after
its publication. As I have not been able to examine the reviews
I can only surmise that the critics were mystified by the collaboration, ignored Ford's major share in it and treated it mainly
as a new work by Conrad. Conrad, in any case, seems to have
been very well satisfied. Writing to John Galsworthy on 30th
November, 1903, he says that "adverts are appearing of the first
edition being exhausted just one month after publication. That
is better than anything of mine has ever done. Eh *voilà!* What
a Romance!" To H. G. Wells he wrote: "*Romance's* gone into
2nd ed. I hear. That, no doubt, does not mean much, but still
it is better than any of my other books did do."

Behind the scenes in all the complicated literary affairs of Ford
and Conrad was the tireless figure of J. B. Pinker. Pinker was,
in his way, one of the most remarkable men who ever adorned
the trade or profession of literary agent. Without much education
or any pretensions to culture, he had a flair for good writing and

courage, enterprise, and persistence in backing his fancies. He exerted himself to place his clients' works to the best advantage and to secure them profitable contracts on both sides of the Atlantic. With Conrad his patience and pertinacity were abundantly rewarded. The £50,000 which Conrad left behind him was at least partly due to his astute business management and commercial acumen. Even with Ford, who, in England, was never destined to get into the best-seller class, he was fairly successful. In a letter to Norman Douglas, dated 18th October, 1905, Conrad remarks: "Hueffer's work was kept off for three years and now it is all going as easy as can be. Some of this stuff has been in Pinker's drawer two years now."

From the extracts from Ford's letters to Pinker which appeared in a New York periodical, *The Saturday Review of Literature*, on 2nd August, 1941, it may be permissible, as it has already appeared in print, to reproduce here a passage which illustrates the nature of Ford's financial arragements with Conrad. The letter was addressed to Pinker in 1914 and concerns the cinema rights of *Romance*, which ultimately, after the conclusion of the then impending war, brought him in, as his half share, about £400.

"As far as I am concerned," Ford writes, "I am ready to agree to the terms you mention. But I should like to make a preliminary query as to the respective shares of myself and Conrad. On the original book we shared equally but on the rights of the cheap editions Conrad took two-thirds to my one. I did not mind this at that time because Conrad was very hard up. If his financial position is now secure—as to which you must be better posted than anyone else—I think we ought to revert to the original shares, since C. does owe me a certain amount of money and I am not a millionaire and have a good many people dependent on me. Of course, if Conrad is not yet straight I don't want to exact this but if he is, I think I ought to. This, of course, is in strict confidence and I am quite ready to leave the decision to you."

Apart from this work with Conrad, Ford in the year 1900 published his *Poems for Pictures*, which received favourable notices, also his large and handsome volume *The Cinque Ports*

which appeared through Blackwood and was lavishly illustrated
by William Hyde. In connection with this work Ford had an
admirable excuse for exploring the part of Kent and Sussex which
he particularly loved. He must have keenly enjoyed these
expeditions. Though the book contains some fine descriptive
passages much of the writing is immature and some of it so
sloppy as to suggest that it was done hastily or against the grain.
Perhaps it was regarded as in the nature of a "pot-boiler".
Experts on the Cinque Ports assure me that the chapters on Rye,
Winchelsea, Hastings and New Romney are better than those
on Sandwich and Deal, to which he seems only to have paid
hurried visits. There is no doubt that his work with (and for)
Conrad exhausted the greater part of his nervous and creative
energy, and his wife's complaints, already referred to, were not
without foundation. Both men were engaged in teaching themselves their trade, both gained from their joint efforts, but as
Conrad says, in a letter to Edward Garnett, "the expenditure of
nervous fluid was immense".

In a cheerful letter to Walter Jerrold, written from Stocks Hill
on 17th March, 1900, Ford says he has been "working like a
galley slave until just yesterday. My colossal book on the Cinque
Ports is hung up waiting for the war—the Conrad-Hueffer novel
(*The Inheritors*) went off to the printers on Friday; that too will
appear in the autumn if serial arrangements permit. I've got a
volume of verse, too, coming out next month, Macqueen being
the happy publisher, the others being Blackwood and Heinemann".

In the summer of 1900 Ford and Elsie Hueffer, with their
daughter Christina, went to Belgium for a holiday and to escape
for a time from the "atmosphere" of the Boer War. To "decent"
English people, of every kind of political and social background,
the South African war was indefensible, and one of their greatest
shocks was the discovery of how few in numbers, among the
middle and upper classes, the "decent" people were. In public-
school circles "pro-Boers" in 1900 were looked on as social
pariahs, and were ostracised in much the same way as, twenty
years later, "pacifists", "bolsheviks", and people who held

"views" were treated in the same circles. Abroad, in Germany, France and Belgium, and in the United States, where Anglophobia is endemic, dislike of the English ruling classes was widespread. Ford on one occasion was shocked, while walking in Bruges, to be greeted with shouts of "*A bas les Anglais!*"

In an undated letter to Walter Jerrold, written from the Grand Hotel de la Plage, Knocke-sur-mer, Ford says he has been there with the Conrads for the past six weeks and mentions that he is returning on "Thursday". He adds that "if you want a really cheap place you couldn't beat this . . . terms range from three francs to five francs a day per person and one and a half francs per kid and railway fares are insignificant". In his book *Ancient Lights*, written ten years later, Ford says the South African war, besides establishing the Rand millionaires in Mayfair, led to a tremendous increase in the cost of living and the enormous increase of the public indifference to anything in the nature of the arts. This last—and possibly both of these factors—began, he says, with the firing of the first shot in the Boer War. "That was the end of everything—of the pre-Raphaelites, of the Henley gang, of the New Humour, of the Victorian Great Figures, and of the last traces of the medieval superstition that man might save his soul by the reading of good books."

Ford's hatred of the Boer War is interesting on account of its having been his first recorded emotional reaction to world events. Theoretically, he very strongly held the view that the artist should be above the political battle and remain aloof from public controversy. He was destined to live through forty years of world history which made this attitude, however justifiable in principle, for a "decent" man untenable in practice.

On his return to Aldington Ford became friendly with H. G. Wells, who was then living at Sandgate. Wells had written an appreciative notice of one of Conrad's books in the *Saturday Review*, in 1896, and two years later Conrad wrote to express his "jubilation at the thought we are going to be nearer neighbours than I dared to hope a fortnight ago. We are going to live at Pent Farm which is only a mile or so from Sandling Junction". In a letter to Garnett, written in August, 1902, Conrad says: "I see no one from month to month. Four or five months ago G. B. S., towed by Wells, came to see me reluctantly and I nearly bit him. Since then—barring Ford—there has been no one."

In the eyes of Wells, Ford and Conrad were regarded as inseparable at this time. Both propounded the same literary gospel of the paramount importance of technique.

In his *Experiment in Autobiography* (vol. 2, page 615) Wells, who never took kindly to this alien doctrine, gives a fascinating picture of the two friends which is all the more valuable from its complete detachment. In the light of the controversy which broke out, after Conrad's death, about the nature of their collaboration, his testimony is important, and may fittingly close this chapter. After mentioning Henry James and Stephen Crane, Wells says: "Two other important men of letters were also close at hand to present the ideal of pure artistry to me rather less congenially. These were Ford Madox Hueffer and Joseph Conrad, of whom the former—through certain defects of character and a copious carelessness of reminiscence—is, I think, too much neglected, and the latter still placed too high in the scale of literary achievement." Of Conrad he writes that he at first impressed him, as he impressed Henry James, as the strangest of creatures. "He was rather short and round-shouldered with his head as it were shrunken into his body. He had a dark retreating face with a very carefully trimmed and pointed beard, a trouble-wrinkled forehead and very troubled dark eyes, and the gestures of his hands were very Oriental indeed." He thinks it was the fine, fresh, careful, slightly exotic quality about Conrad's prose, "that 'foreign' flavour which the normal Anglo-Saxon mind habitually associates with culture", that blinded criticism "to the essentially sentimental and melodramatic character of the stories he told". Wells says that Conrad's humour in *The Nigger of the Narcissus* is "dismal" and that you may "search his work from end to end and find little tenderness and no trace of experienced love or affection. But he had set himself to be a great writer, an artist in words, and to achieve all the recognition and distinction that he imagined should go with that ambition, he had gone literary with a singleness and intensity of purpose that made the kindred concentration of Henry James seem lax and large and pale. *The Mirror of the Sea* was his favourite among his own writings, and I think that in that he showed a sound critical judgment".

Wells records that "he came into my ken in association with Ford Madox Hueffer and they remain together, contrasting and inseparable, in my memory. Ford is a long blond with a drawling manner, the very spit of his brother Oliver, and oddly resembling George Moore, the novelist, in prose and person. What he is really, or if he is really, nobody knows now and he least of all; he has become a great system of assumed personas and dramatized selves. His brain is an exceptionally good one and when first he came along he had cast himself for the rôle of a very gifted scion of the pre-Raphaelite stem, given over to artistic purposes and a little undecided between music, poetry, criticism, the Novel, Thoreauistic horticulture and the simple appreciation of life. He has written some admirable verse, some very good historical romances, two or three books in conjunction with Conrad, and a considerable bulk of more or less autobiographical unreality".

He mentions an occasion when Ford took him to see Conrad at the Pent, where Conrad, he says, "wrote on a desk that may have creaked to the creative effort of *Goblin Market*". Wells's first impression of Conrad was "of a swarthy face peering out and up through the little window panes". The conversation, he says, was "mostly of adventure and dangers, Hueffer talked criticism and style and words, and our encounter was the beginning of a long, fairly friendly but always rather strained acquaintance. . . . We never really 'got on' together. I was perhaps more unsympathetic and incomprehensible to Conrad than he was to me. I think he found me philistine, stupid and intensely English; he was incredulous that I could take social and political issues seriously". Conrad never understood England or the English, was unable to see anything *in* Jane Austen, possessed not a gleam of humour and was unable to see the funny side of himself or anybody else. Wells, on the other hand, as he tells us, was then trying to see

himself as far as possible without pretences. "I eschewed dignity,"
he says. "I found therefore something as ridiculous in Conrad's
persona of a romantic adventurous un-mercenary intensely artistic
European gentleman carrying an exquisite code of unblemished
honour through a universe of baseness as I did in Hubert Bland's
man-of-affairs costume and simple Catholic piety . . ."

Conrad conceived an intense dislike of Bernard Shaw and
once nearly came to blows with the famous dramatist. Wells
intervened tactfully and drew Conrad away. " 'It's humour,'
I said, and took Conrad out into the garden to cool. One
could always baffle Conrad by saying 'humour'. It was one of
our damned English tricks he had never learnt to tackle." On
a later occasion, in his rôle of Polish aristocrat, Conrad urged
Ford to challenge Wells to a duel. "If Conrad had had his way,
either Hueffer's blood or mine would have reddened Dymchurch
sands. I thought an article Hueffer had written about Hall Caine
was undignified . . . Hueffer came over to tell me about it.
'I tried to explain to him (Conrad) that duelling isn't done,' said
Hueffer."

Wells says that in those days "Hueffer was very much on the
rational side of life; his extraordinary drift towards self-dramatisation . . . became conspicuous only later, after the stresses of
the war. In the light of that his last book, *It was the Nightingale*,
is well worth reading".

In regard to the collaboration Wells disposes of a good deal
of the nonsense on this subject which appeared in the British and
American press after Conrad's death. "I think Conrad owed a
very great deal to their early association," he writes. "Hueffer
helped greatly to 'English' him and his idiom, threw remarkable
lights on the English literary world for him, collaborated with
him on two occasions and conversed interminably with him
about the precise word and about perfection in writing."

As a footnote to this account of H. G. Wells's impressions of
Ford, the writer ventures to quote from an interesting letter
addressed to him by Mr. Wells on 30th May, 1945. "Your
story of F. M. H. misses one primarily essential fact. In the
1914–18 war he was a bad case of shell-shock from which he

never recovered. The pre-war F. M. H. was tortuous but under-
standable, the post-war F. M .H. was incurably *crazy*. He got
crazier and crazier. Fill in that gap and you will have your
story complete." He adds: "He wrote some good verse which
I undervalued."

As Ford produced the best of his work between 1920 and
the time of his death, it is scarcely possible to subscribe to
Mr. Wells's view that he was "crazy", though his last two
volumes of reminiscences may, to his contemporaries, have
seemed so fantastically inaccurate as so justify this suspicion.

CHAPTER VII

Winchelsea—and Henry James

FORD WAS only twenty-seven and his wife two years younger when he first established himself in the cottage known as Stocks Hill. Here his second daughter, Katharine, was born and in spite of the "mud and muddle" caused by their incorrigible hospitality—at one time Ford's mother, his sister Juliet and Mrs. Conrad's sister Ethel were all in the cottage together—the "young lovers", as they were locally called, were as happy as all young people ought to be. There was constant coming and going between Stocks Hill and the Pent, the visits to the latter being accomplished with the aid of a pony and trap. The pony, Tommy, one of several remarkable animals owned at different times by Ford and Conrad, had a penchant for backing the trap into ditches, so that the babies had to be strapped into it. There were bathing excursions to Dymchurch, frequent visits to the Martindale "in laws" at Glebe Cottage, Winchelsea, games of bridge with Mr. Rayner, the "literary grocer" of Aldington, who, before meeting Ford, had read and admired the works of Conrad and Henry James. At this time also, while staying at Winchelsea, Ford wrote to Henry James a letter of the most exaggerated flattery and was permitted to begin an acquaintance with the Master which lasted very pleasantly for nearly ten years.

Both Ford and his wife were keen gardeners and there can be no doubt that by their joint activities they used the ground available at Stocks Hill to the best advantage.

In spite of the view over the marsh, in spite of the charm of the stream which ran past their door, and the beauty of the garden and orchard, they yielded eventually to Dr. Martindale's argument that the primitive conditions under which they were living put too great a strain on Elsie Hueffer's health. Dr. Martindale owned an attractive, two-storeyed weather-board cottage at

Winchelsea, called for some reason "The Bungalow", close to his own beautiful Tudor house, and he persuaded them to leave Stocks Hill and occupy it. It stands in a quiet road leading only to the grounds of the Priory. It has been rechristened The Little House and is now occupied by Ford's school friend, Mr. Charles Kinross.

The move entailed many changes in the social life of the young married couple. They ceased to be surrounded by the peasants of the Marsh, whom Ford knew so well and described with so much poetic appreciation, and adjusted their lives to the upper-middle-class conventions of their neighbours, among whom were Mr. and Mrs. Arthur Marwood, and, most impressive of all, Henry James. They lived well, were waited on by servants and went out to dinner parties. Although Ford's "Winchelsea period" lasted, in time, only a few years and was marred by his own ill-health and by a serious fall suffered by his wife, who pitched down the steps leading up to the "look-out" at the entrance to the village and broke an arm, it was as usual packed with interest, creative activity, and mental and emotional excitement. His love for his two little girls, which might almost be described as a devouring passion, reveals itself in the well-known lyric "Christina at Nightfall" and in the now almost unobtainable volume of fairy stories called *Christina's Fairy Book*, published by Alston Rivers in 1906 in a series called The Pinafore Library.

The Bungalow was constantly filled with visitors, Ford's devoted sister-in-law, Mary Martindale, being for a time almost one of the household, and there were the usual contacts with the Conrads, and frequent meetings with Henry James, who used to walk over from Rye, accompanied by his dachshund, Maximilian.

Ford was always extremely deferential to James, for whose work he had a prodigious admiration, but most of his literary contemporaries he treated with a kind of indulgent patronage which might have suggested a superiority complex, but was more likely due to a secret self-distrust. Many people, too unperceptive to realise Ford's essential generosity of character, his real goodness of heart, were intensely irritated by his manner and disliked him accordingly. One such, a friend of Stephen Crane, wrote to Crane complaining about Ford's *arrogance*. Crane's reply was: "You must not mind Hueffer; that is his way. He patronises me, he patronises Mr. Conrad, he patronises Mr. James. When he goes to Heaven he will patronise God Almighty. But God Almighty will get used to it, for Hueffer is all right." With James, however, Ford always comported himself as "*le jeune homme modeste*", so much so that, probably to Ford's secret annoyance, James never seems to have taken him seriously, as an author in his own right. Modesty has its drawbacks.

Mrs. Elsie Hueffer, though less versatile and many-sided than her husband, shared to the full his literary interests, but remained faithful to the William Morris–Walter Crane tradition of arts and crafts which Ford subsequently discarded but in which she still excels. In July, 1902, in spite of her many domestic cares, she undertook the task of translating a volume of stories by Maupassant. In a letter to Ford, enclosing a cheque for £10 to be credited "as against Interest and Rent", Conrad starts off with his usual lamentations. "I am most desperately unhappy and harrowed by the awful task of trying to get the *mood* of my *End of Tether*. Ford—it is terrible!" He goes on to express his delight in Elsie Hueffer's project. "She shall tackle M. I consider her by temperament eminently fit for the task and her appreciation of the author guarantees success." He adds that he is always at her disposition with pleasure and pride—"if I am allowed to take upon myself the office of an intelligent dictionary". We must, he says, "get into a closer heap together when she is ready to commence—if not sooner! I want you and have wanted you for some time". He goes on to observe that it will be a splendid thing for her and "not a bad thing for us. For it is clear that while such a work is going on we shall all *think* Maupassant. *C'est forcé.*" (It may be noted in passing that neither Conrad nor Ford ever realised the social implications, in the eyes of public-school-educated Englishmen, of the use of the word "commence".)

The letter was no doubt a prelude to one of the Conrad family's frequent descents on the Hueffers and it is probable that the project increased the growing annoyance of Conrad's wife, who found herself, perforce, left out of the literary discussions. Mrs. Jessie Conrad, as devoted to her husband as he was to her, had admirable gifts as wife and mother, but as a plain sea captain's daughter her outlook and her education had alike been restricted. This fact is very evident in the book she wrote about her husband after his death—*Joseph Conrad as I Knew Him*. It is saddening to reflect how many literary friendships have been undermined and finally destroyed by the possessive jealousies of authors' wives.

In November, 1902, Conrad wrote to Elsie Hueffer after a visit to London and remarked that "Jack (Galsworthy) and his little world are excited at the prospect of the Maupassant translation, of which I have made no secret *dans les salons* to which I have had access". No opponents of "log-rolling", it may here be remarked, were more ardent in its pursuit than Ford and Conrad in their early years.

Conrad, as the letters in Mrs. Hueffer's possession make clear, nobly fulfilled his promise to give aid and advice in the translation. In one letter he points out, with unconscious humour, that "the French Reporter did not write 'baisait', but *embrassait*. For reasons I am ready to explain privately to Ford he could not use 'baisait' like this". The volume, when completed, earned Conrad's commendation. "My sincerest congratulations," he writes, in an undated letter. "It is indeed a first-rate translation. Your toil, a very honest and unselfish toil, has not been thrown away. There are whole pages upon pages, rendered with an amazing fidelity of tone." The translation, with a preface by Ford, was published in the following year, 1903, by the firm of Duckworth, through the good offices of Edward Garnett who had recently become Duckworth's literary adviser. The selection remains one of the best introductions to Maupassant for English readers and deserves the compliments which Conrad bestowed on it.

Although the friendship with Henry James, the growth of which the series of letters from the Master, kindly placed at my disposal by Mrs. Elsie Hueffer, discloses in some detail, may be considered one of the most interesting events of Ford's Winchelsea period, his friendship with Arthur Marwood, who subsequently provided most of the capital behind *The English Review*, had a more fruitful influence on his career than either James or Conrad. From the circumstances of their upbringing and the quiet life they led at Aldington, Ford and Elsie Hueffer, though familiar with "celebrities", creative artists, several of them foreigners like Stephen Crane, Henry James and Conrad, though well-travelled and themselves highly cultivated and gifted, had had little social experience of a general sort and few contacts with conventionally educated members of the British ruling class. In Marwood Ford discovered what was, to him, a new species of Englishman: for certain purposes, the "real" Englishman. Facts about this enigmatic personality are difficult to discover, and the writer on whom, in the course of several meetings in 1909, he made no impression which has remained at all clear, has been unsuccessful in searching the memory of others. He *may*, as Ford often alleged, have been a Yorkshire "squire", he was certainly educated at a public school, Clifton, from which he undoubtedly secured an Exhibition at Trinity College, Cambridge. Archibald Marshall, who was a Cambridge contemporary, states in his book *Out and About*, that Marwood fell ill in his second year and was never, as Ford used to assert, in the running for a Senior Wranglership, as he went down without a degree. Marshall admits that he had an "encyclopaedic mind" and there is evidence in a paper which Marwood contributed to *The English Review* outlining a scheme for National Insurance that he had a good mathematical brain. No doubt he had a share of the reticence and stoicism, and the habit of not putting his goods in the shop window, common to his class and type. He was a sick man when Ford first encountered him at Winchelsea, devotedly looked after, Marshall records, by his wife. We can take it for granted that, in sharp contrast to Conrad, he bore his afflictions in silence or made a joke of them. He was certainly not the sort of man to cry out "Oh, the heartbreak!" whenever something went wrong or he felt a twinge of pain. In this respect Ford must have found him a wholesome corrective influence. In

Ford's eyes, at any rate, Marwood shone as *par excellence*, the "English gentleman", and thus provided him with a new "persona". It is certainly from the Marwood period that Ford began to invent for himself an imaginary public school background. In 1908, when the writer first encountered him, Ford was modestly content with Westminster, but in the U.S.A. and in his later books he used to hint more or less openly at Eton. In *Mightier than the Sword* (1938) for example, he says: "On the other hand, going to one of the great public schools on whose playgrounds the battles of Waterloo were fought, I had had no education at all, except that, at the end of the birch rod, I had acquired a prodigious facility at writing Latin verse so that to this day I can write it faster than English prose." That Ford possessed the facility he claimed is certainly true. But it is extremely improbable that his aunt Lucy Rossetti, from whose tuition he probably acquired it, ever wielded a "birch rod" on him. In an imaginary conversation between himself and E. V. Lucas, recorded in *It was the Nightingale*, it is permissible to trace some lingering remains of Marwood's influence. Ford asked Lucas why it was that he (Ford) could not appreciate Charles Lamb and Lucas replied: "Because you are not really English." That, says Ford, "hit me in the face like a discharge from a fireman's hose. I said: Why am I not English? I play cricket not quite as well as you do, but with as much pleasure. I play golf more often, if not so well. I went to as great a public school as yours. I take a cold bath every morning. . . . I drop my aitches before words derived from the French. My clothes are made by a Sackville Street tailor who made for my great-grandfather and has never fitted me too well . . ." It would be unkind to dissect this characteristic passage too carefully. Ford never really had any instinct for clothes and if his evening tails and other garments did not fit him too well it was probably because, at all events in his *English Review* days, he had them made not in Sackville Street but by a German jobbing tailor who lived near his office. E. V. Lucas was, like H. G. Wells, a product of Midhurst Grammar School and probably "English" enough to be proud of it. Marwood—Tietjens might quite likely have

John Galsworthy

Ford Madox Ford
by Frederick Carter, A.R.E.

taken a cold bath every morning, if his health permitted, but the
only time I myself saw Ford in his bath it was very hot indeed.
It would be foolish and unjust to upbraid a poet, a vivid day-
dreamer, a creator of enchanting fairy stories, for indulging in
such fantasies. Many great, as well as many less great, imaginative writers have been notable for similar weaknesses. Hugh
Kingsmill, in his biography of Frank Harris, tells us that the ex-
cowboy "sported an Eton tie at times and talked of the 'old
days' at Rugby." There now seems little occasion for the
merciless censure of some of Ford's literary contemporaries for
his "impressionist" flights of fancy.

The fact that Ford's Tietjens was undoubtedly a "projection"
of Marwood, gives Marwood a more secure place in English
literary history than the fact that he was an uncle of the gifted
creator of *The Constant Nymph*. Ford, like Ouida, never got the
hang of English University life and his description of the way
in which Marwood deliberately avoided becoming Senior
Wrangler, through his dislike of ostentation, resembles Ouida's
immortal account of an Oxford boat race, in which all rowed
swiftly but "stroke" rowed swifter than any. The secret of
Ford's fantasies, which enraged so many of his contemporaries,
is to be found in the fact that he was, as completely as any
Gauguin-Strickland, Van Gogh, Maupassant or Baudelaire, an
artist. In his book, *The Summing Up* (page 236) W. S. Maugham
gives the fullest and most lucid description of the kind of bird
the artist is, and the sort of way his mind works, that I have so
far come across. "The images," he writes, "free ideas which
throng his (the artist's) mind, are not guides but materials for
action. They have all the vividness of sensation. His day-dreams
are so significant to him that it is the world of sense that is shadowy
and he has to reach out for it by an effort of will. His castles in
Spain are no baseless fabric, but *real castles that he lives in*." I
have put the concluding words of this sentence in italics because
they provide the essential key to Ford's autobiographical impres-
sionism. In regard to the artist's effect on and relations with
women, Maugham's general comments apply with singular
appositeness to Ford. After pointing out that women, with

G

their shrewd sense, are on their guard against the artist, he adds that "they are attracted by him, but instinctively feel that they can never completely dominate him, which is their desire, for they know that somehow he escapes them. . . . The artist is ill to live with. He can be perfectly sincere in his creative emotion and yet there is someone else within him who is capable of cocking a snook at its exercise. He is not dependable".

The course of Ford and Elsie Hueffer's acquaintance with Henry James can be traced in the series of letters printed in the following chapter. After the collapse of Ford's married life, his loss of *The English Review* and his strange *collage* with Violet Hunt (who was an older and more intimate friend of Henry James than Ford ever claimed to be) the fastidious and rather old-maidish American novelist hastily joined the chorus of Ford's detractors. He was in poor health and had an increasing dislike of being "mixed up in things". Ford claims to have met him on 14th August, 1915, in St. James's Park and to have made it up with him after he had joined the Army and was about to leave for France. This was a week after James had taken British nationality when, as Archibald Marshall points out, he was ill and confined to his flat. We can therefore sympathize with Marshall's disbelief that the meeting ever took place or that James ever used the words Ford attributes to him: "*Tu vas te battre pour le sol sacré de Mme de Staël!*"

In 1913 Ford published a critical study of the novels of Henry James, which remains, for the student, one of the best introductions to the work of this very great but now rather "dated" writer. Their relations, by the time it appeared, had evidently become so strained that Ford did not venture to send him a copy of it. Marshall quotes a letter on the subject, written to him by James from 24 Carlyle Mansions, Chelsea, on 18th January, 1914. "You commiserate me," he observes, "for my exposure to the public assault of F. M. Hueffer, but I assure you that though I believe this assault has been perpetrated I have not the least difficulty in remaining wholly unconscious of it. I am vaguely aware that this book is out, but he has at least had the tact not to send it to me, and as I wouldn't touch it with a ten-foot pole nothing is simpler than for it not to exist for me—and this even I hope (as I do) that it may exist for himself to some purpose, pecuniary or other, not to be by me conceived. Any approach to felicity in life in this impossible age rests, to my sense, almost wholly on what one succeeds in *not* being aware of—and that is a delightful art, susceptible of perfect cultivation." Marshall records that for some years before his death James had kept Ford "at arm's length" and says that a reference he made to Ford was "very coldly received". Later James mentioned something that might have the effect, as he said, of "bringing that young man down upon me again" and ended very emphatically, "I said to myself No! And again, No!"

Marshall's comment is that: "Henry James was a very great gentleman and quite beyond Hueffer's power to depict." The short answer to this is Ford's portrait of Christopher Tietjens. Marshall, who had quarrelled with Ford (after having been launched by him into literary circles which James frequented) was undisguisedly animated by malice; but it is difficult to feel that the Master himself comes very well out of the episode. The correspondence makes clear that over a period of years James was on friendly terms both with Ford and his wife and I have never seen it disputed that the character of Densher, in James's novel, *The Wings of the Dove*, was a projection of Ford as he then appeared to one who knew him well. The inclusion of short stories by Henry James, in *The English Review*, in association with most of the great figures of contemporary English literature, was extremely flattering to the self-esteem of our American guest and added to his prestige at a time when he was neither so well-known nor as highly thought of as he later became. One might suppose that even if James had never troubled to read any of Ford's books, the magnificent tribute Ford paid him in the first number of *The English Review* would have established a claim on his loyalty. Bernard Shaw, another "very great gentleman", never went back on his old editor, Frank Harris, although Harris became far more blown upon, socially, than Ford ever did.

CHAPTER VIII

Letters from Henry James

THE LETTERS which follow, covering a period of thirteen years, are reproduced by kind permission of the novelist's nephew, Mr. Henry James Junior of New York, who is the owner of the copyright. Although somewhat guarded in tone, they corroborate Ford's claim to have been a fairly frequent visitor at Lamb House and to have, as frequently, received Henry James as an honoured guest at Winchelsea. At the same time, the reader may form the impression, from the references to Conrad, that James was really more interested in Conrad, both as a writer and a personality, than in Ford. It is, however, on record that the three men had long discussions and disputations on the perennial theme of literary technique and there is also a legend that the conversations at Rye sometimes verged on the improper! In any case, it is beyond dispute that before the Master dropped him from his circle of acquaintance, his relations with Ford were cordial and that Ford had many opportunities of observing him at close quarters.

Friday.   The Vicarage,
                                  Rye.
                          Sept. 11, '96.

DEAR SIR,

I shall be very glad to see you and talk with you—and am not insensible to the compliment of your wish. I am at home in a free condition more nearly at 2.30 to 3.30 o'clock, than at most other hours—but should be glad to hear from you as to when you will come. If *Monday* at 2.30 wd. suit you, let us take that occasion. I go out, later (for exercise) and don't get in very early.

                              Believe me, yours very truly,
                              HENRY JAMES.

34, De Vere Gardens,
W.
December 30, '97.

DEAR MR. MADOX HUEFFER,

Many thanks for your information about Mr. Hyde. The no. of the *Artist* has not yet arrived, but I will with pleasure, when it does come, read the paper on him. But let me in the meantime put in a general confession. I mean say, frankly, on the question of one's being illustrated, that I don't cultivate it, in general, at all—though it may be sometime imposed on one. I like so my prose, such as it is, to stand by itself, that I almost dread a good illustrator more than a bad one. But, in magazines, one *has* often to accept the general circumstances, and so far as one can exercise a pressure, I shall be glad to remember your friend. Congratulate me: I have just taken on a long lease (for May to November occupation) a charming old house at Rye. I hope to see you there and am yours very truly,

HENRY JAMES.

Envelope: Ford Madox Hueffer Esq.,
Pent Farm,
Postling,
Standford, *Hythe*, Kent.

Lamb House,
Rye,
Sussex.

16th May, 1901.

MY DEAR F. M. HUEFFER,

I am overwhelmed by your letter, touched by your sympathy, and almost appalled by your munificence: in the light, that is, of my fear that my crude pleasantries, my reckless and accidental levity on the subject of your brave Book may have seemed (while you evidently sought, or awaited, but a pretext for kindness) to put a kind of pressure on you in respect of my deprived state. I thank you none the less cordially, but I feel embarrassed and confused; as if I were really inhuman to consent to receive from you an offering of such value. Let me, when it comes, at all events, keep it, tenderly, gratefully, very carefully for you; swagger about the possession of it to my friends; and hold it subject to your order. I shall otherwise feel as if I had received from you the present of a maison montée or of a carriage and horses. For the rest I respond very gratefully to the charming things you tell me in relation to your so friendly acquaintance with things of mine. I'm delighted, this sentiment and this history—which you so happily express—exist for you; and only a little alarmed—or a little depressed—as always—when my earlier perpetrations come back to me as loved or esteemed objects. I seem to see them, in that character, shrink and shrivel, rock dangerously, in the kindly blast, and threaten to collapse altogether. I am always moved to say "Wait"—but I suppose I ought really to be thankful about anything that helps you to wait! Meantime, too, I can't but feel that at Winchelsea you and your wife are beautifully placed for doing so. I fall again to stoking my furnace as I think of you there, and to trying to produce some approach to the right metal. This is one of the reasons why I am glad you have come—I *shall* read the Ports[1] —I can't possibly not; and I shan't promise not to write to you again. But I shall see you again before I do so, and I am with very kind regards to your wife and renewed thanks for your beautiful letter,

Yours most truly,
HENRY JAMES.

Envelope: Ford Madox Hueffer, Esq.,
　　　　　　The Bungalow,
　　　　　　Winchelsea.

Hatley St. George,
Torquay.
March, 19th 1902.

MY DEAR HUEFFER,

I am sorry you should be burdened with questions of the order of the one you quote from Garnett—that is in relation to any

---

[1] " The Cinque Ports " by Ford Madox Hueffer. Illustrated by William Hyde. Blackwood 1900.

wares of mine. Will you kindly, when you have occasion to write to him, say that I am afraid, with my thanks, that my case is just now simple enough for me not to have to seek G. D.'s[1] protection against the penalties of indelicacy—for I pray still to be enabled to be indelicate when I want to, or, more gracefully perhaps, need to. But a kindly tolerance in the trade seems as yet not to threaten to fail me. In short, my work is just now promised as far ahead as I'm ever able to look. And if it were not irrelevant and this message were not already too long for manners, I should add that a series, a "Library" of whatever coloured back, is, sniffy as it may sound, never my "form". Thanks for your sympathy with the rather dismal month—11th February to the 11th March—that I spent at Lamb House mostly in bed. I went up to town only to fall immediately ill and scramble back in a fever, to save my skin by being nursed at home. But I am solidly better now, and this place is beneficent to me. I return home, however, by mid-April. Let me take this opportunity to express to your wife and yourself my friendly participation in your late bereavement. It made me think of you with anxious interest and I hope it doesn't at all displace you at Winchelsea.

Yours very truly,
HENRY JAMES.

Lamb House,
Rye,
Sussex.
September 9th 1902.

MY DEAR HUEFFER,

I thank you ever so kindly for your letter, which gives me extreme pleasure and almost for the moment makes me see the things myself, not as a mass of mistakes with everything I had intended absent and everything present blotched! Such is the contagion of your charming optimism. There is something, I suppose, by way of leaven in the lump; but I have been feeling as if I had deposited in the market place an object chiefly cognisable

---

[1] Gerald Duckworth.

and evitably *as* lump. Nothing, all the same, is ever more interesting to me than the consideration, with those who care to see, or want to, of these bottomless questions of How, and Why and Whence and What or in connection with the mystery of one's Craft. But they take one far, and after all, it is the doing it that best meets and answers them.

The book had of course, to my sense, to be composed in a certain way, in order to come into being at all, and the lines of composition, so to speak, determined and controlled its parts and account for what is and what isn't there; what isn't, e.g. like the "last interview" (Hall Caine would have made it large as life and magnificent wouldn't he?) of Densher and Milly.

I had to make up my mind as to what was my subject and what wasn't and then to illustrate and embody the same logically. The subject was Densher's history with Kate Croy here with him, and Milly's history was but a thing involved and embroiled in that. But I fear I even then let my system betray me, and at any rate I feel I have welded my structure . . . of rather *too* large and too heavy historic bricks. But we will talk of these things, and I think I have a plan of getting over to Winchelsea some day next week, when I shall no longer have my American cousins staying with me, and 2 others at the Mermaid! But I will consult you telegraphically first. I am hoping you have been able to pass the book[1] on to Conrad.

Yours most truly,
Henry James.

Lamb House,
Rye,
Sussex.
Sep 18th '03.
Thursday p.m.

Dear Mrs. Hueffer,

Most kind your note and most tempting your invitation. I *should* extremely like to bring my three friends (for the third has now turned up) to Winchelsea next Monday, and I would engage on the spot to do so were it not that a complication

---

[1] *The Wings of the Dove.*

threatens in the form of the further arrival at the Mermaid (to-morrow) of three *more* (Mrs. Poultney-Bigelow and her two daughters) who will be more or less on my mind and my hands, and whom, not improbably, we others shall not for common humanity like to leave languishing here when we undertake our pilgrimage. And yet I don't like to ask you for tea and bread and butter for 6 (six!) American ladies at once and that is five and a young priestling, who counts almost as one through his long skirts. Please let me say therefore that I will bring with pleasure as few of the party as possible, and that we will beleaguer the Bungalow as soon as possible after we have profaned the Friars.

Believe me yours very truly,
HENRY JAMES.

Lamb House,
Rye,
Sussex.
Oct 26, 1903.

DEAR HUEFFER,

I ought already to have thanked you for the handsome present of the Romantic Volume, the offer of which I take very kindly. I may not, for many impediments, fall upon it instantly—it looks like a store of romance to keep on the shelf like one would keep a large chunk of bride cake for earnest but interspaced and deliberate degustations. I lamented my loss of you and of Conrad two or three days ago, and longed, as usual, to have known you were coming. That can't always be done, I know—and I fear our friend has quitted you again but I hope you will kindly let me hear of it if he is to be with you again before you go abroad —if you *do* go: which I devoutly hope for you *par un temps pareil*. Since saying which I have *been* nibbling the bride cake and have my mouth already full, yet am proceeding to fill it further. It seems most excellent rich stuff.

Yours ever,
HENRY JAMES.

Lamb House,
Rye,
Sussex.
Jan 8th, 1904.

MY DEAR HUEFFER,

I thank you kindly, even from a prostrate posture which forbids my doing ought but dictate, for your letter of advice about your migration—on which event I heartily congratulate you.

Many things have happened since I last saw you—among them that I have been to London, and then have scrambled back thence to tumble into bed with a beastly little inconvenient attack of gout which is waning, but has reduced me to dependence on various kinds of machinery, and not least on this.

Mountain for mountain, you strike me as having made really, for these coming dull weeks, a happy exchange: I have never thought of the tip-top of Campden Hill[1] as of a *gaieté-folle*, but it is certainly the centre of the social maelstrom compared with the eminence you have quitted. May it yield you every innocent beguilement and satisfaction; and may it in particular minister effectively to Mrs. Hueffer's restoration.

Now that the question is—settled, I think I may whisper that it must be *really* more amusing than even St. Jean de Luz, haunted with the ghost of poor Gissing. The only hitch I see is that perhaps A. G. don't provide for Conrad, whom I have ever, quite solidly, on my mind. But perhaps on the other hand they *do*—in which case I shall think of them as akin to the Gardens of Eden.

I scarcely expect to get to town myself before the first days of next month; but then I will come, on some early opportunity, and ascertain what the truth of this urgent question may be.

Yours very truly,
HENRY JAMES.

[1] Referring to Ford's proposed migration to 10, Airlie Gardens, Campden Hill, Kensington.

The Reform Club.
Feb: 19th, 1904.

DEAR MRS. HUEFFER,
On Wednesday 15th with great pleasure, at 7.30.

Yours very truly,
HENRY JAMES.

Envelope: Mrs. F. M. Hueffer,
10, Airlie Gardens,
Campden Hill,
W.

Reform Club, Pall Mall, S.W.
April 14th, 1904.

MY DEAR HUEFFER,
Lord bless you, it is all right about your book,[1] of which I am delighted to hear. Go on with it to felicity and fortune and let it take my hearty benediction with it. Mine is a thing of the far, though not of the contingent future. I agreed nearly a year ago to do for the *Macmillans* (no Heinemann-Pawling) two (wide-printed illustrated) vols. to be called *London Town*, to be illustrated by J. Pennell, and to be of the general type of Marion Crawford's *Ave Roma*, etc. But the essence of my understanding is free margin of *time*, and I haven't *touched* the work yet.

I go to America five months hence (scarce that) and stay there some eight, and while there shall not be able to think of the subject—to do anything but get away and away from it. This means that I can't even begin to "think of" my book for at least a year hence, and when I do begin to think I must collect a great many impressions (by reading) before I can begin to write. So there it is. My work is relegated to a dim futurity. Go on with yours never dreaming of my job. Bring yours out and find all comfort, pride and profit in it; the sooner the better; then I shall be able to crib from you freely—yet shall [be] demurely acknowledging.

All greetings and good wishes.

Yours ever,
HENRY JAMES.

[1] "The Soul of London."

Reform Club,
Pall Mall, S.W.
Thursday 25th [——?], 1904.

DEAR MRS. HUEFFER,

I have both your sad letter and Hueffer's kind telegram (I came back from 3 days of gout, in bed at Rye on Tuesday p.m. in time to keep, grimly, an engagement to dine that night!) and they give me a lively sense of your associated and complicated troubles—of which the one redeeming feature appears to be (?) the sociable turn, among yourselves (?) that they have been taking. Poor little Xtina's combustion manquée will surely have accounted for any peccant humour in you and Hueffer. But I rejoice heartily that you are all saved and improving and I could come with pleasure on *Thursday next*, today week. On that Wednesday and that Friday, as happens, I am engaged, but I will [be] doing nothing with Thursday till I hear from you.

Yours most truly,

Envelope: Mrs. F. M. Hueffer,   · HENRY JAMES.
          10, Airlie Gardens,
          Campden Hill, W.

Lamb House,
Rye,
Sussex.
August 11th, 1904.

DEAR MRS. FORD MADOX,

Oh yes, I *must* acknowledge your interesting and touching letter, for which I thank you kindly; but you must bear with me if I take this form for doing so—my pressure just now being considerable, and the sight of my demoralised and decrepit "hand" having become so detestable to me that I can face it only under rigid coercion.

What you tell me of your husband's condition, past and actual, excites my liveliest sympathy for both of you and affects me as a very pathetic story indeed—even as an almost tragic one. I think that, for that matter, I was really all the while, from quite a time back under the impression of it, and though I didn't know the detail of all your worriments the sense of them in the air was not at any moment far from me, little as I could intervene to lighten any of your burden. You had, together, the sad fortune, inevitable at certain moments of life, that things—things of hard friction—accumulated on your exposed heads and spent their fury—that is I hope they *have* spent it. Don't doubt that they will now have begun to pass on, and hurl themselves at other victims; for if worriment sometimes all but wears us out, we also wear it (by rubbing) a little in return, and it ends by having enough of us.

I rejoice that Hueffer has meanwhile found a thorough asylum —just the right one as I should suppose; the office of good German life being assuredly to muffle and pacify our intenser and finer vibrations. Keep him there as in a beatific doze, and let no reminder of any responsibility penetrate his good thick super-incumbent eiderdown. Give him my friendliest remembrance and benediction when he can bear it, but don't be precipitate even about that. I jump to meet your fairly good news of Conrad, but my days and hours think so, while my unperformed duties don't, that I fear my fondly-fancied visit to him will have to reduce itself, at the most, to a poor abashed and inadequate note.

I like to think that you are about to re-enter the blessed little circle of the pair of hilltop towns, and though I shall have gone off before you re-appear I become thus enabled to spare myself a sigh through my general sense of knowing the worst that Winchelsea can do to you. You will be able to bear that now, since I take it to be really over, and I hope I shall find your whole existence happily reconstituted when I come back in the spring.

Believe me yours most truly,

HENRY JAMES.

The Reform Club,
March 17th.

MY DEAR HUEFFER,

I write to Comyns Carr by this post—and as in a period of thirty years I have never asked of him anything whatever perhaps he will go and see (invite) your friend's work. In fact I am sure he will and I hope some real good may come thereby to Mr. Bohm.[1]

I have the *Fifth Queen* just to hand to thank you for very kindly. How you flame with vivid production. I shall "go for" the poor Fifth one at the earliest opportunity.

Yours ever,
HENRY JAMES.

Lamb House,
Rye,
Sussex.

Jan. 23rd, 1906.

DEAR MRS. HUEFFER,

I go up to town to stay on February 5th, and I go up to-morrow to a melancholy funeral. (Back only Friday, I fear.) But I want you and Hueffer [to] come over some day *next* week to tea? *Any* day—if you will but give me a hint.

Yours very truly,
HENRY JAMES.

PS. Wouldn't this coming Sunday do?

Envelope: Mrs. Ford M. Hueffer,
       8, Girdler's Road,
       Hammersmith, W.

Lamb House,
Rye,
Sussex.
October 10th, 1907.

DEAR FORD HUEFFER,

Just a word to say that I hope very much you will come down for your Winchelsea books and by that same occasion

---

[1] American Artist. Inside this letter is a note from Ford to his wife saying that the "enclosed is the great man's reply to an epistle in which I begged him to get Comyns Carr to invite the great Bohm to contribute to the New Gallery—yes, my dear thing, your prayers for my success have been answered. As for my health I have been going through a bit of a relapse—but I'm taking more care of myself and fattening up (D. V.) again. The children went back to the convent again this morning, very well and cheerful, and we reached here at eight to-night."

come over to tea with me and give me a little more of your news, especially as it brightens (as I guarantee you it will). Only please make me some sign beforehand, so that I don't miss you —for the hurly-burly of life in this place is most damnably growing and one now really never knows from day to day what trap may not be laid for one.

Believe me,
Yours ever,
HENRY JAMES.

Envelope: Ford Madox Hueffer Esq.,
    84, Holland Park Avenue,
    London, W1.

Lamb House,
Rye,
Sussex.

July 12th, 1908.

DEAR MRS. HUEFFER,

I am very glad indeed to hear from you, in spite of your sad history, by which I am greatly touched—though your account of recent events certainly qualifies—all happily—the dark record. I knew you were unwell—and feared you might be gravely so —but it's a long lane that has no turning. You must have been through dreary days and I congratulate you on the blest relief you express. May this better order widen and weighten and restore you completely to activity and felicity. My own annals are much less dramatic and consist mainly of my having been absent hence—partly in Paris, but mainly in town, for a good many rather strenuous weeks—till the other day. I am having a good deal to think of, attend to and generally deal with (as almost always at this season) by reason of an affluence of near relations (from America) who have been, are, and are still to be, much with me and whose presence adds itself, as a claim on my time (and space) to the constant appeal of a very prolonged and still unterminated job of work. My brother and his wife and son and daughter—with a steady flow of cousins bringing up the rear—people in short my foreground and make it rather intensely undesirable I should leave home this month. I should like much, however, to come over to see you in August, and nothing would be more interesting to me than to do so while Conrad is near you. This I will achieve, taking a day with you for the purpose—short of some insurmountable (and as yet incalculable) bafflements. I don't quite geographically *place* you—but I will work it out. Charmingly you describe your elements of beauty and salubrity. I trust they will lead you to a convalescence of long strides. Give my friendly remembrance to Ford Madox—I hope he is in good heart and good case. I never go to Winchelsea now—and it seems twice as far away. Major Stileman is dead—the Friars are to be presently put up at auction—and we hear that Mrs. Freeman is frantic to outbid everyone—which I shouldn't think would—for her—be difficult. Rye meanwhile is going to the dogs—with increase of population, villas, horrible cheap suburbs, defacements, general ruinations. I rejoice for you in the happy cloisterment (in so demoralised a world) of your little girls. But good night. Will you kindly make me some *sign* in August of the Conrad approach? I am too horribly in his debt. Believe me yours most truly,

HENRY JAMES.

Lamb House,
Rye,
Sussex,
12. 10. 09.

DEAR MRS. HUEFFER,

I have already delayed too long to acknowledge your hand-some novel[1]—in which I none the less at once felt a welcome sign of remembrance. I was tumbling into bed with a vicious attack of gout at the very moment it arrived, and have only now picked myself up again and begun to deal with letters. I shall place your so engaging-looking volume on the shelf that already shines with the serried fiction that has flowed from the Hueffer fount—and cultivate a closer acquaintance with it on the first

---

[1] "Margaret Hever" by Elsie Martindale, Duckworth 1909.

H. G. Wells

Henry James
From a painting by J. S. Sargent now in the National Portrait Gallery

symptom of a lapse in the uncanniest feature of my accumulated age and disillusionment—my almost insurmountable inability to persist in the perusal of any wanton Fable at all—which works as a safeguard against my loss of the personal influence that enables me to persist in the wanton perpetration of such works. I have to choose—by a strange elderly law—between reading and writing stories and I can't do both; and there are stern reasons that preside at my choice. If I could only make my fortune a little I would do nothing *but* read Hueffers (including Martindales—and on opportunity, Conrads) I have just had, by the way, a very touching and interesting letter from the bearer of that last romantic name—to whom I must even now write.

I hope your admirably placed village brings a measure of peace and ease to all of you. Rye continues to be admirably placed, but *I* haven't had a very easy or peaceful year. However, a better turn seems to promise, and I invoke all good omens on Hueffer and yourself. You have left a great gap at Winchelsea —to which I now never go.

Yours most truly,

HENRY JAMES.

H

CHAPTER IX

Nervous Breakdown

THE EFFECT on Ford's highly sensitive nervous system of various events which occurred in 1903 and 1904 culminated in an alarming nervous breakdown. For a long period, he roamed about the Continent, going from one spa to another in search of a cure, but without success. He has given an amusing description of his experiences in *Return to Yesterday*, which, allowing for characteristic exaggerations, can be accepted as a reasonably truthful impression of what he went through, particularly as the main outlines of his story are corroborated by the letters of William Michael Rossetti. It is impossible to trace all his movements, particularly as there were evidently "bright intervals", spent probably in London among his literary friends, which mitigated his general depression and morbid lack of self-confidence. His wife's accident had been a severe shock and the reception of *Romance*, in spite of the rapid call for a second edition, as I have mentioned in a preceding chapter, seems to have been a great disappointment to him. At the more profound causes of his spiritual and mental malaise we can only make a guess. The long and nerve-racking collaboration with the always wailing and bemoaning Conrad no doubt had pernicious after-effects. It could hardly be otherwise in view of Ford's easily impressionable nature. Again, both as a writer and as a man, he had not yet found himself. He was still much influenced by the aesthetic movement in which he had been brought up and by Madox Brown's vision of the colour and romance of medieval England. This he did not get out of his system until after he had written his magnificent trilogy of historical novels, *The Fifth Queen, Privy Seal,* and *The Fifth Queen Crowned*. His studies for these works began after the publication, in two vast volumes, of the private letters of Henry VIII. It was originally his intention to write a Life of this monarch, but when he found that another historian had preceded him in this field he used his material as the basis for his trilogy. His researches led him also to make an important contribution to art criticism, through a monograph on *Hans Holbein the Younger*, which was published by Duckworth in 1905. For at least two years, however, his normal productivity was held up by his illness. In 1902, he had published a little book on Rossetti through Duckworth, but nothing new came from his pen in 1903 and 1904 except a small volume of poems called *The Face of the Night*, issued by John Macqueen in the latter year. In 1905, however, apart from the book on the younger Holbein referred to above, his novel *The Benefactor* appeared through Brown Langham & Co., also the first of his books to be issued by the firm of Alston Rivers. This was *The Soul of London*, the first of three monographs on English life and character, the others being *The Heart of the Country* and *The Spirit of the People*. The three books were issued in New York in 1907, in an omnibus volume called *England and the English*, almost his first appearance on the American literary scene, apart from *The Inheritors*. The flattering welcome accorded by the reviewers to *The Soul of London* no doubt largely helped, by affecting Ford's "state of mind", to complete his cure.

A series of letters sent to Ford and to Mrs. Elsie Hueffer by William Michael Rossetti, between November 1903, and October 1904, reveal their writer's generous and kindly nature, his unfailing sympathy with Ford's misfortunes and his active interest in the work on which Ford was at the time engaged. In a letter written on 10th November, 1903, after sympathizing with Elsie Hueffer's serious accident, "a fall down ten feet of stone steps seems a shocking thing merely to hear of", he offers to lend Ford a complete set of photographs of Holbein's famous English portraits in Windsor Castle, which "used to belong to Gabriel". He says he is reading *Romance*, by Ford and Conrad, which he finds "most truly clever and vivid, and the 'sutures' between the 2 collaborators hardly apparent to any reader". In a postscript he remarks that the phrase "all serene wh. I see two or three times in *Romance* is, I am sure, an anachronism. I can myself quite recollect when this phrase first came into use—wh. may be towards 1858 or so. Previous generations were happily ignorant of that refinement of English speech".

Writing again, three days later, he discusses the character of Katharine Howard who, he fears, was "a slightly scabreuse female"; refers to the "rather shabby observations in the *Athenaeum*" (presumably a review of *Romance*) and thanks Ford for giving him "news of poor Elsie: bad news, yet not the worst that might have been. Your Father (I suppose at Hythe in 1883) had a nearly similar accident under my own eye: it gave him a shaking but did not entail anything grave". In the spring of 1904 Ford and Elsie Hueffer decided to migrate to London. The months which Ford spent in the large and most inconvenient house on Campden Hill, referred to in the Henry James correspondence, had disastrous consequences to his own and his wife's health. In the hope of recovering he stayed for some weeks in the summer of 1904 in a village in the New Forest, on the recommendation of W. H. Hudson. While there, he seems to have become seriously ill, and, as already mentioned, went abroad by himself in search of a cure for his neurasthenia and chronic depression.

Earlier, in the autumn of 1903, Ford seems to have spent some time in London, seeing various literary friends and acquaintances, among them John Galsworthy. When Ford was interested, "taken out of himself", he was always able to forget his worries, illnesses and all the serious complications of his life. Thus even at his most harassed and despairing moments, he almost invariably presented an outward appearance of cheerfulness and normality. He was naturally reticent about his private affairs and did not obtrude his afflictions, at least outside the domestic circle. During his visits to London, therefore, it is unlikely that anyone noticed anything wrong. On the subject of literary technique he was always able to talk and correspond, with complete absorption in his favourite theme. His connection, never a very close one, with John Galsworthy, was due principally to Conrad, who was, in a sense, Galsworthy's protégé and always his devoted friend. While in London Ford had rooms not far from Galsworthy, and the two writers, for a brief period, formed the habit of "dropping in" on one another to discuss their books. These conversations resulted in correspondence, of which the following letters from Galsworthy form a part.

> 16a Aubrey Walk,
> Campden Hill, W.
> Oct. 26th [1903].

MY DEAR HUEFFER,

Your welcome writing and the still more welcome volume within came this morning, and was warmly and gratefully taken in. As you know, I think, I have only read the last few pages of the book and the first few, and I have a thirst for what lies between. I wish you a great success.

Please tell your wife from me how much I enjoyed and appreciated her translation of Maupassant's stories. I thought it very good, and especially *The Return* and *Night*, which by the way I think the most powerful of the collection. . . . What are *you* doing now? I have just revised my book *The Pharisees* for Heinemann, coming out in January; and am full of a novel, which however makes no progress.

Let me know when you are coming up to town.

> Ys very sincerely,
> JOHN GALSWORTHY.

By the way I'm dropping my *nom de plume*.

Address on envelope:

> Ford M. Hueffer Esq.,
> The Bungalow,
> Winchelsea,
> Nr. Rye,

Sussex.

> 16a Aubrey Walk,
> Campden Hill, W.
> Ap. 14th 04.

MY DEAR HUEFFER,

I feel like a pig and an impostor for having by a slipshod annotation opened the flood gates of your wrath and let out so much of your vital energy, especially as I agree with nearly every word you say. The fact is my note was meant to say (I can't remember what it did say) that: *talking of the third state which you mention* (man looking out of club window all which I took to mean an important quiescent enjoyment of things going on round you) non-artists would feel IT, i.e. third state when they were slightly drunk and artists at other times as well. You have turned my note to psy-turvy. I quite agree with you that non-artists feel, more deeply, more personally, and pathetically than artists, because they lack the impersonal, analytic, philosophic element; or at all events they feel more deeply for all practical purposes because they have nothing outside the personal to compare with their suffering and through which to fritter down the edge thereof.

You are evidently so sick for personal reasons of the word "artist" that I regret to have employed it, and perhaps we do not mean the same thing by the word (which I used for lack of a better). After all in your book, and in this discussion we are trying to talk philosophically, that is to really fix the essential main difference in the constitution of human beings, which is by the way of course, only a question of degree [unreadable] two sides of an invisible line approaching thereto till they merge. So that let us assume that you sink for the moment the natural indignation against all the snobbish cant that is talked by painters and men of letters—d—n their eyes.

I use the word "artist" to include roughly people with more of the outside eye, habit of impersonal reflection, analytical spirit, and incidentally in some cases power of expression, than the rest of mankind. I don't exalt these people, I merely say that I think they form the one half of mankind—a smaller half than the other of course.

This may be too wide a definition of the word "artist" but it will serve as well as any other for the purpose of a discussion, for it fixes a definite meaning to a definite word which we are using.

I think these people are those who are given to generalities in thought, i.e. not parrotwise; and I think on the whole they form a smaller proportion in the English nation than they do in some others, most others. I remember that W— wrote to me after reading *Villa Rubein* and told me he did not believe in the "artistic temperament"—I suppose that he also was suffering from revolt. I have heard just enough cant talked to know that I also should suffer if I heard more; but all this personal revolt is beside the mark. The possession of the impersonal eye in a greater or less degree is the quality which marks mankind off to one side of the line or the other (and this is incidentally what lies behind the much overpraised and much over-abused "artistic temperament").

That *feeling* and the *impersonal eye* are the very antitheses is fairly obvious; but here again we are likely to get into a tangle over the word "feeling", and perhaps I had better close down for the present.

I'm so glad you're settled in comfortably, but I shall miss you very much—it was nice to feel one could "drop-in". If I ever do any more "Forsytes" I will send it to you, in the meantime why not send me Chap V and risk some more slipshod annotations? You see I thought I was going to talk the thing over with you, rubbing out any remarks as I went along. All good wishes to yr wife.

Ever yrs,
JOHN GALSWORTHY.

A writer for whom Ford had an intense admiration was the American-born naturalist, W. H. Hudson. When the symptoms of his nervous breakdown first became apparent, Ford, as already recorded, seems to have thought that a change to the seclusion of the New Forest, which Hudson knew so intimately, might benefit his health. Accordingly he wrote to Hudson to ask if he could recommend a place to stay in and received the replies which follow:

Martin,
Salisbury.

April. 2

MY DEAR HUEFFER,

I am in Wiltshire as you see, in a village ten miles from Salisbury. I have stayed here before, also in other villages and towns in the county, but always in inns or cottages, so I do not know, and have not stayed in any farmhouse. There's no inn here, but being resolved to find a place to stay in I was at length accommodated in a cottage, and have a big room with a ceiling which I can touch with my head and a brick floor. It is the best room in what was anciently a farmhouse. The bedroom is rather difficult of access as the way is up a winding stair, which threatens to collapse as I go up. But apart from the difficulty of finding rooms to live in here—and I mean in this downland country of S. Wilts—I cannot think it would have any attraction for you and Mrs. Hueffer at this season. It is so bare and bleak, almost treeless, and I should think very depressing to anyone who was not enamoured of solitude. The farm where I have stayed often in Hampshire is

Rollstone,
Southampton

and you go to it from Beaulieu Road Station, eight or nine miles. If you arrange to go there the farmer, Mr. Snell, goes with his pony cart to meet you. Unfortunately you have to put up with very coarse fare, as the farmer's wife is absorbed in her proper work and does not trouble much about the stranger in her gates. Another much better place is Roydon House, a pretty little old manor house half way between the two nice villages of Brockenhurst and Boldre. It is in the woods close to the Boldre or Lymington river, and the rooms are nice—the people—Hooker by name—very attentive and kind and open to do things. I can't tell you about the terms, as I have always lived with them as one of the family when I have been there, getting up to prayers and breakfast at seven in the morning and so on. It is not a farm although they keep a few cows in the meadows belonging to the house. It is a pretty spot, and the two villages near have the two best of the old New Forest churches. From Roydon you walk through Brockenhurst park to go to the village. If you should think of trying that part the best way wd be to write to

Mrs. Hooker,
Roydon House,
Lymington,
Hants,

for particulars. But I must warn you that you cannot smoke a pipe with Mr. Hooker as he is agin all the things which the unregenerate man loves. You wd have to smoke your pipe all alone by yourself.

Another nice spot in Hampshire where I have been several times is Bronsbury close to Longparish, on the Test. It is a hamlet by the river, and if not too wet is a delightful spot. One stays at the inn—"The Sheepcrook and Shears" kept by a remarkable woman, Mrs. Bliss, who knows how to cook, and is most attentive and—very entertaining. We that know Mrs. Bliss smile when we mention her, but we love her. Her terms to the wealthy angler are high but she takes me and other persons I know at quite moderate terms. Close to the Crook and Shears there are some interesting British earthworks called the Ansdyke, and Longparish and Cherwell are near. The Longparish station on the L.S.W. is quite near to Bronsbury. I wish I knew of more good places to tell you, but I really can't recommend the cottages where I have been in such out-of-the-world villages as this.

With kind regards,
Yours sincerely,
W. H. Hudson.

Martin.

Friday evening (late).

DEAR HUEFFER,

A thousand thanks for the book which I found this evng on coming back from a six hours' ramble on the windy downs —dead tired. And there was a paper to be gone over and corrected too, which had to be done at once as I wish to leave here in the morning. You couldn't have sent me anything better. Yesterday it was in my mind when you spoke of the London book to ask you why you didn't write more verse, but something put it out. I have always liked your verse very much, and I love poetry. If you are serious in saying you can't read verse then I'm sorry for you. I am like Minermus—with a difference. He was all for Aphrodite and the bed of desire, and cried that when these naughty things failed him he would be ready to die. When I can no longer read verse then let *me* die. I know Yew Tree House very well, tho' I never stayed there, and as for the Common, there's not a whin bush on it I am not intimate with. You will be within a very easy walk of good old Roydon House, and I wish you wd go with Mrs. Hueffer and the children to see it, and that you will go in and see the Hookers, especially Maude, my chum, and give them news of me.

Yours cordially,
W. H. HUDSON.

Martin,
Salisbury.

Sunday evening.

MY DEAR HUEFFER,

I am here still—or here again, and shall stay until Tuesday, when I go up. I have to be in town this week, and with the weather as it is it seemed idle to go on to those lonelier high downs beyond the Nadder which I had intended visiting. I must do my business and come down to those parts in a little while. Yesterday I had a long day in an interesting part of Dorset, between Cranborne and Venwood, and at Hinton Martel spent an hour with an old shepherd of eighty-four who was born here —son of a shepherd who died here aged eighty-seven. These Martinites are tough people.

To-day, after morning service, I enjoyed reading your poems, which are all good, but I like those in dramatic form best. Perseverance D'Amour is a fascinating piece. And where I should like to know did you get that legend of St. Aethelburga if not in the wilderness of your own brain! That quotation with no author named looks suspicious. It is a beautiful idea, and is similar to Olive Schreiner's in one of her "Dreams"—"The White(?) View", the best thing she ever did, I think, excepting some of "An African Farm". After writing "The Mother" it is rather absurd of you to try to believe that we can ever live healthy happy lives apart from nature. No we can't in spite of the Jews. By the way, a large proportion of the Jewish aliens who come to us, and whose children are so much healthier than those of our poor native Londoners, are from villages, and they too will perhaps deteriorate even as our country people do when they settle in the towns. Do you know, I think the author of *Thanks whilst Unharnessing* ought to be a member of the Society for the Protection of Birds. An annual subscription—any amount from a shilling—sent to the Secretary, 3 Hanover Square, W.I, would be all. I mean you *two*—the poet and his wife who discussed "Grey Matter". I am sending the book to a friend to read—one who loves poetry and is ever eager for something fresh. Do you know young Coventry Patmore's verse: he has just published a small collection: but he will not, I fancy, rise to the height of old C. P.

Yours,
W. H. Hudson.

19 Birkenhead Avenue,
Kingston-on-Thames.
June 10

Dear Hueffer,

Thanks for your letter, but I assure you I do not know any blade of grass at that place. Nor can I tell you of a guide-book. One or two of the Salisbury guides mention some of the villages and places near, but I never used them and I fancy you will have to be your own guide in that remote and unconsidered district. I wish I could get away before it gets too late in the season for [unreadable] birds and spring flowers, but I fear I am stuck here for some time. I have some business to finish before I can leave Kingston where I've been these six weeks past.

Here is a copy of my last work[1] hot from the press. This three-colour process is still in the experimental stage and the colours can't be got quite right. They come out rather too strong in

---

[1] "A Linnet for Sixpence."

the linnet—in the red of the breast especially, and in the green of the furze.

In the original drawing the colours were very true—soft and brilliant.

Perhaps before the summer is over I shall drop in to see you one day, but all my Wiltshire plans are pretty well knocked on the head.

My best regards to Mrs. Hueffer.

Yours,

W. H. HUDSON.

Address on Envelope: Ford M. Hueffer, Esq.,
        Bridge House,
        Winterbourne Stoke,
        nr. Salisbury.

The village in which Ford subsequently found what he wanted and in which he spent some weeks with his wife and daughters before going to Germany, as the address on the envelope of the last of Hudson's letters indicates, was Winterbourne Stoke.

During his absence abroad Ford managed to pull himself together sufficiently to write to Conrad who, as the following replies show, proved helpful and sympathetic, in spite of his usual preoccupation with his own afflictions. The reference to Pinker in the first letter, suggests that both Ford's novel *The Benefactor*, a "projection" of his father-in-law Dr. Martindale, who had died in 1902, and also *The Soul of London*, were already completed and in his agents' hands before his health broke down.

The Pent.

5th Sept. 1904.

MY DEAR FORD,

Don't imagine I have not been thinking of you in all the concern of the sympathy and affection which exist between us. Four days ago I finished the book. I wrote to no one—except to Elsie in answer to a letter I had from her. I spoke of your last missive to me favourably. That was the true impression. Distinctly favourable.

I received it just as I was starting to see Pinker about my own deplorable affairs.

I was unable to see Dunn that day. Perhaps it's just as well. The idea of correspondence from Germany has been very much in my mind even in my half delirious state of finishing *Nostromo*. I have meditated upon it since. But of evil, great evil, some little good may spring. To expect much good out of anything is useless; though cases have been known. . . .

Of course your illness is a serious matter, you must not be worried. But I've been struck by your letter, it contains much promise. Why not correspond in that tone? And even correspond with me—if you like; if you think that the idea of a concrete recipient of your prose may help you in the least. Write *currente calamo*. Trust me to have the thing properly typed. And if points are to be made I'll attend to that. In the state of nerves from which you suffer any mention of Pinker may be exasperating. But it is unavoidable. So I'll only say that the man says and repeats that he has always been, still is, and intends to continue in a state of readiness to handle your stuff. He says he will make special efforts. The fact is my dear boy that without understanding you in the least the man likes you personally. He also nurses in his mind a by no means irrational idea of your usefulness. You are for him the man who can write anything at any time—and write it well—he means in a not ordinary way. His belief in you is by no means shaken. He admits in effect that he has failed both with the London and the novel. But he does not admit that he has failed finally. The things are not topical. They exist. They are not lost.

Write then (if you can and only when you can) the German correspondence, with remarks on Authors, Landowners, Officers —Officials—and the language.

Write down what you see; and if you are well enough to put your tongue in your cheek, put it there and fire off a general consideration or two upon the rôle of Germany in the future of Europe. Raise a whisper of German peril—or German blessing

—what you will. Something for the great stupid. But mainly describe. And if you can write twaddle——! So much the better.

Directly I get something I shall make a sort of expedition—a crusade.

Phoo! I am weary. For more than a month I have been sitting up till three a.m.—ending with a solid thirty-six hours (in the middle of which I had to wire for the dentist and have a tooth drawn! . . .) It broke! ! . . ! ! Till at 11.30 *I* broke down just after raising my eyes to the clock.

Then I don't know, two blank hours during which I must have got out and sat down—(not fallen) on the concrete outside the door.

That's how I found myself; and crawling in again noted the time; considerably after one.

But I've finished. There's no elation, no relief even. Nothing. Moreover I've yet a good fortnight's work for the book form.

The miserable rubbish is to be shot out on the muckheap before this month is out. I'll send you the book. I am weary! Weary.

As soon as I recover I shall try and write something sensible to you. If this letter irritates you, you must forgive me. My mind runs on disconnected like the free wheel of a bicycle.

I feel going downhill as it were.

Love from us all,

Ever yours,

J. CONRAD.

22nd November 1904.

MY DEAREST FORD,

I am bitterly ashamed of my criminal remissness in writing to you; but you know me enough *à fond* to understand my state of utter exhaustion after finishing the accursed *Nostromo*. Do you know my dear fellow that the almost full half of that book has been written in five months! From end of March to end of August. All September was taken up in revision and writing up at high pressure. And what energy that was left after that bout had to be used for writing on and on infernal things for sale.

And still it has to go on though I feel half dead mentally and very shaky physically with a sort of choking fit every day which I hope is nothing more than asthma.

We came here about five weeks ago. Got into this flat. Then the doctors got to work upon Jessie. Her general state is not satisfactory but the great matter was the knee.

And the matter has dragged. She has been a week now in a Nursing Home near Harley Street with Bruce Clarke the joint specialist Surgeon, lecturer at Barts., in charge of the case.

Various rather horrible things have taken place. The examination under chloroform was made four days ago, and would you imagine? the mischief was not located—it was not even found. As a matter of fact B. Clarke (as good a man as there is) took his patient for a pampered silly sort of little woman who was making no end of fuss for a simple stiff joint. You may imagine to what horrible pain he put her acting on that assumption. I daren't trust myself to write it. *Assez.*

The long and short of it is that he found his mistake. The cartilage is displaced and must have been so for thirteen years since her first accident when she was seventeen! That no disease of the bones was set up Tebb[1] (and also Clarke) accounts for by the large quantity of fluid always present which prevented the displaced cartilage from granulating and as it were infecting the bones.

Clarke owned up his mistake the day before yesterday, like a man. Yesterday he wired for me and told me he had no doubt now; he could feel the displacement now; had felt it on three separate occasions. "I can put my finger on it every time," he said (I felt as if I could strangle him).

His compunction was very visible. What would you have! He is a good operator with a great reputation for carrying his cures through. The operation is fixed for the day after to-morrow, Thursday, at noon.

Voilà. And all this time I have been writing! I've written since we came here a thing on H. James, a paper on London River (for the *World's Work*) and [an] imbecile short story

---

[1] " The doctor, friend of W. M. Rossetti, admirer of your grandfather."

(2,500 words) for the *Strand*. To-day even I did 500 words dictating to Miss Hallowes. But I could not muster courage enough till now to sit down and write you a letter, though there is not a day you haven't been in my thoughts.

This is all for to-day or rather for to-night. I shall write you a *real* letter in a few days. I've been meeting a few men lately. The sound of your name is not allowed to die out of the land. But I can't enlarge just now; the natural egoism of a suffering man will not allow it at present. Jessie and Borys, your great friends, send their love. As to mine it is always with you.

Yours ever,
CONRAD.

A reference to Ford's illness occurs in a letter from William Michael Rossetti dated 3rd October, 1904. After praying Ford to think no more "about that tin", presumably a loan which he says Ford is to regard as a free gift, the kind and generous old man continues: "Your letter has filled me with concern—but it allows me to infer that you have now turned the corner, and are on the high road to recovery. I had not known anything about your disheartening condition until 21st Sept., when Olive Garnett, calling here, gave me some information regarding it."

Writing to Elsie Hueffer on 22nd October, he says "it relieves my mind not a little to learn that Cathy (Ford's mother) has gone off to look after Ford. Some such step was I think highly requisite, and likely to produce as good an effect as anything else cd do. I am glad too that the account of him wh you give is even a *little* better."

The problem of the financial insecurity of the independent artist was one which had always weighed heavily on William Michael Rossetti's mind and in this letter he again returns to it. "The question whether Ford shd get, or try to get into some regular *groove* of writing, apart from pursuing a wholly speculative career of authorship is," he remarks, "again a ticklish one. My own opinion is—yes. I (having always earned a settled income, small and then increasing) cannot but regard as very anxious and risky the position of a man with a family who has nothing beyond his talents as an author to rely upon; for the remuneration of those talents depends, not upon their being real or even fine, but upon the capricious likings of the public. I myself shd always have liked to be a literary personage, doing literary work of my own, as best I cd: my position did not allow of this, and what I had to be was a Government clerk giving his spare hours to newspaper critiques, etc."

A few days later, after hearing from Ford, his anxiety was increased and he was in two minds whether or not to reply. Writing to Elsie Hueffer (28th October, 1904) he says: "Consequent on your letter of yesterday, I thought I might just as well send a few friendly words to our dear Ford—as per enclosed. I enclose them to you, to dispatch or not as you see the more fitting. Probably the safest course might be for you to transmit them to Cathy, for her to deliver or not according to the dictate of the moment.

"I certainly think (replying to a point in your letter) that the immediate cause of Ford's gloomy self-estimate is depression, rather than serious illness. The serious illness has been there to cause the depression and I suppose still is there—but I shd very much hope both curable and abating."

In the letter to Ford, referred to above, he pointed out that "so young a man as you, with so many talents, is surely warranted in looking upon matters from the brighter side. There must be tens of thousands of people going about, 'from China to Peru', or from Port Arthur to the Dogger Bank, who have had severe nervous breakdowns, and under proper treatment have recovered, and do all their work as well as ever. I cannot but assume that the treatment wh you are now undergoing is judicious, and your Doctor's assurance sincere—so there is every reason to hope". It is not recorded if it was judged advisable to pass on to Ford these friendly words. His state of mind must have been morbid in the extreme if it was thought they could do him harm.

Any attempt on the part of a biographer to trace the movements of Ford and his wife during the years 1904 and 1905, to provide dates for their frequent journeys or to place their changes of habitation in correct chronological order, would now be doomed to failure. All we can say with certainty is that they retained the Bungalow at Winchelsea as their base of operations, that Ford almost continuously and Elsie Hueffer for long periods, was very ill, and that, in the spring of 1904, they made their ill-fated move to 10 Airlie Gardens on the top of Campden Hill. Apart from this, Mrs. Hueffer paid a long visit to Rome, by herself, where she met her Italian uncle-by-marriage, who had the title of Baron and lived in a "Palazzo"; while Ford's mother stayed in Germany with the invalid. "Cathy" took Christina and Katharine with her and it was in Germany, no doubt more to please the rich relations than because Ford took the religion of his fathers very seriously, that his daughters were received into the Roman Catholic Church. A summer visit, as before mentioned, was paid to Winterbourne Stoke, and, after Ford went abroad, William Michael Rossetti invited Elsie Hueffer and the children to occupy 3, St. Edmund's Terrace during his absence, while alterations were being made to the Bungalow.

It was, no doubt, to their attempt to set up house-keeping in London while some of the uncle's legacy still remained, that many subsequent misfortunes must be attributed. By a strange coincidence, of which Ford seems to have been unaware till later, a previous tenant of 10 Airlie Gardens had been his brother Oliver who, had he known in time, would certainly have warned him against it. The few months which Ford and his wife spent in this "heart-break house", were punctuated by severe attacks of influenza and every kind of minor adversity. On one occasion, through the carelessness of a maid, Ford's elder daughter's hair caught fire and a serious accident was only narrowly averted. The house was tall, ugly, badly designed and impossible to run without a large staff of servants. The effort to cope with her house-keeping difficulties resulted for Elsie Hueffer in a serious illness, through which her mother nursed her. Of Ford's collapse details have already been given.

What, we may suppose, contributed as much as anything to his recovery was the success of his book *The Soul of London*, which appeared in 1905.

From Winchelsea we find him writing to Walter Jerrold telling him that he was instructing Alston Rivers to send a copy of this book to the *Observer*. "The rather overpowering reception of the work over-excited me a little and has knocked me over a little, so I can't write letters and have hundreds to write—— But let us talk when we meet." Jerrold seems to have gone to stay with Ford at the Bungalow, in Elsie Hueffer's absence. In another undated letter, Ford writes from 226 Finchley Road, N.W., to say he is "still alive—and the least said about my miseries, no doubt the better—though your sympathy is good . . . I rejoice that you're all right. It makes the world seem a better place". Among the "miseries" referred to was probably, though the lack of dates makes this guess-work, the serious illness of his wife. In a letter headed "93 Broadhurst Gdns. N.W." he says: "the above address points to the fact that Elsie was taken very much worse after you left and had to be removed to her mother's house to be nursed". He goes on, "she asks me to ask you whether you could or would take a day or two off with me— say at Winchelsea. I have represented to her that you're a busy man and so on—but she insists I shd make the request. It's difficult for me to find a congenial companion—though I'd willingly pay expenses and so on. If you cd manage it, it would be delightful for me: if you couldn't, do you know of anyone—that one could talk to—who could? It would be an extreme service!"

More interesting to the reader than the details of Ford's ill-nesses are the glimpses we can get of his London social life. At the beginning of the century the National Liberal Club was prominent as a centre for rising politicians, publishers and men of letters. Ford was a member of it from 1904 to 1908, when he joined the smaller Author's Club, also in Whitehall Court. Among his other friends and acquaintances who were fellow-members of the Liberal stronghold were C. F. G. Masterman (1903–1927), H. G. Wells (1901–1932), Walter Jerrold (1906–1913), and Ford's close friend and publisher, R. B. Byles (1901–1908). Byles was manager of the firm of Alston Rivers of which the Hon. Lancelot Bathurst and Archibald Marshall were directors.

Other publishers who were members were T. Fisher Unwin, who used to give evening parties on its terrace, and T. Werner Laurie.

More important as a meeting place for authors was an anonymous luncheon club which met every Friday in the Mont Blanc restaurant in Gerrard Street. I am indebted to Mr. Philip Tilden, F.R.I.B.A., for the following account of these remarkable gatherings.

"I first went to the Mont Blanc with Gerald Bishop in 1906," Mr. Tilden writes. "It was the only time I ever knew Gerald Bishop to go there after he took me there. The Mont Blanc had been chosen for its utter emptiness, and the fact that it was central and cheap. Edward Garnett had chosen it with Edward Thomas. They liked it because we got all we wanted to eat for about 10d. to 1s. 1d. a time. Edward drank no wine. The round-faced Swiss proprietor had a fine-looking dark-haired wife who sat in the box and received our pennies and a pretty little daughter used to take mysterious people upstairs—one of those 1680 barley-sugar stairs varnished over and very dark. (Most of the visitors were young men.) When I went there in 1906 the luncheons had not long been started and the only visitors were *always* Garnett and Thomas (the latter was living at Steep near Petersfield), W. H. Hudson about every month and Archer about the same. Another name has come into my mind: March Phillips. I don't think that Garnett liked Ford (physically, I mean). I think that a sort of fleshly dislike upset our talks, for we must remember that all these men were of very definite character. Hudson, so modest and unassuming, Archer, very quiet and looking unlike what one expected of him. By the way, it was over the lunch table that Edward Garnett told W. Archer to write a play that would fulfil his own critical demands of the playwrights. The result was *The Green Goddess*. I went to live with Edward Thomas and his wife for six months in 1908 and by that time many more people had joined the lunches. I think I mentioned W. H. Davies, Stephen Reynolds, the fisherman novelist (whom I quarrelled with all the time), Baerlein and I know there were others." In another letter Mr. Tilden recalls that of "the permanencies" Ford was one of the chief ones. "I remember that blond hair of his so well and his blue eyes—he reminded me in very great measure of the Prince Consort . . . Conrad used to come at intervals."

Mr. Tilden recalls that, in the *English Review* days (1909) Edward Garnett was "terribly snappy with Ford M. H. across the table. They had a row about something that Edward wanted Ford to put into the *English Review*, and which never got there".

"All this seems terribly rambling," Mr. Tilden adds, "but I can say that: (*a*) Edward Garnett and E. Thomas chose the Mont Blanc (later Taglionis). They liked the shop opposite—I've forgotten the name, but he was a 'sword maker'. (*b*) E. G. and Ford quarrelled over some work for the *English Review*, and it just put the extra grain on to the donkey's back, for they really never liked each other. Edward told me one day that Ford was 'too blond for him'."

On the occasion when the writer, then a tongue-tied youth of twenty-one, was taken by Ford to one of these exciting meals, W. H. Hudson, Conrad and Garnett were certainly present, possibly also Henry Baerlein and Edward Thomas. The others I did not know by sight or name. To me, at so impressionable an age, they might have been veritable Dr. Johnsons, Goldsmiths, Hazlitts, and Leigh Hunts, and I noticed that they were all intimate enough to be extremely outspoken to each other.

Another group of literary men of which Ford was a member at this period, met for dinner once a month over a restaurant in Fleet Street. G. K. Chesterton had been, if I remember right, the founder. Its name was "The Square Club" and most of the members, as Edgar Jepson records in his *Edwardian Memories,* were literary critics of the heavy academic type. When I was taken to dine there one evening, by my editor, it was apparent that Ford was somewhat out of his element.

In 1906, after Ford had established a more or less permanent foothold in London, he and his wife entertained numerous guests at week-end parties in their Winchelsea home. Mr. Ferris Greenslet, a Boston publisher and literary critic, in his autobiography *Under the Bridge*, recalls a visit paid to the hospitable Bungalow.

"I week-ended at Winchelsea," he writes, "where Ford Madox Hueffer, later Ford, freeholder of the Cinque Ports, who could wear his hat in the presence of the King, was advising both Conrad and Galsworthy in their early efforts. There I heard talk of a different flavour from any I had known in Boston and Cambridge. We drove over the marshes to Rye to pay respects to Henry James, but when the long white Georgian door opened inward from the village street a dour housekeeper, Mrs. Bathsheba Paddington, informed us: 'He isn't home. I sent him away for my spring-cleaning, and I'll not have him back till it's entirely transacted'."

Mr. Greenslet, whose leg Ford could rarely resist pulling, as the nonsense about keeping his hat on in the King's presence indicates, may have encouraged Ford to pay his first visit to the United States. In any case, Ford and Elsie Hueffer set sail for the U.S.A. at the end of July, 1906, were greeted with the usual American hospitality and made a number of friends and acquaintances before returning to England towards the end of October. Like so many British tourists before them and after them, they arrived impressively in a crack liner, the *Kaiserin Augusta Victoria*, which had a thousand passengers on board. After spending much more money than they anticipated, they returned, less impressively, on the Atlantic Transport liner *Minnetonka* which carried a thousand cattle, a dozen race horses and only sixty passengers. In his book *Return to Yesterday* (1931) addressed principally to an American audience, Ford, in order to emphasize his American sympathies and curry favour with his readers, invented a story to the effect that, when a boy of less than twenty, he had spent a year in the Deep South, studying farming on his uncle's estate. It was no more than a daydream; indeed there is no evidence that he ever saw the "oncle d'Amérique", a small share of whose wealth he inherited.

At some period in 1906, during the Times Book Club controversy, the dynamic "stunt" expert, Lord Northcliffe—populariser of standard bread, sweet peas and *Daily Mail* hats—decided to take up literature in a big way, in rivalry to the *Times Literary Supplement*. The *Daily Mail* venture was called *Books* and had an office of its own in Sackville Street. The services of the highly respected Edmund Gosse were secured as director of this publication and Mr. Archibald Marshall was appointed his assistant. Among the contributors were Robert Ross, Austin Dobson and P. G. Konody. Gosse, for a variety of reasons, had long been Ford's *bête noire* and his dislike was actively reciprocated by the editor of *Books*, who would not print, or have anything to do with, Ford at any price. Gosse's open antagonism prompted an amusing practical joke, over which Ford scored heavily. Using his brother Oliver's *nom de guerre*, "Jane Wardle", Ford submitted a poem which Gosse accepted and published. After six months Northcliffe got rid of Gosse and promoted Marshall to succeed him. Marshall, at that period, had a great admiration for Ford, who had been of service to him in many ways, particularly by introducing him to Conrad, Henry James, and other literary figures, and at once called him in as a regular contributor. Ford took no part in editing the paper, Marshall asserts, but suggested ideas for brightening it and wrote a weekly "feature" article consisting of a character sketch of some contemporary writer. These were to have been illustrated by Max Beerbohm, but the arrangement fell through. Marshall maliciously states that Ford pinched two of Max's cartoons and walked off with them. As Max subsequently contributed to the *English Review* and showed no sign of resentment against its editor when the writer was sent to call on him, the charge reveals more about Marshall than about Ford. For several months, Ford, Marshall, Thomas Seccombe, the historian, Stephen Reynolds, and various other critics and men of letters not only enlivened the columns of *Books* but made its office the centre of much social intercourse and informal literary discussion. Of Reynolds, Ford had a high appreciation, both as a man and a writer. He had been educated at Manchester University and taken a degree in science. After a severe illness he went to live in a Devonshire fishing village, in the home of a longshore fisherman called Bob Woolley, and soon became an acknowledged authority on Fisheries. He was a big, stocky man, wore spectacles and always a blue suit. As he was usually hard up, his visits to London were not very frequent, but Ford admired his work, serialised his novel *The Holy Mountain* in the *English Review*, and wished to make him a sort of assistant editor. Their mutual respect did not prevent them from indulging in violent arguments.

For some reason or other, probably temperamental, Ford proved too much for Thomas Marlowe, editor in chief of the *Daily Mail*, and Northcliffe, with whom Ford had had only one interview, finally sacked him. Ford threatened an action, claiming two years' pay, but was sensible enough to drop it. The incident, which occurred during the years in which his friend R. B. Byles of the firm of Alston Rivers was his principal publisher, evidently left a deep and probably painful impression on Ford's mind, for a quarter of a century later we find the whole affair made the basis of an entertaining piece of fiction in *Return to Yesterday*. Archibald Marshall asserts that practically all Ford's stories about Alston Rivers, R. B. Byles, his interviews with Lord North-cliffe and the nature of his association with *Books* are apocryphal, and it would be unwise not to accept this. Ford says he met Byles accidentally, in a train going to Rye, Byles being on the way to interview Henry James in the hope of securing one of his works for publication by his firm. Marshall denies this flatly and says that "the possibility of our publishing the work of Henry James never entered our heads, and Byles never took the slightest part in procuring manuscripts or interviewing authors. Actually Ford met Byles in a train going to Walham Green, and he told him we were hoping to get hold of a novel by Ranger Gull". The probability is that Ford owed his connection with Alston Rivers to the activity on his behalf of J. B. Pinker. What is undoubtedly true is that he took a great liking to Byles, no matter how their first meeting took place, and that Byles remained his devoted and loyal friend until his death. He was an extremely pugnacious, warm-tempered and dynamic little man and while he remained with Alston Rivers the rows and discords in the office seem to have been more or less continuous, especially as Bathurst—not "Hervey" as Ford calls him, but "Lancelot"—was not merely a phlegmatic pipe-smoker but, according to Mr. Grant Richards, had "heaps of decisive energy".

The books by Ford which Alston Rivers issued before Byles left them and the business was discontinued, were *The Soul of London*, already mentioned, which came out in 1905, followed by *The Fifth Queen*, *The Heart of the Country*, and *Christina's Fairy Book*, in the Pinafore Library, all in 1906; and *Privy Seal*, *From Inland*, a paper-covered volume in "The Contemporary Poets Series", and *The Spirit of the People* in 1907. In 1907 Ford also published, through Methuen, a novel called *An English Girl* and a monograph on *The Pre-Raphaelite Brotherhood*, in Duckworth's series of little books on art. The third of the "Fifth Queen" trilogy, *The Fifth Queen Crowned*, appeared through Eveleigh Nash in 1908.

This burst of productivity, concentrated in three years, though none of the books achieved a large sale, established Ford in the position to which he was entitled, that is to say, in the front rank of the younger generation of writers. The "Fifth Queen" trilogy and the three monographs on England and the English had an outstanding *succès d'estime* both in the press and among his fellow-writers. A small handful of the discerning, among them H. G. Wells, also recognised in him an admirable yet strangely unappreciated poet.

When *The Soul of London* appeared, Conrad was staying in Capri and Ford sent him an advance copy which evoked an enthusiastic reply. In a letter beginning "Dearest Old Boy", written on 9th May 1905, Conrad says:

"Hurrah for the Soul of London. Brute as I am by nature and training, I was touched by the sight of those pages so familiar in a way and so strange now, when far away from you I went off following your thought overleaf from page to page. . . . It was very dear and good of you to have sent it on without waiting for my return—which is now only a question of days."

On 20th February, 1908, after the publication of *The Fifth Queen Crowned*, Conrad wrote to John Galsworthy saying: "Ford's last *Fifth Queen* novel is amazing. The whole cycle is a noble conception—the swan song of Historical Romance—and frankly I am glad to have heard it."

At this moment Ford was fully entitled to consider himself on the crest of the wave. After many years of struggle his efforts had brought him the sort of recognition which every writer requires if he is to accomplish his best work. His long toil with Conrad, followed by months of illness which in turn had been followed by the excitement and liberation of London life had been at last amply rewarded. In 1908 he was thirty-five years old, no longer a *jeune homme modeste* but, in the estimation of others besides himself, a *jeune maître*. It was a thrilling moment in Ford's career; but success, like failure, makes severe calls upon a writer's character and capacity for self-control.

CHAPTER X

The English Review

FORD's account of the genesis of the *English Review*, repeated with little variation in several of his autobiographical works, ascribes the initial conception to Arthur Marwood, who was incensed to discover that all the existing literary periodicals had rejected a long poem by Thomas Hardy on account of the supposed indelicacy of its theme. This poem, "A Sunday Morning Tragedy"—not one of Hardy's best—undoubtedly filled the first four pages of the first number of the review, thus to some extent corroborating the anecdote. It is probable, however, that Ford's quarrel with the *Daily Mail* over his dismissal from the staff of *Books*, had a good deal to do, if only subconsciously, with his eagerness to assert himself in an editorial capacity. Marwood, if an excellent mathematician, was evidently as inexperienced in business matters as Ford. Although enthusiastic about the literary side of the undertaking, as the Hardy incident suggests, he seems also to have imagined that his contemplated investment might prove financially profitable. Whether Conrad and H. G. Wells, both of whom were extremely shrewd in regard to money matters, shared this strange illusion we have no means of knowing. The probability is that, from the first, they and others—knowing Ford's uncommercial character and outlook—had their doubts. Conrad's affection for Ford and respect for his literary gifts certainly made him anxious lest his adventure in editorship should impede his productivity as a creative artist. Whatever may have been the secret misgivings of Ford's inner circle, their belief in his ability, as well as the advantages to themselves which might accrue if his project materialised, combined to assure him of their moral support, at least to the extent of agreeing to contribute to the new venture. It was Ford's idea, from the start, to make it as far as possible a co-operative undertaking, with himself as a kind of director and co-ordinator. Advice was therefore sought from every approved quarter and preliminary discussions were, we may be sure, carried on at enormous length with all the members of Ford's group, from Conrad to Stephen Reynolds, from John Galsworthy to Edward Garnett, from Gerald Duckworth (the original publisher) to that experienced survivor of the "Henley gang", P. Anderson Graham, the editor of *Country Life*. The walls of the upper room in the Mont Blanc restaurant where the luncheon club already alluded to held their Friday reunions, must have resounded again and again to heated arguments, suggestions and criticisms.

The title of the review is said to have been suggested by Joseph Conrad. It had been used before by T. W. H. Crosland and Lord Alfred Douglas, as the title of a little-known periodical which had been allowed to lapse. When the gossip reached their ears that their title was to be revived, an effort was made by these two journalistic buccaneers to establish a claim to compensation. Whether they succeeded I cannot now remember, but the incident caused some anxiety, before it was closed. By the early summer of 1908 preparations were sufficiently far advanced for Ford to look about for a sub-editor. What he wanted was a youth who was experienced in proof-correction, and willing to undertake all the sub-editorial tasks without expecting to contribute. Accordingly he called one morning on Anderson Graham at the office of *Country Life*, to explain his requirements. Graham, with the speed of a conjurer producing a rabbit out of a hat, called in the junior member of his staff, myself, and before I understood what it was all about I found myself engaged. The arrangement was that I was to go to Ford's office in the evenings, after leaving *Country Life*.

My first assignment was to spend a week-end at my new chief's cottage at Aldington, where my first job was to take down, in longhand, a letter to Thomas Hardy, couched in terms of almost obsequious respect, asking permission to publish "A Sunday Morning Tragedy" in the first number of the new review and offering to pay £20 for it. After this incident, a hitch seems to have occurred in the financial arrangements and operations were

suspended until the autumn. I was then charged with the somewhat alarming task of finding Ford a secretary and, by great
good fortune, managed to secure the services of a remarkably
competent lady who, in after years, served Mr. Lloyd George
in a similar capacity. There followed hectic weeks of turmoil,
scurryings to and fro (on the part of the sub-editor), proof-
readings, consultations, correspondence, the production of a
"dummy" by the printer, discussions with the publisher, tele-
phonings, calls from contributors, calls from beggars, tea parties,
dinner parties, supper parties, and a thousand other excitements
and distractions, the whole terminating in a descent—by editor,
sub-editor and secretary—on the household of Joseph Conrad
who was then living near Luton. As these events have already
been described by the writer in *South Lodge,* there is no need to
elaborate them here.

The first number of the *English Review,* dated December 1908,
a stalwart, bulky affair in blue paper covers, came out, punctually,
after prodigious exertions in which Conrad had a share. It
provided the literary reader with more first-class writing than
had ever been collected before in a single issue of a monthly
periodical. A list of the contents will be sufficient to establish
the validity of this claim. Hardy's poem was followed by a
long short story by Henry James, called "A Jolly Corner."
Then came an instalment of Joseph Conrad's *Some Reminiscences,* a short story called "A Fisher of Men," by John Galsworthy, an essay on Stonehenge by W. H. Hudson, the first
part of a story by Tolstoi, newly-translated by Constance
Garnett, called "The Raid," and a long instalment of H. G.
Wells's new novel *Tono-Bungay.* This concluded the main
section of the review which was devoted exclusively to *belles-
lettres.* At the end there was an editorial section, devoted to
current events, containing comments by the editor and com-
munications from various writers on topics of the month. In
the first issue, apart from Ford's editorial exordium there were
articles by R. B. Cunninghame Graham and W. H. Davies on the
unemployment problem, the first part of "A Complete Actuarial
Scheme for Insuring John Doe against all the Vicissitudes

of Life" by "A.M." (Arthur Marwood), a study of the "Personality of the German Emperor" by an anonymous German diplomat, "Notes on the Balkans" by Henry W. Nevinson, a review of Anatole France's *L'Ile des Pingouins* by Joseph Conrad and one of Swinburne's *The Age of Shakespeare* by Dr. Levin Schücking of Göttingen University. I may perhaps be forgiven for interjecting that the task of reading the proofs of such a collection of new, unpublished work, by masters of their craft, was an unforgettable experience for a youth of twenty-one, the thrill of which is still easily recalled after a lapse of nearly forty years.

Ford's editorial paragraphs, which now seem rather pompous and over-elaborated, were mainly devoted to erecting a pedestal on which to stand the possibly embarrassed figure of Henry James. "The *English Review*," he says, "is a periodical devoted to the arts, letters and ideas and—to continue the 'freighter's' simile—with our passengers in the stern now we consider the horizon—for topics of the month!

" For a periodical devoted to arts and letters, to those fine things the humaner letters, the topics of the month are the production of a well-flavoured book, the commencement of a historical series, the production of a play not too shallow, the chronicling of a symphony, the opening of a gallery containing fine etchings. Thus to a review devoted—and let us emphasize the point—to the arts and to letters the publication of the first volume of Mr. James's collected edition is the topic of the month."

Although, as we have seen, James subsequently repudiated Ford and told Marshall that he would not touch Ford's book about himself at the end of a barge pole, it is extremely unlikely that even the Master was insensible to the respectful appreciation bestowed upon him in the columns of England's foremost literary periodical.

The references to the *English Review* in Conrad's published correspondence, throw interesting sidelights on its early days. In October 1908, after Ford had implored and cajoled him into beginning *Some Reminiscences*, he writes to Pinker to say that his literary reputation has already enough substance "to weigh favourably in the scale for the success of a *personal* book. This seems the psychological moment—and the appearance of a new *Review* is a good determining factor. My friendship for the editor (which is known) is a sufficient motive," Conrad goes on to say that it may be "so to speak, the chance of a life-time—coming neither too soon nor yet too late," for, he says, his acceptance as an English writer is now "an accomplished fact."

Conrad was the means of introducing his friend Norman Douglas to Ford, who accepted an essay by him for publication in the *Review*. Writing to Norman Douglas from Someries, Luton, on 29th September, 1908, Conrad says that Douglas's "Isle of Typhoeus" has been accepted for publication. "Hueffer, the editor (and my *intime*) asks you most heartily to call on him in a friendly way at 84 Holland Park Avenue as soon as ever you arrive in London. They have enough capital to go on for four issues. Then if the thing shapes well it will be continued—and may become a permanent outlet for your work. If the public does not respond to the new monthly magazine devoted to Art, letters and ideas—the publication will end with the fourth issue."

On 12th December, 1908, in a letter to Edward Garnett, Conrad asks: "Do you see the Editor [Ford] as of yore? He seems very busy. The *E.R.* looks noble and I hear from all sides that the first No. has gone off very well, remarkably so. Is that a fact? I am anxious to know, for I am anxious for Ford to make a success." Garnett evidently replied criticizing the way in which the *Review* was being conducted and four days later Conrad writes agreeing with his remarks. "Yes! You speak words of wisdom as to the *E.R.* That is the way. I've already said something to the same effect; but I don't want to appear as if I wished to meddle: the more so that I can't pretend to any experience—tho' I may have some 'sense'—of affairs."

How little sense of "affairs" Ford had at this period is demonstrated by a comic squabble with Arnold Bennett. If we may try to analyse Ford's attitude in the matter, it seems evident that he regarded all first-rate writers, among whom he naturally included himself, as being, at least potentially, on terms of easy familiarity with one another. This attitude may have been a remnant of that pre-Raphaelite Bohemianism which thought in terms of artist versus "tradesman", or "philistine". Ford also felt, very keenly, that the *English Review* was so clearly, so self-evidently a non-commercial undertaking that writers should automatically rally to its support by not exacting their commercial "price per thou".

Ford's first letter to Arnold Bennett, addressed c/o. H. G. Wells at Spade House, Sandgate, was despatched on 6th October, 1908. In it he asks Bennett if he has by any chance "a Five Towns story that you think would do for me? If so, would you send it along? I know I am late in writing to you, but that is not from lack of admiration for your work, but simply because I have not the pleasure of your acquaintance, as is the case with all my other contributors". He adds that probably Wells has told him all about the *Review* and signs himself "Yours cordially".

Something in Bennett's reply to this polite invitation seems to have irritated Ford, for on 24th November, 1908, just before the publication of the first issue, he dashed off a letter beginning:

"My dear Bennett, What the devil more did you expect me to write you after I had already written crawling on my belly in the dust before you to tell you that anything you sent would be published?" He goes on to mention a possible serial, which might start in the August number and adds "haven't you a Five Towns short story which could appear before then? Only don't ask me to write letters! I am ready to admire you any amount but though you are the busiest man on the Continent I am three times as busy as the busiest man in England". Bennett, evidently nonplussed by this communication, forwarded it to Pinker with a request for his observations. "I may say," he adds, "I have never met Hueffer."

Bennett left the fixing of terms for the short story he subsequently wrote for Ford—"The Matador of the Five Towns," which is generally conceded to be his masterpiece in this medium—to Pinker. Ford seems to have beaten Pinker down to a considerably lower figure than Bennett was accustomed to receive, which caused that business-like author considerable annoyance. In another undated letter Ford begins "Dear Mr. Arnold Bennett, Why sneer at 'a man like me'? I am really dreadfully busy but of course I will keep the August number open till I see your serial." After asking if Bennett can tell him of anyone who could write him at short notice an article on the International Outlook from a Frenchman's point of view in French, he adds "please remember that I want a short story—of any length as long as it is long, and that I will pay a pretty good price for it". Ford, like Conrad, never mastered conventional English usage, in regard to the way to end letters. Bennett, who was extremely correct in these matters, must have raised an eyebrow when he found Ford signing himself "Yours always".

On 10th March, Ford wrote asking Bennett to come to see him. "I am at home here every afternoon at four." As Bennett was still smarting over the price arranged for his story, he does not seem to have accepted this invitation. When it was renewed, two months later, he wrote the letter which follows, to explain the reason for his reluctance.

37 Clarendon Road,
Putney, S.W.
26 May 09.

The fact is, my dear Hueffer, that I should like to come and see you and have a chat, but the feeling that I have something against you would impair the naturalness of my demeanour.

I consider that either you or circumstances have got the better of me in regard to the story I wrote for you. In settling the price with Pinker you gave him to understand (wittingly or unwittingly) that the original overtures had come from me, that I had begun by offering you a serial and that on declining this you had by way of good nature suggested that you might like to see a short story. Accepting this as a basis Pinker agreed to an absurd price for the story. There was no foundation whatever for all this. The overtures came from you and they were urgent and repeated and quite spontaneously you said you would pay me a good price. I have all the correspondence: I made no mention of a serial until the story was arranged for. A man with your knowledge of the literary world must be aware that my ordinary serial price is at least four guineas a thousand, whereas you are paying me two and a half: Briefly I consider that I am nineteen pounds out of pocket on that story—and I should be surprised to hear that you consider $2\frac{1}{2}$ guineas a thousand a good price for me. Of course what Pinker arranges is final: I should never have referred to the matter if your note of the 10th had not seemed to me to make a little statement on my part desirable—and having regard to that note I am quite sure that you have no consciousness of having negotiated with Pinker on a wrong basis and do not suspect that I have a grievance, so I tell you.

Believe me, yours cordially,

ARNOLD BENNETT.

PS. Many thanks for the extra proofs.

Ford Madox Hueffer, Esq.

This produced from Ford an impassioned and almost illegible reply, the tone of which suggests that he was again on the verge of a nervous breakdown. Beginning "My dear Bennett," he says, "Oh hang! If you negotiate thro' Pinker what can you expect? . . . I am running a philanthropic institution for the benefit of the better letters. I am perfectly resigned to bankruptcy and the sooner you bankrupt me the sooner my troubles with the *Review* will be over. I stand here to be shot at. Shoot! But not through Pinker!" He goes on to say that if the *Review* were a business concern it would be a different matter, "but it isn't: it is a device by wh. I am losing £300 a month—I have so many £300s—when they are gone—finis. And *all* you chaps—*all*, do you understand, are clamouring for this dissolution. Very well—I won't fail you . . . I pay any price any author asks—no more—no less . . . But I fight anybody who has what appears to me the indecency to employ an agent, to the bitter death." He goes on to apologize if he misrepresented Bennett to Pinker "to forward a private grumble", and urges Bennett to prove himself the first generous-minded author that ever existed by coming in "to dinner on Monday with Violet Hunt". He sums up by saying: "This is the position—I am not repentant at having bested Pinker: I am sincerely sorry if I misrepresented you: I am ready to give you (not Pinker) any additional sum you like to ask: so there: and if you can read every word of this letter I will double the price!" Bennett seems to have made a friendly reply to this *cri du coeur*, but apparently did not accept the dinner invitation. Ford wrote again saying "Thank God you consent to bury the hatchet: I don't really deserve it because my letter to Pinker was silly—but I don't agree that the Pinker argument was illogical—not from my standpoint—and in most cases it is one's standpoint that counts". He says he is not commercial, "I cannot be and never will and am not going to try to be. But when a commercial gent comes to me I simply feel it sporting to beat him at his own game". He promises to send on a cheque for the balance of Bennett's claim and asks him not to tell Pinker, who, he says, is a "good creature and I see nothing in the world against him: quite the reverse". He adds that there is in this world so much of "what is called 'Klatsch' in the country we are going to war with" and concludes: "pray choose yr evening and if Mrs. Bennett is with you pray bring her. To-morrow I have some rather pleasant people coming in: come then —the only other day when I have an engagement that I cd not break for you this week is Thursday: so choose".

I was present at the crowded party which Bennett and his French wife attended and thus personally witnessed the meeting at which full diplomatic relations between the editor and the novelist were restored. The whole imbroglio sheds a fascinating light on two contrasted literary temperaments, besides revealing the hectic and emotional way in which Ford played his part as impresario.

No one who knew anything of Arnold Bennett could fail to realize his fundamental generosity of character. At the same time, he was tidy by nature and believed in conducting business in a businesslike way. No one can blame him for it. While he was arguing with Ford about his "price per thou." he was contributing, gratis, under the pseudonym Jacob Tonson, an admirable weekly causerie to the *New Age*, then brilliantly edited by A. R. Orage. In this paper, after Ford had given up the *English Review*, Bennett paid a characteristically generous tribute to Ford's services to English letters. This evoked a heartfelt letter of gratitude from Ford, which makes a very pleasant ending to the incident above recorded. "Many thanks for your kindly reference to me in the *New Age*," Ford writes. "You are a good fellow and the only one I know who has in the least appreciated what I have been trying to do and that I have been disinterested in the effort. At the same time, I wish you had not mentioned my name." He goes on: "I have all along tried to suppress any public reference to my connection with the *Review* and I don't in the least desire funeral tears from people who—with the sole exception of yourself—did all they could to impede and bother me. And please, please, no talk of public recognition. I did only what it was the simple duty of someone to do and let that be the end of it . . ."

By June 1909 not only had the *Review* run into all the financial and other difficulties which some outside observers foresaw, but Ford himself, apart from his editorial worries, was driven half crazy by domestic anxieties. Rumours that all was not going well at Ford's flat, which also served as his editorial office, had evidently begun to circulate in London literary circles. Conrad got to hear of them and in a letter to E. V. Lucas, quoted by his biographer, G. Jean-Aubry, he is at pains to dissociate himself from a periodical which already seemed headed for disaster. "In this connection," he writes, "let me mention (for I don't know what you may have heard) that I have been in no sense associated with the *E.R.* except that I wished Hueffer well in his venture. I showed him the Douglas MS. I had by me, which to say the least was being as kind to the *Review* as to Douglas. And of course there are my own contributions, which obviously I could not have placed elsewhere—not because they are improper but for other reasons, one of them being that editors are not falling over each other in their eagerness to get at my stuff —oh dear, no! This is absolutely the whole extent of my connection."

Evidently a coolness had now arisen between Ford and Conrad, at a moment of crisis in Ford's life when he was most in need of the steadfast loyalty of his friends. Trouble of every kind was blowing up, and as we do not know all the circumstances it would be unjust to blame Conrad for keeping out of it. In a later letter Conrad writes to Garnett: "I fully share your opinion of the *E.R.* My *Reminiscences* have come to an end now, and of course the fate of the *E.R.* is very uncertain I hear. So I don't suppose I'll ever appear in its pages any more."

While the most agonizing domestic drama was in progress behind the scenes, such was Ford's reticence about his private affairs that a surface observer could have gained no hint, from his manner, that anything was seriously wrong. I saw my chief almost every evening, while Ford remained in editorial control, and did not discover till much later what had actually been happening. This may be accounted for partly by a youth's natural absence of curiosity about the private life of an Olympian employer, but more because of the continuous excitement centring in the *Review* itself and in the unending stream of literary visitors who passed in and out of the office and enjoyed the editor's hospitality. In retrospect the twelve months of Ford's editorship appear like a continuous "wild party", except that, unlike the wild parties of the 'twenties, the people who frequented it were almost all in their various ways, celebrated, distinguished or, at least, interesting. Ford's discoveries among the then unfledged writers included P. Wyndham Lewis, Ezra Pound, D. H. Lawrence, and H. M. Tomlinson. If Norman Douglas was Conrad's "discovery", Ford was the first to introduce his work to the public. Of the various contributors who later achieved fame, the one who has left behind him the most generous tribute to Ford's encouragement is D. H. Lawrence. In the introduction to his collected poems, re-published in the posthumous volume *Phoenix*, Lawrence writes: "The first poems I had published were 'Dreams Old' and 'Dreams Nascent' which Miriam herself sent to Ford Madox Hueffer, in 1910 (1909) I believe, just when the *English Review* had started so brilliantly. Myself, I had offered the little poem 'Study' to the *Nottingham University Magazine*, but they returned it. But Hueffer accepted the 'Dreams' poems for the *English Review* and was very kind to me, and was the first man I ever met who had a real and true feeling for literature. He introduced me to Edward Garnett who, somehow, introduced me to the world."

As already recorded, by the middle of 1909 the finances of the *Review* were in such a precarious condition that more capital was urgently needed. For reasons connected with his domestic affairs Ford was unwilling to approach his original backer, Arthur Marwood. Eventually his brother-in-law, Dr. Soskice, head of a Russian Law Bureau in Lincoln's Inn Fields, was called in to reorganize the business side of the undertaking. The issue of August 1909, however, betrayed no sign, either to the general public or to the young man who read the proofs, of any financial instability. It is as bulky as its predecessors while the high literary standard established in the first issue is maintained unimpaired. In addition to the names of writers already famous, such as Walter de la Mare, Henry James and C. E. Montague, there are several of those who were destined to become so. Among the latter are Norman Douglas, with an essay on "Tiberius", and P. Wyndham Lewis, who contributes a character sketch called "Les Saltimbanques". The issue also contains a charming essay on "The Art of Dining" by Ford's accomplished wife, who signs herself Elizabeth Martindale, the first instalment of his own new novel, *A Call*, the usual editorial paragraphs, an article, singularly interesting to present-day readers, on "The Persian Crisis", by Professor Edward G. Browne and a long and appreciative review of C. F. G. Masterman's book *The Condition of England*. The most important absentee is Joseph Conrad.

The thirteenth issue of the *English Review*, the last over which Ford exercised full editorial control, shows certain evidences of change. Duckworth's imprint has been replaced by that of Chapman & Hall and the section devoted to current affairs has been expanded to occupy an equal number of pages to the opening half reserved for *belles-lettres*. The political half contains important articles by J. A. Hobson and H. N. Brailsford and two valuable papers on the current Russian dispute with Finland. In the diminished literary section we find the first instalment of a new novel by Violet Hunt, *The Wife of Altamont*, poems by Ernest Rhys, John Freeman and Frederic Manning and prose contributions from Professor Gilbert Murray, Edwin Pugh, G. Lowes Dickinson and Gilbert Cannan. In spite of the increased emphasis on political topics it cannot be said that, while Ford remained in the editorial chair, the standard of excellence of this historic periodical was ever lowered. Ford has many titles to a permanent, indeed a prominent, place in the long record of British literary achievement. He qualifies for his "niche" as poet, as critic, as novelist, as *belles-lettrist*. But if he had done nothing else but edit the first thirteen numbers of the *English Review*, his title to lasting fame would be assured. Great Britain has never seen a literary magazine which can be compared with it, either before or since.

People used often to ask how it could be done for the money, a mere half-crown. The short answer to this question is that it couldn't. In England, then as now, there was only an extremely limited public capable of appreciating the best in contemporary literature. Whereas in France culture is so widely diffused that a literary periodical like the *Mercure de France* can find readers in remote country towns and among all classes of society, such has never been the case in England. There are now welcome signs that this situation is changing for the better, but in 1909 the *English Review*, unfortunately for Ford, was several decades in advance of its time.

By the end of 1909, the only way of securing continuity of publication for the now bankrupt venture was to sell out. Violet Hunt who, by this time, had become closely associated with Ford, had a large circle of friends and acquaintances in Society (as she was accustomed to put it) and among these were a number of wealthy Jews including the Liberal politician, Sir Alfred Mond, afterwards Lord Melchett. On the political side, the *Review* had become Liberal in attitude and Mond was induced by Violet Hunt to take it over. The exact amount paid for the good will has not been ascertained, but it was referred to at the time as "derisory". Mond's first action, when he became proprietor, was to dismiss Ford and Violet Hunt and instal Mr. Austin Harrison, a former correspondent of the *Daily Mail*, as editor. No doubt Ford gave his successor every assistance while the change-over was taking place, and Norman Douglas, who succeeded the writer as sub-editor, helped to maintain the continuity of the literary standard which Ford had established. But by the beginning of 1910 Ford had not only lost his review. His marriage had collapsed, he was completely penniless, some of his closest friends had deserted him and he was in deadly fear that the affection of his daughters would eventually be alienated. Moreover his always highly sensitized nervous system was again giving way under the strains which constant anxiety, disappointment and a bitter feeling of injustice had put upon it.

CHAPTER XI

"No Villain Need Be . . ."

FORD and Elsie Hueffer had taken the "upper part" of 84 Holland Park Avenue, which was to become famous as the editorial office of the *English Review*, in 1907, about a year before the inception of that enterprise. Mrs. Hueffer's health did not make it advisable for her to live permanently in London, so they divided the furniture between them. Later the Bungalow at Winchelsea, which was Mrs. Hueffer's property, was sold and she bought two cottages at Aldington, then known as Hurst Cottages, together with the land surrounding them. The children slept in one of the cottages and the grown-ups in the other. They were afterwards united, by additional building, to form a very attractive small house called Kitcat, which, like Stocks Hill, commands a superb view over Romney Marsh. Before moving back to Aldington Mrs. Hueffer was taken seriously ill, her life being only saved by a major operation, performed in the nick of time. Both before, and after, this catastrophe, there had been a long history of ill-health on the part of both Ford and his wife and there can be little doubt that this cause contributed in large measure to exacerbate their normal disagreements into major clashes. The artist, as Maugham has pointed out, however sincere and deep-rooted his affections may be, is never "dependable". If he is a man of genius he is possessed by, and must be obedient to, what D. H. Lawrence called "the demon". On the other hand, it is inborn in the nature of any devoted wife and mother to be, whether she is aware of it or not, possessive. The demon, alas, cannot be caged and the least hint of possessiveness on the part of wife or mistress, however deeply loved, is apt to drive it to the extremities which Maugham describes in *The Moon and Sixpence*. To strong characters—single-hearted, single-minded, instinctively honest and truthful—the instinct to "thrash the matter out", when there is cause for grievance, seems the most natural thing in the world. But the effect of this plain-dealing on such a complex and highly sensitized nature as Ford's was almost lethal. He could not bear "scenes" of any kind, with Conrad, with his wife, or with anyone else for whom he cared deeply. They drove him distracted and there is little doubt that he believed that, if continued, they would kill him. The reason why a divorce first presented itself to Ford as a way out of his difficulties seems to have been the idea that if he and his wife were legally separated, that is to say if she no longer "possessed" him, the barriers between them would be broken down and their mutual affection would thus continue undisturbed. It was hardly to be expected that Elsie Hueffer would look at the matter in this light, particularly after the nervous strain of a serious illness. Rumours of Ford's "goings-on" in London came to her ears and the inevitable misunderstandings arose on both sides. These were not lessened by a country woman's lack of experience in the ways of the metropolitan world, by the well-meant advice given her by friends and relatives, or by the appearance on the scene of Violet Hunt.

As Violet Hunt, in her book *The Flurried Years*, and the present writer in *South Lodge*, have both dealt fully with an imbroglio which, at the time it occurred, was dramatically publicized by the middle-aged literary heroine, there is no need to repeat the details here. They are of great interest to women novelists and students of the psychology of literary people and, if the interest still taken in the stories of Bulwer Lytton and Rosina, of George Sand and Musset, is anything to go by, they are likely to remain so, unless human nature changes. For Ford, his connection with Violet Hunt was a case of out of the frying-pan into the fire. She was eleven years older than himself and, in spite of their community of interests, their mutual love of parties, the pre-Raphaelite background which they shared, in temperament and outlook they were diametrically opposed. For whereas Violet was incapable of reticence, had indeed discussed her personal affairs all over London, to the acute embarrassment of her friends, for the past quarter of a century, Ford's instinct to keep his private concerns strictly to himself was no less deeply ingrained.

If we may attempt to analyse the basic motives for their strange association we shall find on Violet's side an overmastering ambition to be married and made respectable. She had had an unfortunate love affair with a married man, in her girlhood, and when this individual was at last free to make an "honest woman" of her, in the Victorian sense, he preferred to marry someone else. She was therefore determined, at all costs, to provide herself with a husband as a suitable background to her South Lodge salon and Ford, had his divorce gone through, would have suited her purpose well enough. On Ford's side, though he was already beginning to sicken of the pre-Raphaelite circle which meant so much to Violet, the fact that she had money, had come to his rescue in a moment of black despair, when the control of his *Review* was slipping out of his hands, possibly weighed less than the fact that she appeared to open the door to what, for him, was a new kind of social world. He was exceedingly tired of living in the country, in an atmosphere of Arts and Crafts. He needed a change and the prospect of appearing in London "Society", under Violet's wing, may have had its attractions for a man with so little normal social experience. Old Mrs. Alfred Hunt, who had been a great social figure in her day, was still alive and her house was still frequented by numbers of people who were either in "Society" or on its fringes. Meanwhile, Ford was desperately in need of money, in the grip of neurasthenia due to his worries and incapable of putting his affairs in order. He lived on in his forlorn flat in Holland Park Avenue, amid the ghosts of his once crowded parties, surrounded by reminders of the *Review* which had been snatched from his hands, deserted, as he supposed, by most of his literary friends whose fame he had done so much to promote, and cut off from the daughters whom he adored. In strict regard for the proprieties, while waiting to be served with his divorce papers, he saw Violet only in the evenings, when he dined at her mother's house.

In making his preliminary dispositions for his impending divorce Ford acted in accordance with all the accepted rules of

honourable conduct. To protect Violet's name and to save his
wife from humiliation he hired the usual "official" co-respondent
to provide the "evidence of adultery" on which our antiquated
Divorce Laws then insisted. Unfortunately in this particular, as
in most other things connected with his personal affairs, Ford
contrived to muddle the whole business. Had he consulted a
lawyer experienced in Divorce Court procedure he would doubtless have been put in touch with a respectable clergyman's widow
who, for a suitable fee, would undertake to share a room with
him in an hotel and to spend the night playing double-dummy
bridge, repairing to bed only a few moments before the appearance of the chamber-maid. This time-honoured device is, of
course, rendered safer and more effective if there is a certain
amount of collusion on the part of the plaintiff to avoid publicity.

The course which Ford took was to pick up a little German
girl of the "unfortunate" class and let her live in his flat and eat
at his expense. She used to slink about at night, in the *English
Review* days, but made so nebulous an impression on me that I
had forgotten her existence, until my memory was jogged by
reading about her in Violet Hunt's *The Flurried Years*. I then
recalled that Ford once explained to me that she was the daughter
of a German-Jewish tailor in Nottingdale, who had been turned
away from home, and that he let her sleep in the spare room
because she had nowhere else to go. This story was doubtless
invented on the spur of the moment, but that there was ever
"anything between" Ford and the pallid waif never occurred to
me when I saw them together. After a lapse of nearly forty years,
I still think it rather improbable. I once found a poem in the
editor's handwriting, in the office waste-paper basket, on *English
Review* writing paper. It was addressed "To Gertrude" and
signed "G. Angel". I asked Ford if I might keep it and received
his permission to do so. It is before me as I write. It is not a
good poem, on "Jennie kissed me" lines, which is no doubt why
Ford discarded it, but is interesting, revealing and oddly sentimental. It reflects the Victorian cult of the "fallen woman" of
which Mr. Gladstone was, in his day, a leading exponent and
which inspired such poets of the 'nineties as Arthur Symons and

Ernest Dowson. The same romantic attitude was common among Oxford undergraduates half a century ago, as readers of Compton Mackenzie's period novel *Sinister Street* will remember. The picture drawn for us in the poem of the weary harassed man of genius, paternally comforting the poor little street-walker and bidding her disclose "the little budget of your woes", both of them having "much ancient work to do", the girl selling "worthless love", the poet "modern rhyme", dates it as a "period piece". Though it has little literary value, it is definite about the "purity" of the relations between the poet and his protégée, which are those of a father and a substitute daughter, united by suffering.

It is improbable that this serio-comic episode, when rumours of it percolated to Kent, presented itself to Elsie Hueffer in the light in which it would be regarded by a man, or woman, "of the world": that is to say, as a device for saving a lady's name from being mentioned in Divorce Court proceedings. To adopt such a device was, in fact, very honourable and gentlemanlike, very much the "done thing" by Society people when faced with a similar problem. When her services were not required, the German girl was despatched to Königsberg, with a "solatium".

Eventually the long-expected papers were served, the case came before the Court on 11th January, 1910, and the evening papers of that day placarded the result. "Mr. Hueffer Ordered to Return in Fourteen Days." Mr. Hueffer, naturally, did not return, and in the normal course the "decree nisi" would have followed after a brief interval. It did not follow because Mrs. Hueffer, when it was represented to her that her daughters, being Roman Catholics, would suffer grave injury if their parents were divorced, abandoned her suit. This action on her part effected a profound change in Ford's character and altered the whole course of his life. It put an abrupt end to what may be described as his "first period", and filled him with a burning sense of injustice. He knew that over the whole business, he had behaved like a civilized and honourable man. He had gone to the extreme limit of his financial capacity, almost beyond it, in making arrangements to support his wife and family. If divorce, at that time, was not so common in England as it was in the United States, thousands of other men had managed to change partners without any reflections being made upon their personal character. The Court, at the Restitution suit, had made the usual formal order, requiring Ford to pay £3 a week to his wife, *pendente lite.* As he had, from the first, been paying his wife nearly three times this amount, Ford registered his indignation, when he discovered that the case was not to be proceeded with, by refusing to submit to legal pressure. As a "gesture", therefore, he allowed himself to be incarcerated in Brixton Gaol, rather than pay up. It was a foolish gesture, and a painful one: even as an "experience" it was hardly worth it. Violet Hunt, who, though confused about her dates, is a fairly reliable witness, tells us in *The Flurried Years* that his ill-judged attempt to influence his wife's decision, had unexpected repercussions. ". . . When I thought he could bear it," she says, "I gave him some heavy news from Germany. Two days ago his Aunt Laura had died. She was his very rich aunt. Her will, altered an hour before her death, made her so well-rubbed-in, thumping legacy to her nephew doubtful until January 1911, and contingent on his good behaviour. So, through her sudden death—she had had a shock, news from England, *on dits* about her favourite nephew—he had lost quite a lot of money in hand and his children's future." The aunt had died two days after he had gone to gaol. So far as the writer is aware Ford did not receive any further legacies from any of the German members of his family. Throughout his life he was, indeed, singularly unlucky in everything to do with money.

It was the businesslike Violet who took charge of Ford's financial affairs after the collapse of the *English Review.* Without her aid, which was undoubtedly generous in spite of the fact that she could not restrain herself from talking about it, he would have been unable to support either himself or his wife and daughters. To provide immediate petty cash, Violet Hunt and Ford's sister-in-law, Miss Mary Martindale, sorted out Ford's extensive library, returning borrowed books to their owners and selling the rare volumes and valuable first editions. Later Violet took out a Bill of Sale on his furniture and pictures, dated 8th

October, 1910, which enabled her to raise £1,500 from her trustees for his immediate needs and the support of his family. When the divorce suit was abandoned, these possessions were removed to South Lodge and remained there until Violet Hunt's death in January 1942. (They were sold by auction with her other possessions, so that a portion, at least, of the money advanced was recouped by her heirs.) The maisonette at 84 Holland Park Avenue was evacuated and Ford removed to South Lodge nominally as the "paying-guest" of Mrs. Alfred Hunt. This house remained his headquarters until 1919, when he finally severed his connection with Violet.

South Lodge may thus be regarded as the background of Ford's second period. Before he embarked upon it he wrote a farewell to the past called *Ancient Lights and Certain New Reflections*, which was published by Chapman & Hall in 1911. From certain passages in the dedicatory letter to his daughters Christina and Katharine, which forms a preface to this volume, it is easy to see that the impetus behind it was to make an appeal to his children's loyalty in the hope of retaining their affection. Like so many fathers in a similar position, Ford was obsessed by the fear that his children's minds would be poisoned against him, as a result of his quarrel with their mother. I have been assured by one of them that nothing of the kind was ever attempted and, from my knowledge of Mrs. Elsie Hueffer, I have no hesitation in believing her. That the fear existed, that Ford's fevered imagination was tortured by it, is also undeniable.

Ford starts off by telling Christina and Katharine that "I made for myself the somewhat singular discovery that I can only be said to have grown up a very short time ago—perhaps three months, perhaps six. I discovered that I had grown up only when I discovered quite suddenly that I was forgetting my own childhood". He says that his childhood was a thing so vivid "that it certainly influenced me, that it certainly rendered me timid, incapable of self-assertion, and as it were perpetually conscious of original sin until only just the other day". In a later passage he adjures his "dear children" not to desire to be Ancient Lights. "It will crush in you all ambition; it will render you timid, it will foil nearly all your efforts." He urges them, when in doubt, to act on the lines of their "generous emotions" and reminds them that their ancestors, whatever may have been their defects, were "never cold, they were never mean, they went to shipwreck with high spirits".

In the course of the book there is a passage which reveals some of the bitterness with which, owing to the collapse of his marriage, Ford was at that time regarding his early years at Aldington and Winchelsea. As previous chapters have disclosed, they were undoubtedly very happy years, full of movement and literary activity, enlivened by collaboration with Conrad and enriched by the interesting social life which centred in the "Rye Circle", of which Henry James was the focus. In retrospect, he dwells, not without a good deal of truth, only upon one aspect of his period of rustication. "I lived entirely or almost entirely, among peasants," he says. "This was of course due to the idealizing of the country life which was so extraordinarily prevalent in the earlier 'nineties amongst the disciples of William Morris and other Cockneys. It was a singularly unhealthy frame of mind which caused a number of young men, totally unfitted for it, to waste only too many good years of their lives in posing as romantic agriculturists. They took small holdings, lost their hay-crops, saw their chickens die, and stuck to it with grim obstinacy until William Morris and Morrisism being alike dead, their feelings found no more support from the contagion of other enthusiasms. So they have mostly returned to useful work, handicapped by the loss of so many good years, and generally with ruined digestions, for the country with its atrocious food and cooking, is, in England, the home of dyspepsia."

If the last sentence is to be read as an oblique reflection upon his wife's abilities as a cook, it was quite unwarranted. Ford's dyspepsia was due to his "state of mind", to the disturbance of his subconscious caused by the struggle for emergence of a new "persona". On the spiritual plane, the process was as painful as the growth of a new wisdom tooth.

CHAPTER XII

Flurried Years

THE SITUATION caused at South Lodge first by the publicity attending Mrs. Hueffer's application for Restitution of Conjugal Rights and secondly by her failure to follow it up, can easily be imagined. Ford, as we have seen, regarded himself as the victim of a cruel injustice and, as an honourable man, he felt that having involved Violet Hunt in a mess it was his duty to get her out of it. Accordingly, his ingenious brain evolved a scheme by which, as he believed, he could attain his ends. In retrospect the whole plan seems perfectly crazy and it is only fair to remember that Ford's "state of mind" during this period of frustration and disaster was hardly conducive to sound judgment. As for Violet, her romantic and emotional temperament made her a willing accomplice in anything he suggested. In brief, the idea was that Ford should return to the bosom of his father's family, apply for German citizenship, obtain a divorce —which was apparently feasible, under German law—and marry Violet in Germany. An additional and characteristic flourish was the possibility of reviving a barony to which Ford was supposed to have a right, and of securing his claim to some legendary estates. Between their daydream of returning proudly to South Lodge as "Baron and Baroness Hüffer von Aschendorf"—thus scoring off all their enemies—and the fulfilment of their "wish" by making the fairy-tale "come true", a host of practical difficulties, including vast entanglements of teutonic red tape, had to be surmounted. Ford set out bravely on his Quixotic adventure, enlisted the support of his titled Aunt Emma, established himself in the dreary little University town of Giessen, while waiting for his naturalization to go through, and poured out money to a grasping and avaricious attorney who seems to have created more difficulties than he overcame. As Violet Hunt has left us, in *The Flurried Years*, an account of these long, involved and tortuous proceedings which I did my best to clarify in *South Lodge*, there is no necessity to recapitulate the details. It is sufficient to say that, when the delays and complications became intolerable, Ford and Violet decided to take what appeared to be the easy way out. In other words, they agreed to *pretend* that their plans had gone through, and to return to London, ostensibly as man and wife.

When they came to this unfortunate decision they were staying at Spa, in Belgium, with some friends of Violet's. By ill-luck they were interviewed there by a *Daily Mirror* correspondent, to whom Ford, in a moment of aberration, unbosomed himself. The interview duly appeared in the issue of the paper for 11th October, 1911, and a copy was shown to Mrs. Elsie Hueffer, in her cottage in Kent, by her gardener. It was her turn to feel outraged when she saw Violet Hunt referred to as "Mrs. Ford Madox Hueffer" and read such sentences, so uncharacteristic of Ford, as: "I don't want to advertise myself but it happens that both my wife and myself have books appearing . . ." The interview concluded with the remarkable statement: "I am heir to large, entailed estates in Prussia and have therefore retained my German nationality." A similar "publicity paragraph" appeared, later, in a Society weekly called *The Throne*, of which René Byles was manager. Mrs. Elsie Hueffer immediately embarked on actions for libel, for which, in the circumstances, she can hardly be blamed. The *Daily Mirror* sensibly withdrew their interview and apologized, but *The Throne* contested the action, which came up for hearing in February, 1913. They lost their case, in which neither Ford nor Violet was called upon to give evidence, and were mulcted in substantial damages. The effect of the resulting scandal on Violet's relations, on the older and more distinguished friends of her family, on Mrs. Elsie Hueffer's friends, on Conrad, on Henry James, on the Rossettis and the Garnetts, was in the highest degree embarrassing and generally disturbing. The fastidious Henry James, who was then too old and failing to be involved in messes, was careful to keep right out of the whole affair. Others, if not quite so firm in their attitude, declined invitations or showed their disapproval by a graduated coldness.

Meanwhile, if old intimacies lapsed, if "stuffy" relatives behaved in a Victorian manner, if "circles" which had once seemed so indestructible were broken up by the scandal resulting from the libel action, the effect on the social activities of South Lodge was outwardly only one of change and rejuvenation. As host and hostess, Violet and Ford had few equals in literary London during the brief interval before the outbreak of war, and their South Lodge parties, though they lacked the Society element and became more purely literary and Bohemian, were no less crowded and brilliant than those over which Mrs. Alfred Hunt had presided. The place of the late Victorian celebrities and socially distinguished figures was taken by "les jeunes" of the *English Review* circle, among whom Ezra Pound, P. Wyndham Lewis, Rebecca West, the Compton Mackenzies and W. L. George were prominent. Of Violet's older literary friends, May Sinclair, Ethel Colburn Mayne and H. G. Wells remained loyal, while Ford never lacked friends and admirers even if he did not always keep them. A distinction must be drawn between Ford's relations with the people with whom he associated, and his "life of the mind". His personal affairs might be in an agonizing muddle but his intellectual detachment and devotion to the arts he practised or appreciated, never faltered. Nothing, unless he was actually incapacitated by illness, deflected him from his work, although he found stimulus in social contacts, and always enjoyed parties. In front of South Lodge there was a garden containing a tennis court, which could be hired by the tenants of the houses opposite. Violet, at Ford's instigation, made arrangements to use this court, and on almost every fine afternoon, in the summer months, Ford and "les jeunes" played on it. Another amenity was Violet's seaside cottage—the Knap Cottage, Selsey—which became the centre of lively week-end parties. A number of friends, particularly the brilliant Liberal politician, C. F. G. Masterman and his wife and the beautiful Mrs. Bridget Patmore and her husband, went to Selsey to play golf and either stayed at the Knap Cottage or were constantly in and out of it.

One of Ford's and Violet's friends at this period was Mr. Ralph Cope who has kindly furnished me with some notes of his impressions. He got to know them through the Patmores, with whom he went down to Selsey for a golfing week-end.

"I was bad enough at golf," he writes, "to make a good enough game with Ford against Mr. and Mrs. Masterman, who was not plus 4; though one day she distinguished herself by holing a long putt which so delighted the enraptured Masterman that he embraced her before us all, caddy included. There must have been some zest about that particular match. It was delightful at Selsey; after the game I found it so entertaining to sit and listen to Ford and the Cabinet Minister talking about various things. . . . At Selsey there seemed none of the stress or strain which there must have been at times over the association. Violet told me once how Ford returned from prison with his socks sewn up in balls with which he used to while away his time in his cell.

"Violet once or twice discussed a legal point with me and when, arising out of it, I asked the date of her marriage, I think she was not forthcoming and I did not realise the exact position until the libel action. Life down there seemed to go as smoothly and happily as if we were as free from matrimonial complications as 'the angels in heaven'. Masterman in his once white flannel suit and a lock of hair over his forehead, duly portrayed in *Punch* . . . Ford like an adventurous schoolboy trying to make his way round the drawing-room without touching the floor. (This happened one night when we had dinner at the hotel.) . . . There is a nostalgic flavour about those days. I was very lonely in London and going to South Lodge was always something to look forward to. I used to play tennis in the garden opposite with Ford and Ezra Pound in his green shirt which, after the game, Violet would have liked covered up by a coat, when in the drawing-room! Ezra asked me to dinner once but I thought I would not know what to talk about with a poet so refused. Ford took me to that Sloane Square Theatre [the Court Theatre] once when the Irish players were there and introduced me to Lady Gregory: I used to stay in Co. Galway somewhere near her home but never met her before. After that Ford and I had supper in some little restaurant with another poet, W. B. Yeats. I felt I would like at any rate to simulate some literary intelligence so I introduced the subject of George Moore. (I knew a man mentioned in one of his books.) That was a fruitful topic for Yeats . . . I am left with a memory of their [Ford and Violet's] kindness and an oasis in a city of solitude. I have quoted Ford's remark that 'God is a magnificent entertainer'. As far as mortals can imitate this lofty benevolence, I have to make my acknowledgements to Ford and Violet—though I never called them that."

It is worth while drawing attention to Mr. Cope's reference to Ford's "kindness". The word occurs over and over again, in their recollections of him by people younger than himself. Kindness and generosity, particularly to the young and shy, were outstanding features of Ford's character and, as is so often the way, they were frequently rewarded by malignant spite and mean misrepresentation. It is a curious and horrible thought how many people there are who detest and distrust kindness. The reason may be that the possession of this quality acts as an unspoken criticism upon those devoid of it.

Violet's account of the period between her return to England as "Mrs. Hueffer" and Ford's departure to join his regiment after the outbreak of war, given in her book *The Flurried Years*, provides a breathless, disordered but extraordinarily vivid rendering of her own and Ford's experiences as she recalled them in later life. She was undoubtedly subjected to intense nervous strain, but underneath her emotional garrulity, her impetuousness and folly, there was a quality of North Country toughness which carried her through, while her strong sense of drama and combative instinct made some people suspect that she secretly enjoyed her woes. There is little attempt at precision either as to dates or details in her reminiscences but, though a literary "impressionist" rather in the Ford manner, she never loses her respect for the factual or strays into the realms of pure fantasy. When she is not telling the truth, she has very good reasons for not doing so. She never, as the saying is, "kidded herself". On the whole, I believe her story is fairly trustworthy as a general picture.

In addition to *The Throne* libel case, referred to above, Violet found herself involved in a law suit with her two married sisters in regard to her administration of her mother's estate. After her mother's death, in the autumn of 1912, the will was put into Chancery, which involved a further heavy drain in lawyers' fees. Meanwhile, Ford was facing the prospect of passing through the bankruptcy court, which wounded his self-esteem for, as Violet put it, "a bankrupt can hardly use the grand manner" and to Ford, "the grand manner" was a necessity. Financial difficulties were increased in 1913 by the action of Ford's old friend Arthur Marwood who wrote and demanded the repayment of £440, lent for the purpose of defraying the cost of the major operation on Mrs. Elsie Hueffer. "It was paid," says Violet, "on the nail", but Ford believed the suddenness of the demand was due to the recent libel case in which counsel for the plaintiff, to prejudice the jury, had implied that he had neglected to pay for the upkeep of his daughters. The charge was monstrous and as Violet rightly says, neither Marwood nor anyone else who had known Ford, "could or should have let themselves believe it". There is no evidence that Marwood did so. He was a sick man, foresaw—rightly, as it happened—that another illness would kill him and thought it advisable, for the sake of his dependants, to put his affairs in order.

In the Christmas following her mother's death Violet says that "by Christmas Day we were all, Ezra Pound—taking great interest in the cooking of a sucking-pig—Mary, Joseph Leopold [Ford], his sister and I, installed in a haunted cottage at Farnham Common which had been lent to me. I was poor. My mother's money, on which I had lived and on a share of which, augmented by my earnings, I was to live in future, was not immediately forthcoming. It did not come for four years—a contested will—sisters of the same bed masquerading as strangers—heads averted—the sneer courteous—macabre scenes such as one reads of in Victorian novels".

As an indication that Violet's memory for details was not always dependable the following account of what was evidently the same party, from Faith Compton Mackenzie's book *As Much as I Dare*, may be quoted, for comparison.

"I once spent Christmas with the Hueffers at a cottage near Burnham Beeches," she writes. "My contribution to the household was a Sudbury ham, which was fallen upon with greedy enthusiasm by the other guest, Ezra Pound, who talked without ceasing throughout the festival. On Christmas Day Ford could only be approached through the keyhole of his bedroom, in which he was securely locked against all comers. The cause of this retirement was not made known, but it gave spice to the party, since Violet was continually running upstairs to entreat him, speculating loudly as to why he was up there at all, and giving a touch of drama to the whole affair, so that the trumpery little cottage (which was only lent) achieved a sort of sublimity as the setting of a scene in history. Meanwhile Ezra's monologue went on without serious interruption.

"Ford, releasing himself from bondage on St. Stephen's Day, descended upon us with his store of intellectual energy unimpaired by festive excesses, full of benevolence, good cheer and lively conversation; in short, he was himself again. And Violet, her great eyes blazing, carved the turkey and what remained of the ham with more than her usual dexterity, her cheeks flushed at the excitement of his restoration. It was a really notable Christmas, for I was, and have always been, devoted to Ford and Violet."

Although Violet mentions her own poverty and Ford's bankruptcy, there is no sign of their freedom of movement or their way of life ever having been impaired through lack of funds. Besides keeping on the Selsey cottage, they were able to make a long journey through the South of France and to visit Corsica (which Ford disliked) in the spring of 1913 and, when at home, they entertained continuously.

In the summer of 1913, in spite of the libel case, the social activities at South Lodge continued almost, but not quite, as usual, and a touch of bravado can be detected in Violet's account of them. "Home, and my yearly garden-party never so well attended. Cabinet Ministers, by Jove! Dinners in the House. Fêtes champêtres at the Monds and in Lowndes Square, Henley with the Harmsworths, the Cabaret Club and all the charming artist rabble who were on the top of the vogue, and then to the cottage we rented at Selsey. A gorgeous season. I wished my poor old mother had been there to see it."

The "Cabinet Ministers" were presumably C. F. G. Masterman and his wife, who had by now become intimate friends and with whom, in the hot summer of that year, they went for a tour through parts of Germany. The atmosphere, on the eve of the war, was already hostile and the people silent and suspicious. Masterman was very anxious to see the battlefields of Sedan, Gravelotte and Mars-la-Tour. The arrangements were eventually made for the excursion but, according to Ford, a plain-clothes policeman accompanied them wherever they went. Later, Ford invented a fairy story to the effect that the Germans had mistaken the Mastermans for Mr. and Mrs. Winston Churchill! That Ford realized his position as a would-be German subject was, however, clear from his reluctance to accede to Violet's request to visit Giessen, where he was supposed to have been naturalized.

"I felt," says Violet, "that there was something uncomfortable about it, something not quite final, and repeated my request in the evening. Then he said, still more languidly:

" 'Do you want me to be shot or forced to fight against France? If you're prepared for that, dear, we'll go.' "

Of course, Violet was not prepared "for that", nor was Ford. Hatred of Prussian barbarism was traditional in his family, France was his spiritual home, Provence the part of it he loved best, and England, in spite of its divorce laws, the country in which he had his deepest roots. His *native* land. When the war broke out in the following year it evoked in him a simple "schoolboy" patriotism not very far removed from Rupert Brooke's. Of all Ford's numerous "personae" the Teutonic one was, paradoxically, the least convincing.

In spite of all the domestic strains and agitations to which Ford was subjected, his capacity to isolate himself in the world of his creative imagination never failed him. "Joseph Leopold," as Violet observes in a revealing passage, "seemed to the naked eye, to take it all pretty calmly—his own troubles and mine. He sat there in the Futurist room" (the first-floor writing room at

South Lodge which had been decorated in a violent shade of red by Wyndham Lewis and for which he also painted a large abstract picture to surmount the chimney-piece) "neatly and with aplomb dictating his daily screed of pages. He preserved at least his literary balance, the pendulum of his thoughts ticking backwards and forwards with an even motion. Great man! He could concentrate. His inner commotion was subdued by the superior claims of Literature on its votary. Perfect copy flowed from his mouth. No corrections were made or apparently needed. He scorned to look over a manuscript after his secretary had typed it. And why—since the line was cleared for an express train? No alarums or excursions were allowed to interfere with its mass produce. As for the quality—the avoirdupois—that must be left with the critics, whom he little regarded, except perhaps Edward Garnett."

Two of the dominating influences at South Lodge in the brief pre-war interval were Ezra Pound and Percy Wyndham Lewis who, with other *avantgardistes*, including the young French sculptor Gaudier-Breszka, were busy establishing a Rebel Art centre in Bloomsbury, writing manifestoes for the new movement, Vorticism, and developing their plans for the launching of *Blast*, a quarterly periodical of huge dimensions which broke out in the summer of 1914.

The stronghold of Rebel Art was established in one of the old houses in Great Ormond Street, and Ford once lectured there "absent-mindedly, in a tail coat". In all the Vorticist activities Ford and Violet were both patrons and collaborators. Lewis, as has been mentioned, was commissioned to vorticize the study at South Lodge, while *Blast* printed in its first issue a long instalment of a story by Ford, later developed into the novel called *The Good Soldier*, which ranks as the finest achievement of his "second period".

Ford, Violet and all the Vorticists and their friends frequented an amusing cabaret in a basement in Heddon Street, called The Cave of the Golden Calf, the walls of which Wyndham Lewis had decorated with mural paintings. Here, on one occasion, Ford produced a shadow play. The cabaret was run by one of

Strindberg's widows, a formidable lady who quickly created a
legend which still forms part of the mythology of the
period.

Although caught up in the whirlpool of hectic social gaiety
which preceded the outbreak of the first world war, the strains
and stresses of their relationship were already beginning to tell
on both Ford and Violet. The latter was too old to adapt herself
to the new conditions and, at the bottom of her heart, hated
having to exchange Ford's circle of young and noisy iconoclasts for
old and valued associations. She suffered bitterly when her niece,
Rosamond, to whom she was devoted, was restrained from staying any more at South Lodge, and did not hesitate to reproach
Ford for all the social rebuffs, snubs and cold-shoulderings, for
which she held him responsible. She lacked his adaptability and
his readiness to adopt new "personae", as Wells called them. All
the same, although as regards the quality of his work, his "second
period" hardly compares with either his first or his subsequent
periods, it is probable that Ford derived some literary benefit
from the association. Violet was an experienced as well as an
accomplished novelist and her best books had a quality of smoul-
dering passion and a depth of feeling which were absent from
Ford's novels before he wrote *The Good Soldier*. Violet once
informed me that, when he had completed this novel, Ford, in
a fit of neurasthenic depression, consigned the MS. to the dust-
bin. According to her story, which may or may not be true, she
rescued it, had it re-typed and was responsible for getting John
Lane to issue it.

The list of Ford's publications, between 1909 and 1915, contains several pot-boilers, some of them written under the pseudonym "Daniel Chaucer", and other books which, with sound
critical judgment, he subsequently made no attempt to revive.
A survey of his productions between the collapse of the *English
Review* and his joining the Army in 1915, establishes at least his
versatility and his amazing capacity for concentrated effort in
the midst of domestic worries. The titles are *The Half Moon*
(Nash, 1909), a minor historical novel; *Songs from London* (Elkin
Matthews, 1910); *A Call* (Chatto & Windus, 1910); *The Portrait*

(Methuen, 1910); *The Simple Life Limited,* by Daniel Chaucer (John Lane, 1911); *Ancient Lights* (Chapman & Hall, 1911, published in U.S.A. as *Memories and Impressions*); *Ladies Whose Bright Eyes* (Constable, 1911), a successful return to his historical vein, partly written when he was staying with Violet at Fordingbridge; *The Critical Attitude* (Duckworth, 1911), elaborated from editorials contributed to the *English Review; High Germany* (Duckworth, 1912), a small volume of poems; *The Panel* (Constable, 1912. Published in the U.S.A., 1913, as *Ring for Nancy*), a very amusing and still readable farce; *The New Humpty-Dumpty,* by Daniel Chaucer (Lane, 1912); *The Monstrous Regiment of Women,* 1913, a pamphlet written for the Women's Freedom League of which Ford and Violet were enthusiastic supporters; *Mr. Fleight* (Howard Latimer, 1913); *The Young Lovell* (Chatto & Windus, 1913); *Collected Poems* (Max Goschen, 1913), and *Henry James* (Secker, 1913). *Mr. Fleight* has a history which I suppose must be unique in the annals of publishing. The ever faithful René Byles had become manager of a new firm of publishers and was determined to use his opportunity to put Ford over "in a big way". Accordingly a most tremendous, even sensational, advertising scheme was worked out and partially put into execution. Unfortunately the firm had little or no financial backing and expired before Ford's novel ever got into circulation. As far as I know the book was never put on sale and all trace of it has now disappeared.[1] Ford seems to have borne the shock with equanimity. At all events, he made no effort, even if he himself possessed a copy, to get it re-published either in England or America. The issue of the *Collected Poems* was an act of piety on the part of the writer who was then acting, like Byles, as a publisher's manager. It was well produced and printed, but the sales, alas, were negligible. Why the British literary public refused to take Ford seriously as a poet has always been a mystery to me. His poetry was appreciated by a handful

---

[1] In a letter written to Mr. Percival Hinton on Nov 27th 1931 Ford says "I don't think Mr. Fleight was ever completely published. I understood from Byles that it was seized by the sheriff's officer immediately after copies had been sent out for review and the copies thus seized were sold to someone—Bell, I think—who used them for a Colonial edition. I may of course be mistaken but I do not remember ever having seen a copy other than that of the Colonial edition referred to".

of people, among them H. G. Wells who, in *Boon*, was vocal
on its behalf, but the public did not listen.

To the above list of Ford's productions should be added a
volume of short sketches, written in collaboration with Violet
Hunt, called *Zeppelin Nights* (John Lane, 1915). He also wrote
the preface to a re-issue of Mrs. Alfred Hunt's novel *The Governess*
(Chatto & Windus, 1912) which Violet revised; and contributed
a preface and two additional chapters to Violet Hunt's novel *The
Desirable Alien* (Chatto & Windus, 1913).

CHAPTER XIII

British Officer

THE MAJOR events in Ford's life, in the two years preceding
his joining the Army, were his development, as novelist
and poet, displayed respectively in *The Good Soldier* and
the *vers libre* poem "On Heaven", addressed to "V.H. who asked
for a working Heaven". Seen in perspective, in spite of the
welter of nagging personal worries in which he was constantly
involved, all the "major events" of Ford's life centre round his
books and the particular inspirations and "states of mind" which
enabled him to produce them. On this point the women most
closely associated with him seem to be agreed. In the personal
relationship the fact that his art was his Way of Escape which,
in all possible situations, never failed him, rendered him exasperating.

The Good Soldier is Ford's first really adult novel, the first with
"heart" in it, the first in which pity and passion and resulting
tragedy are the themes which make their demands on his now
fully developed technical equipment. Violet Hunt quotes Miss
Rebecca West, then one of England's most youthful as well as
most penetrating literary critics, as saying that "behind it is a
force of passion which so sustains the story in its flight that never
once does it appear as the work of a man's invention. . . .
Union of inspiration and the finest technique . . . is the only
reason it can bear up under the vastness of its subject". In the
"dedicatory letter" which precedes the American re-issue of the
novel, published in 1927, Ford gives us an extremely interesting
account of the genesis of this book, which he regarded as his
best book of a pre-war period.

It would be possible, but unprofitable, to examine Ford's
emotional life during the ten years which preceded the writing
of *The Good Soldier* for events which were ultimately sublimated

in a perfect work of art. It would be possible to search for "originals", as Violet Hunt has done, for the three heroines, to speculate on the effect on the author of a passing infatuation for the beautiful secretary to whom it was dictated and express views as to whether the contrasted characters of Dowell and Edward Asburnham are, as Violet suspects, two aspects of Ford's own character. All books can be "taken to pieces" in this way, by persons who claim some knowledge of the author's private life, but the central fact, the mystery of creation, inevitably defies such investigations. Ford tells us that he started work on *The Good Soldier* on 17th December, 1913, his fortieth birthday, and reveals that it was his first attempt to extend himself or, in other words, "to go all out". "I had never really tried," he says, "to put into any novel of mine *all* that I knew about writing. I had written rather desultorily a number of books—a great number —but they had all been in the nature of *pastiches,* of pieces of rather precious writing, or of *tours de force.*" So on his fortieth birthday he sat down to show what he could do and *The Good Soldier* resulted. He fully intended that it should be his last book and even took "a formal Farewell to Literature in the columns of a magazine called *The Thrush*", being, as he tells us, prepared to stand aside in favour of Ezra Pound, T. S. Eliot, Wyndham Lewis, H.D., "and the rest of the clamorous young writers who were then knocking at the door". His ambition was to do for the English novel what, in *Fort Comme la Mort*, Maupassant had done for the French. "One day I had my reward, for I happened to be in a company where a fervent young admirer exclaimed: 'By Jove, *The Good Soldier* is the finest novel in the English language!' whereupon my friend Mr. John Rodker who has always had a properly tempered admiration for my work remarked in his clear, slow drawl: 'Ah yes. It is, but you have left out a word. It is the finest French novel in the English language!'" The book was not published until 1915, when its original title, *The Saddest Story*, was changed, at John Lane's request.

The long poem in *vers libre* "On Heaven", which first appeared in England in a volume called *On Heaven and Poems Written on*

Active Service, published by Lane in 1918, dates from the spring of 1914 and was written at Selsey. It was printed in the American magazine *Poetry* and Ford at first intended to suppress it as being "what I should now call 'too sloppy' ". It was, however, immensely admired by Ezra Pound and a number of young poets who were then experimenting with free verse and who recognized in Ford a master of their chosen medium. "*Vers libre*," says Ford in his Preface to the 1918 volume, "is the only medium in which I can convey any more intimate moods. *Vers libre* is a very jolly medium in which to write and to read, if it be read conversationally and quietly." "On Heaven" may be said to have inaugurated his second innings as a poet. His first had aroused little interest among the British public: the second was to secure him a full measure of appreciation in American literary circles.

When war broke out, Ford and Violet were staying in Scotland with the American novelist "Mary Borden" who later married General Spears. Wyndham Lewis, who was painting their hostess, was a fellow guest. After their return to London they went to Selsey which, being only eighteen miles from Portsmouth and "scheduled to be razed to the ground by the town's guns the moment the German fleet got anywhere near" was, as Violet says, "most unpleasant". A number of Violet's Selsey friends had, from the first, resented the intrusion of Ford. They now, so Ford believed, took a mean advantage of the war situation to denounce him to the police as a German agent. I have been unable to discover precisely what happened, but the rumour current at the time was that Ford had been interrogated on the golf course, in the presence of his friends, by a couple of detectives, who asked to see his birth certificate. Such incidents were very common at the time, all over England, and anyone with a German name or German connections was liable to be subjected to what the authorities called a "routine check-up". In Ford's rather difficult situation, due to his having publicly given out that he had "resumed" his German nationality, the "check-up" was only to be expected, although the police seem to have chosen an unnecessarily offensive way of doing it. Ford evidently suspected that Violet had been talking about him indiscreetly. The incident caused him much humiliation and distress of mind and was certainly one of the causes which ultimately led to the open breach between Violet and himself. In a letter to C. F. G. Masterman, written in June 1919, shortly after his demobilization, he refers to it. "I gave Violet the choice between my leaving South Lodge or her giving up the acquaintanceship of certain people whom I regarded as my enemies. I found that she had been entertaining at Selsey the various gentlemen whose chief claim to patriotic activities, as you know, had been the denouncing of myself to the police as a German agent; and I also found that various other gentlemen were stating, on her authority, various other untruths to my disadvantage. This simply meant my absolute ruin."

Either before or after the police enquiry, Ford consulted Masterman as to his civil status and was at once reassured. Masterman had been given by the Government the important task of countering the propaganda begun by the Germans in the United States. Most of the leading authors and publicists of the day were called into conference and promised their services. In her biography of her husband, Mrs. C. F. G. Masterman says that "Mr. Ivor Nicholson records that early in the war, when the work was only just begun, Masterman warned his staff that the work must be secret, that they would be subject to attacks just and unjust and unable to reply and that, when it was finished, it was highly probable it would go completely unrewarded and unacknowledged". Mrs. Masterman adds: "I imagine this was received without any particular resentment. Already in certain circles there was a kind of *chic* in a civilian refusal to benefit by the war." The Department, being a hush-hush affair, was merely known as "Wellington House", the name of the building in which it shared offices with the National Health Insurance Commission.

Masterman was glad to make use of Ford's literary talents while, at the same time, allowing him an opportunity to prove the sincerity of his patriotism. The two volumes which he wrote, in succession, for Wellington House, *When Blood is Their Argument: An Analysis of Prussian Culture* and its companion, *Between*

St. Dennis and St. George: A Sketch of Three Civilizations, were published by Hodder & Stoughton in 1915, without, of course, any indication that they were officially sponsored. Although written at high pressure, neither book shows any sign of hasty composition, while both reveal Ford's natural gifts as an historian, his wide reading, his accuracy and precision in documentation (in a work where such accuracy is essential) and his capacity for incisive argument. Animating both books is a restrained "passion of the mind" which lends them an extraordinary power of conviction. *When Blood is Their Argument,* apart from its propaganda value at the time it was written, is an historical essay of permanent importance, annotated and documented with scholastic completeness and written in a prose style, compact, virile and sensitive, exactly suited to its purpose. For once in a way the reviewers did full justice to a remarkable achievement. The *Daily Telegraph* said: "A clever, penetrating, caustic style drives home every point, and a sharply whetted memory provides him with perpetual material, which is continually employed with great adroitness and resource. . . . Mr. Hueffer has done a public service by writing this book. . . . It is a book of genuine importance and of a wide significance. It is to be hoped that it reaches Germany as well as Great Britain and the United States." James Douglas, in the *Star,* also expressed the hope that "this remarkable volume" would be read in the United States, "for Kultur has yet to be understood by the greatest Republic on earth." The *Morning Post* stated that: "Nobody knows Prussia and its Prussianised dependencies better than Mr. Hueffer, and his indictment of the form of so-called civilisation which the flesh-and-blood mechanism of German Militancy is now prepared to force on Europe and England is the most effective that has yet appeared. . . . Every patriotic Briton should read it to the end that he may be able to argue more effectively with the enemy inside the gates . . ."

Between St. Dennis and St. George is, in the writer's view, still one of the most sympathetic appreciations of the value to civilization of French culture which has been written in English. As a South German by family origin, Ford may be excused for

M

pointing out that "there is no race barrier and no barrier of creed between the peoples of South Germany and the peoples of France. Racially and historically these people are Franks, and it is only for a century or so that they have been united with Germany or represented by Prussia. . . . I cannot myself see either in common sense, in humanity, or in the light of history any objection to a revival of the Confédération du Rhin under a French protectorate. That such confederations of differently speaking peoples not racially very different can be successful, independent, and harmonious is proved by the Confederation of Switzerland, and I do not mind hazarding the prophecy that in some such confederation the salvation of the world will eventually be found." It is in the Epilogue, called "Félicité", that Ford gives the most eloquent expression to a feeling for France which has been shared for generations by English artists and humanists, though few, if any, have so well explored and clarified the reasons for their liking and respect for the neighbours with whose Government theirs has so often quarrelled. Ford shows his readers why France "in spite of the worst of Governments, retains always, or recovers miraculously soon, her equilibrium". No one who had read Ford's book could, even in 1940, have had any fear that France was permanently down and out. The book, indeed, is as valuable at the present day, and will be as valuable in days to come, as it was when it was written. It was translated into French by a Mlle Marie Butts and published, after Ford had joined the Army, by the firm of Payot. It was received with delight and evoked a warm response from the French public as well as from "official France" and earned its author some well-deserved honours and decorations from learned bodies. But as we shall see when we come to Ford's military career, it did not earn him the Staff job to which he was so obviously entitled. There is a certain "continuity" about War Office methods in the recruiting of personnel for British Military Intelligence. Masterman was right to warn those who assisted him at Wellington House that it was highly probable their efforts "would go completely unrewarded and unacknowledged".

Before leaving *Between St. Dennis and St. George*, it may be useful to quote the concluding sentences because of the light they throw upon the author's outlook, temperament, and deepest convictions. "So, if in the world from now on," Ford says, "there is to be any of the pleasantness that we loved, any of the virtues that we have held made men and women gracious, the cause of France, which is our cause, must prevail. If it do not, there may well be in the world many more machines, many more gilded hotels—but assuredly there will be none of that civilisation of altruism and chivalry which, beginning in that triangle of Provence, has spread pleasantness and light upon the minds of men to the furthest confines of the earth."

Ford was already in the Army at the time when this book and *The Good Soldier* appeared. He was forty-two years old and by no means of strong physique. No pressure of any kind, whether of public opinion or, after 1916, of compulsion, could have been put upon him to volunteer for military service. There is no doubt that, with Masterman's aid, he could, had he wished to do so, have had a "safe" war and drawn considerably more than a subaltern's pay in some Government Department. The fact that he preferred the nobler course and deliberately chose to risk his life in fighting for his country, and for France, as a subaltern in a line regiment, was in simple terms, an act of unselfish patriotism. That, in joining the Army, he also disentangled himself from the nerve-racking domestic atmosphere of South Lodge, is undoubtedly true. But this fact, except in the eyes of the deliberately malicious, cannot be held to detract from his patriotism in joining up when over military age.

That he had plenty of excuse for what some have described as his "persecution mania", cannot be denied by those who know the facts. In certain circles a dead set was made against both Ford personally and against his writings. No doubt, as he was pathologically sensitive in these matters, he exaggerated the importance of the signs of prejudice and hostility on the part of certain fellow-writers and reviewers which still confronted him, even after he had joined the Army. No doubt, he was wrong in supposing that Violet Hunt and her constantly clacking tongue, were the sole or even the principal cause of his evident unpopularity. But that the prejudice and hostility were genuine enough at the time and have even persisted, in some quarters, long after his death, cannot possibly be disputed. Crabbing Ford Madox Hueffer and sneering at his successor, Ford Madox Ford, became almost a tradition in certain London newspaper offices, as the obituary notices revealed. As late as 1943, when *South Lodge* was published, it was evident from some of the reviews that Ford's detractors were still as active as ever.

The mean attacks on Ford by disgruntled poets and soured novelists who, in the *English Review* days, had been only too glad of his help, brought H. G. Wells charging up to his defence. In his glorious literary "rag", *Boon*, published in 1915, "H.G." had made several friendly references to Ford, who he insisted should attend the "World Conference on the Mind of the Race". "Through all the jam, *I* think we must have Ford Madox Hueffer, wandering to and fro up and down the corridor, with distraught blue eyes, laying his hands on head and shoulders, the only Uncle of the Gifted Young, talking in a languid, plangent tenor, now boasting about trivialities, and now making familiar criticisms (which are invariably ill-received) and occasionally quite absent-mindedly producing splendid poetry."

It is interesting to note this later specimen of *Boon's* opinions. "Conspicuous success, and particularly conspicuous respectable success, chilled his generosity. Conrad he could not endure, I do him no wrong in mentioning that; it is the way with most of us; and a score of flourishing contemporaries who might have liked tickets for the Conference special would have found great difficulty in getting them."

When the attacks on Ford reached their climax in a review of *The Good Soldier*, followed by correspondence in G. K. Chesterton's paper, *The New Witness*, Wells's sense of decency was outraged. Maisie Ward, in her life of *Gilbert Keith Chesterton* (Sheed & Ward, 1944) quotes a letter from Wells to G.K.C. in which he says, or rather shouts: "This business of the Hueffer book in the *New Witness* makes me sick. Some disgusting little greaser named ―― has been allowed to insult old F.M.H. in a series of letters which make me ashamed of my species. Hueffer has many faults no doubt, but first he's poor, secondly he's notoriously unhappy and in a most miserable position, thirdly he's a better writer than any of your little crowd and fourthly, instead of pleading his age and his fat and taking refuge from service in a greasy obesity as your brother has done, he is serving his country. His book is a great book and —— just lies about it—I guess he's a dirty-minded priest or some such unclean thing—when he says it is a story of a stallion and so forth. The whole outbreak is so envious, so base, so cat-in-the-gutter-spitting-at-the-passer-by, that I will never let the *New Witness* into the house again.

Regretfully yours,

H. G. WELLS."

It is only fair to interpolate here that Cecil Chesterton, an outstandingly honest and brave man, far from taking refuge in a "greasy obesity", enlisted as a private and was killed in action. To H.G.'s outburst, G.K.C. wrote a mild reply saying that he knew nothing of the book or of Hueffer's circumstances, that the reviewer was "a poor journalist, and I believe a Free-Thinker", and mentioning that Mr. E. S. P. Haynes, who was both on the board and on the staff of the paper, had already put Wells's views, "I cannot help thinking with a more convincing logic". Wells, thereupon, wrote to end the quarrel. "But the Hueffer business," he says in his reply, "aroused my long dormant moral indignation and I let fly at the most sensitive part of the *New Witness* constellation, the only part about whose soul I care. I hate these attacks on rather miserable exceptional people like Hueffer and Masterman. I know these aren't perfect men but their defects make quite sufficient hells for them without these public peltings."

In spite of a certain complacent note of moral patronage (for no one could suppose that Wells himself was "perfect" or lacking in the normal complement of human faults) the correspondence reveals one of Wells's most attractive virtues. Apart from his contemporary and fellow-Victorian, Shaw, I can think of no great literary figure to-day who would be at all likely to spring to the defence of an unpopular colleague when unjustly reviled.

Since the end of the Four Years' War, the American national slogan "there's no friendship in business" seems to have permeated the literary profession. At least I have come across no example among the younger generation of Wells's spontaneous outburst of decent feeling.

Before Ford entered the Army he had been deeply moved by the sufferings of the Belgian refugees. He had witnessed at Charing Cross the arrival of the long, unlit trains with their tragic load of women and children who had managed to escape from Antwerp. The poem on Antwerp, the first and one of the most moving poems in the *On Heaven* volume, records his emotions of pity and admiration for the way in which the common people of Belgium resisted the invader.

By 1915 the war had already become a massacre, particularly for the younger officers whose expectation of life was far less than in the Second World War. The casualties were appalling, and no responsible man could contemplate being sent to the Front without making a will, if he had anything to leave, or at least putting his affairs in order.

Owing to the strong aversion which Mrs. Conrad had conceived for Ford—"hoofing out Hueffer" as she tells us in her memoir of her husband was a task to which, after 1909, she set herself with unremitting energy—owing also to Ford's matrimonial complications and resulting social notoriety, Conrad's feeling for him had evidently cooled, but the close association over so many years had forged a link of friendship between them which, on Conrad's part, could not with decency be altogether broken. As they had never ceased to correspond with the old intimacy, it was natural that they should meet to settle various matters arising out of their collaboration, and that Ford should be anxious for Conrad to undertake some of the duties of a literary executor in the event of his being killed. There is no reason to suppose that there was any lack of cordiality, any failure to respond, on Conrad's part, particularly as Ford's action in volunteering was the kind of noble gesture which, as his novels demonstrate, he was certain to appreciate.

Before joining his regiment it was, of course, inevitable that

Ford should take leave of his two daughters. Readers of *Christina's Fairy Book* and that exquisite lyric "To Christina at Nightfall", now very properly included in the new edition of *The Golden Treasury of English Lyrics*, do not require to be told how he idolized them in their childhood and how greatly he suffered from being separated from them. The efforts he made, when he was himself almost destitute, to pay for their education and upkeep, have already been mentioned. As recorded in an earlier chapter, it was at his instigation, for Mrs. Elsie Hueffer (contrary to the statement of her counsel, Mr. J. A. Hawke, K.C., in the second libel action she brought against Violet Hunt in 1925) has never been a Roman Catholic, that they were received into the Roman Catholic Church. The elder daughter, having a deeply religious nature, had already formed the decision to enter a convent, and although Ford begged her to postpone taking the vows until after his return from the War, the strength of her vocation was too great to allow her to accede to his request. After their parting they never met or corresponded again. This fact lends a tragically prophetic significance to certain lines from the poem referred to above.

> "*When I am weak and old,*
> *And lose my grip, and crave my small reward*
> *Of tolerance and tenderness and ruth,*
> *The children of your dawning day shall hold*
> *The reins we drop and wield the judge's sword*
> *And your swift feet shall tread upon my heels,*
> *And I be ancient Error, you New Truth,*
> *And I be crushed by your advancing wheels . . .*"

With his younger daughter, he continued to correspond regularly until, after his mother's death in 1924, her letters, for some still unexplained reason, remained to her great regret unanswered. Although Ford made several suggestions for subsequent meetings, none, from various causes, ever took place, and after their parting in 1915 Ford never again (so far as the writer is aware) set eyes on the children he had loved so dearly.

Ford secured his commission in the Reserve of Officers in July 1915, and on 16th August a small gathering took place at South Lodge, to bid him good-bye. "Not a party," says Violet's note of invitation to the writer, "only whisky and sandwiches and a few old friends." I cannot, at this distance of time, recall who were present but I imagine that Ezra Pound, possibly Wyndham Lewis, and probably W. L. George, May Sinclair and Ethel Colburn Mayne were among them. Relations between Ford and Violet were already strained, but at the close of the evening the departing guests did not take Ford with them, as seems to have been anticipated. He stayed behind to finish off the remaining whisky with Violet and her secretary, as the latter has since informed me, and, after a violent quarrel, was finally ejected to find his way to bed as best he could. Poor Ford! It wasn't much of a send-off to three years of mud and blood.

CHAPTER XIV

Welch Regiment

"SIR,

With reference to your letter of 6th April, I am directed to furnish, from the records of the Department, the following particulars of the military service of Ford Madox Hueffer.

Appointed to a commission as 2nd Lieutenant,
the Welch Regiment (Special Reserve) . . 14.8.15
Promoted Lieutenant 1.7.17
Relinquished commission on account
of ill-health 7.1.19
London Gazette (Supplement) dated 6.1.19
Served with the British Expeditionary Force
(France and Flanders).
Awarded British War and Victory Medals.

I am, Sir,
Your obedient Servant."

The above, in curt officialese, are the only details of Ford's military service preserved in the War Office records. Through the courtesy of two of Ford's brother officers, who remember him with affection, and the kindness of Mrs. Lucy Masterman in permitting the perusal of letters written by Ford to herself and her husband between 1915 and 1919, I have been able to fill in some of the blanks. Ford's habitual inaccuracy and his habit of romancing about himself and others has made it possible for his detractors to suggest, with no other foundation for their disbelief, that he never heard a shot fired "in anger", that he never went near the Front and that his alleged experiences were mostly fable. For sedentary persons to indulge in this kind of slander there can be no excuse. It prompts the reflexion that Ford was as unfortunate in his choice of enemies as he was, on occasions, in his choice of friends. As an elderly, often over-worked and always underpaid subaltern in a line regiment, his period of service in France and Flanders as well as in various depots in England and Wales, would have been a hard and gruelling experience for any man, however tough, thick-skinned and unimaginative. For a man of Ford's temperament, with his sympathy with other people's sufferings, his innate compassion and what may be termed his cosmic sense, what he saw and endured affected him physically and mentally, till the end of his life. Physically because, although not actually wounded, he suffered severely from gas and shell-shock and spent long periods in hospital. His lungs never fully recovered.

The first of the series of letters to Mrs. Masterman was written about a month before the farewell party referred to in the last chapter. "You may like to know," he says, "that I went round to the W.O. after seeing you and got thrown into a commission in under a minute—the quickest process I have ever known. . . . I can assure you, for what it is worth, that it is as if the peace of God had descended on me—that sounds absurd—but there it is! Man is a curious animal!"

Ford was, to begin with, attached to the 3rd Battalion of the Welch Regiment and began his period of training at Tenby. On 28th August, 1915, he wrote to Masterman to say he was "hard at it—6 a.m. to 7 p.m. every day, like any V form boy and at about the same sort of stuff. Literature seems to have died out of a world that is mostly interesting for its contours. (A contour is an imaginary line, etc.) But I am really quite happy except for an absolute lack of social life". He adds: "Pay some attention, will you, to the reviews of *Between St. D.*, etc. The more I think about it the more certain I feel that it is more valuable than *When Blood*, etc."

A few days later, he must have been gratified to receive a letter from Conrad which Mr. G. Jean-Aubry quotes. The quarrel between them which arose in connection with Conrad's contributions to the *English Review* and resulted in a letter beginning "Dear Hueffer", had long been patched up, although Ford's

position as Conrad's admirer-in-chief and head bottle-washer
had been taken, since 1913, by Mr. Richard Curle. Conrad's
letter of 30th August, 1915, starts as usual "My dear Ford" and
ends with "Love from us all here". It is chiefly concerned with
a pair of field-glasses Ford was anxious to borrow, but in the
course of it Conrad remarks: "Yes! *Mon cher!* Our world of
fifteen years ago is gone to pieces: what will come in its place,
God knows, but I imagine doesn't care.

"Still what I always said was the only immortal line in *Romance*:
'Excellency, a few goats', survives—esoteric, symbolic, profound
and comic—it survives."

Early in 1916 Ford was stationed at Cardiff Castle, one of his
fellow officers being Masterman's younger brother "Sixtus". In
a letter written in February he mentions that he goes down to
Porthcawl every Sunday "to play golf with an old major who
is a revolting person" and says that some of these places are
wonderfully beautiful just now and "if I ever wrote poems they
would be full of Celtic twilight". In a letter written on 13th
May he gives an amusing glimpse of the kind of routine duties
he has to perform. One of them was to write a long memorandum
about a lady who got into the Rink at night and "was chased
round and round over the men's beds" and then, "quite illegally,
handed over to the police on an impossible charge". Ford says
he had to exercise a good deal of ingenuity "to get our people
out of quite a nasty scrape" and composed a forcible document
which went up to H.Q. It was returned with the comment
from the Garrison Commander that "the document of the
subaltern, name indecipherable, was illegible and *illiterate* and
must be written over again. I had worried the good gentleman
by using the words *proprio motu*—'the charge would not lie
because the lady had not come into the Rink *proprio motu*—but
had been introduced by Cpl. Plant 5/Welch etc.' And so everybody strafes everybody else in this microcosm and, without
doubt, discipline is maintained."

Ford's popularity with the rank-and-file, about which there
is general agreement, is easy to understand in the light of this
incident.

In the concluding half of the letter Ford says: "I do not seem to get much nearer the fields of France—but I may go suddenly. I devoutly hope so", and adds that "all leave has been stopped here for some months past on account of three Hun cruisers and we have had many alarms and excursions".

A brief reference to the Easter week Rebellion in Dublin reveals a sympathy with the Irish people which was to become more active and defined four years later. "I don't know," he says. "One cannot comment on Ireland: at least, I can't. As for shooting the rebels: I wish it had been done *in situ;* I suppose it had to be done, tho' I don't know why . . . But at any rate it is no business, thank God, of mine to worry about these affairs."

On 11th July he is still delayed in Cardiff, "without the very slightest idea as to when the trumpet will sound or the 'phone ring", and mentions that he is desperately hard up, so hard up that he cannot stir out of the Castle. He says that he has been "writing some silly little lyrics which no one will print" and correcting the proofs of Violet Hunt's novel—presumably *Their Lives*—which he says is "really very good. She seems," he adds, "to be absolutely untouched, mentally, by the war—wh is no doubt a blessed state."

A week later, his letter is headed "3rd Attd. 9th Welch. B.E.F. Rouen", and he tells Mrs. Masterman that "we leave here to-day to join our various units—presumably in the firing line: I don't know where. We are all scattered—which is disagreeable, but, as jollities go, we have had a jolly time till now, on the boat and so on. . . . Sixtus, who is sitting beside me, sends his love".

Ten days after, in the course of one of the longest and most vivid of his letters from the Front, he says: "we are right up in the middle of the strafe, but only with the 1st Line transport. We get shelled, two or three times a day, otherwise it is fairly dull—indeed, being shelled is fairly dull—after the first once or twice". He remarks that of course it is all very interesting—"filling in patches of one's knowledge and so on, but it isn't more than interesting because we get no news". Rumour and gossip take the place of information. They hear that such and such a division has taken such and such a place—then that it

hasn't; such and such a regiment has been wiped out, then that
its casualties are one accident. The landscape he describes as long
downland, "the sun blazes down and then gets obscured by haze,
blazes down and is then obscured again; there are trees in rows;
in little copses—each copse with a name—La Boisselle, Mamets[?],
Pozolies, and so on. But there isn't any village any more, to
bear any of the names". He says that the air is full of sausage
balloons, swallows, larks and occasional aeroplanes. Apparently
the Germans were not very enterprising in the air and rarely
flew over our lines. "I have only seen three since I have been
here and one was brought down." The noise of the bombardment he describes as continuous, "so continuous that one gets
used to it, as one gets used to the noise in a train, and the ear
picks out the singing of the innumerable larks".

Like most soldiers at the Front, Ford was unimpressed by
Lloyd George's bellicose utterances. "The *Daily Mail* has just
come in and I see that we have taken Pozières and that the Rt.
Hon. D. L. G. still has his back to the wall, and will fight to the
last drop of our blood. I wonder what he would say if he were
out here for a week."

The letter concludes with a revealing reference to Violet Hunt.
"Poor V. I wonder what is happening to her. I have not had a
line from her since I started: I don't know what psychological
vagary or manœuvre it implies. But it is a queer way to set
to work." He says he is fairly fit, "but the officers here are a
terrible lot, without a soul that one can really talk to except the
little boys. I have heard nothing of Sixtus since we parted at
Rouen".

In a long letter in pencil headed "Att'd 9/Welch 19th Div.
B.E.F. 23.8.16." Ford gives Mrs. Masterman further details of
his experiences. He says he is fairly cheerful though he does *not*
get on with his C.O. and the Adjutant overworks him because
he talks Flemish. "So I have to buy straw and pacify infuriated
farmers as well as attending all parades and fatigues. Still it is
all very interesting and one learns a little more every day. We
have been out of the trenches since Monday and go in again
almost immediately—but it is quiet here at its most violent,

compared with the Somme." He says that even the strafe that
the artillery got up for George V—which the artillery officers
called "great" or "huge" according to their temperament—
would, for sound, have "gone into an old woman's thimble in
Albert, not to speak of Bécourt or Fricourt". He remarks that
George V, whom he saw strolling about among the Cheshires,
really was in some danger. "At least he was in an O.P. that was
being shelled fairly heavily when I was in it 'for instruction'.
But I guess they squashed the Boche fire fairly effectively while
he was there". He says that the King, all the same, gave the
impression of being "a good plucked 'un" and that the Prince
of Wales, who was quite unrecognisable, was "perfectly businesslike".

Ford quite justifiably felt that he deserved a staff appointment
and mentions in this letter that General Bridges rode up to him
and talked about "*Entre St. Dennis*, etc.", which he took to
indicate that the Staff was "nibbling" at him. "I should not be
really sorry—because I have had my week on the Somme, other
weeks here and a week in Field Ambulance and a week draft
conducting". He says he would naturally prefer going on as a
regimental officer but his C.O., an ex-Eastbourne Town Coun-
cillor, and the Adjutant, an ex-P.O. clerk, annoy him. The C.O.
"says I am too old" and the Adjutant thanks him all day long
for saving the H.Q. a few francs on turnips and the like. "I
don't know which I dislike most!" Otherwise, he says, it is "a
dreamy sort of life in a grey green country and even the shells
as they set out on their long journeys seem tired. It is rather
curious the extra senses one develops here . . ." In an undated
pencil note, he writes to apologize for the gloom of a previous
letter and says that he ought now to share with Mrs. Masterman
his comparative gaiety. "I don't know why I am gay—except
perhaps that the whole army is gayer. Anyhow, there it is. I
have got plenty to do and have been rather commended." He
again speculates as to the possibility of General Bridges recom-
mending him to Plumer for a Staff appointment and concludes
with an incident to show that he gets "a certain amount of fun"
out of himself. "This morning, for instance, I was standing in

a pail like Adam before the fall when some shrapnel burst over-
head—and I was amused to discover that I grabbed for a shirt,
before a tin hat."

On 25th August Ford writes to Mrs. Masterman that "M.
Gérard, 'Ambassadeur de France' and Gabriel Hanotaux are
writing about *Entre St. Den et G.* and, according to the pubr,
the book ought to make me famous in France". He says "isn't
it rather queer and bitter to think that no one—according to V.
[Violet Hunt] at least—will publish my poems—of wh I have
written several out here?" and adds that he wishes C.F.G. would
make some of his editors put them in, "for I rather suspect V.
(tho' I may be unjust) of suppressing them for ends of her own".

He goes on to describe the kind of routine work on which he
is engaged. "With the labour of 184 men I have to-day drained
a considerable portion of this country and I have also marched
twelve miles to bring up a draft. So I have not been idle." He
complains that his C.O. continues to impress on him that he is
too old for this job and seems to want to force him to relinquish
his commission. He asks Mrs. Masterman if she knows of anyone "who cd impress on Gen. Bridges the desirability of
having me in his Intelligence Department", and says it would
be a good action because he is sure he deserves better—even in
a military sense—than to be harassed "by a rather doting Lt.-
Col. who cherishes a special dislike for the Special Reserve". Ford
says that he is "terribly afraid of becoming a bore with a grievance" but that his "grievance" was legitimate and well-grounded
few can doubt who examine his record. The publication of the
French translation of *Between St. Dennis and St. George* was of
considerable importance in furthering amicable relations between
the Allied countries, and it is difficult to think of anyone better
fitted than Ford to act as a liaison officer. His ability to speak
Flemish must also be regarded as an unusual accomplishment and
one for which "M.I." ought to have been able to find a use.

In an undated letter, written in pencil at about this period,
Ford again mentions that he does not get on with his C.O.,
finds the Adjutant disagreeable and is "not vastly happy with the
people here". He infers that he has been in hospital and only

got back to duty by using a great deal of determination, after an incredibly tedious struggle across France. "I rather begin to think that I shall not be able to 'stick it'—the conditions of life are too hard and the endless waitings too enervating." He remarks, however, that it is extraordinarily quiet where he is "compared with the other front; the Germans seem to have nothing but minenwerfers and little or no artillery—only occasionally a shell comes over here—so that it seems wonderfully like Heaven".

In the next letter, dated 6.9.16, written in pencil, evidently in the midst of a bombardment, Ford asks dolefully why it is that nobody writes to him. "Does one so quickly become a ghost? Alas!" He says he has had nothing for a week except notes from Violet "disclosing the fact that I have lost my bicycle and the like—which of course takes one's mind off oneself—and before that no one wrote to me for ever so long. Except French Ministers and poets". He adds that "we are in a h—ll of a noise, just now—and my hand is aching badly—our guns are too inconsiderate . . ." The rest is almost illegible.

Four days later he writes to tell Masterman that the French "Minister of Instruction and of Inventions useful to the War" has asked him to come to see him, "merely as a vague politeness I suppose". However, armed with this letter he extracted week-end leave from the authorities, and went to Paris "where H.E. thanked me very prettily". He says that his book is "really rather booming among the lit. gents and official world of Paris and, to please Payot, [the publisher] I spent thirty-six hours in strenuous work, cutting it down and writing into it in French —a rather pretty epilogue which pleased Payot". The effort evidently exhausted him as he collapsed on his return and was made to see the M.O. "who said I was suffering from specific shell-shock and ought to go to hospital. However, I didn't and got back here".

A month later he was back in Wales and his next letter, addressed to C. F. G. Masterman, was headed "3rd Batt. Welch Regt. Kinmel Park. No. 4 Camp. Rhyl. North Wales. 12.10.16". He says he has been "posted to a Coy—wh. does

Violet Hunt

Arnold Bennett

seem to be a waste of my abilities—otherwise I wd not worry you. Moreover I can't afford it—wh is also a motive—whereas in France I cd be really useful in a dozen ways and could just live." He asks Masterman to try to use his influence to get him a Staff job. A fortnight later (25.10.16) he writes to Masterman in considerable dejection. "No: I have not heard anything at this end and, knowing the W.O. as I do, I don't suppose I shall. I wish you cd have done something—but I never really expected you cd. My luck is too much out." He was evidently in great financial difficulties and saw nothing for it but to resign his commission and "disappear into a decent obscurity". He says he is doing no good at Kinmel Park either to himself or to anyone else and that as the training they are giving the men seems "ridiculously ineffective" he cannot console himself with the idea that he is doing useful work. He tells Masterman that he is not doing any writing, because "to write one must have some purpose in life—and I simply haven't any. You see one has phases of misfortune that get too heavy for one as one gradually loses resiliency . . ." Not for the first time during his war years, he was harassed by the effects of Violet's gossiping tongue, though the details of his complaint are not revealed in a letter on the subject he addressed to Mrs. Masterman on 27th October. In this he again refers to his financial difficulties and intention of giving up his commission. "I could get along personally on my pay—but I have outside liabilities too, you see. And V's campaign of vilification makes people very shy of publishing my work, even if I cd write. So I shd really be much better off if I relinquished my commn and enlisted. It isn't depression, or pique, but just common sense."

On 29th November, Ford writes to tell Masterman that the War Office has sent down an "imperative order that I am to be sent to France! ! !" He says that all he is really anxious about is that he should not go back to the IX Welch, with whose Adjutant and C.O., as earlier letters reveal, he was on very bad terms. "I don't at all want not to be killed," he observes—"but I don't want to be strafed unjustly as well." He says that France, in the meantime, continues to honour him: "Academies and things

offering me ribbons and so on—from the Académie Internationale
Historique—which is probably a bum show—up to the Institut
de France—which isn't." He says also that he has paid a considerable portion of his mess bill out of auction, "which shows
that God is on my side!"

The next letter to Masterman, written in pencil, is headed
"IX Welch. No. 11 Red X Hospital. Rouen. B.E.F. 5.1.17."
He says he has not written before because of unsettlement and
partly because he has been too ill for some time to write cheer-
fully and was tired of writing uncheerfully. When he got to
the base camp he was greeted with the news that he was re-
attached to the IX Welch, which was precisely what he wished
to avoid. He was informed that it was meant amiably but, as
he notes, it did not seem to him very tactful "for if that particular C.O. didn't want me, I still more obviously didn't want
that C.O. So I protested rather vigorously, though unofficially".
While he was waiting to rejoin the battalion he was given
various polyglot jobs such as writing proclamations in French
about thefts of rations issued to H.B.M.'s forces and mounting
guard over German sick. While thus engaged his "lungs intervened", which was hardly to be wondered at as what he was
doing entailed getting wet through and coming in to write for
a couple of hours in a stifling room and then getting wet through
some more and then sleeping in a dripping hut. When a thorough medical overhaul finally became necessary his lungs were
found to be "in a devil of a way, with extensions at the bases
and solidifications and all sorts of things—partly due to a slight
touch of gas I got in the summer and partly to sheer weather".
He was sent at once to hospital and seemed to be "doing very
nicely" when he had a sudden relapse on Christmas Eve. He
says his temperature has been "normal since yesterday", that he
is still "jolly weak", that he expects to be sent to Menton, to
the convalescent home there, fairly soon and would be fairly
contented if he did not chafe at the inactivity. "But of course
I couldn't very well be active", he says—"even at writing proclamations because all day I am as stupid as an owl and all night
I lie awake and perceive the ward to be full of Huns of forbidding

aspect—except when they give me a sleeping draft (sic)". Ford was evidently a very sick man when he wrote this very lucid and interesting letter. He tells Masterman that he sometimes doubts his own sanity, "indeed, quite frequently I do" and adds that he supposes "the Somme was a pretty severe ordeal, though I wasn't conscious of it at the time". As was so often the case with shell-shocked men, the effect of what he had been through was delayed until some time after the tension had been relaxed. He says that he now finds himself waking up "in a hell of a funk" and going on being in the hell of a funk till morning and adds that "that is pretty well the condition of a number of men here. I wonder what the effect will be on us all, after the War —and on national life and the like. I fancy amenity of manners will suffer a good deal—for most of us who were once civil-spoken enough have become arrogant and intolerant. Well, *qui vivra verra!*"

He expresses the hope that Masterman has not lost Wellington House, "for I am sure you could not have done a better 'bit' during Armageddon—and no one else could have done it better, either", after registering his dislike of the recent Governmental changes. "What a Ministry! Everything one has fought against all one's life! Northcliffism, Georgeism, Mondism, Balliolism! If it weren't for Balfour and Robert Cecil—and I don't suppose they cut much ice *dans ces parages*. . . . If I only had a pen and could still use it and it wasn't war time and I wasn't a bit dotty, I wd shew you, my dear, what I cd do as a political writer!" He ends this letter: "Give my love to Lucy and thank her, will you, for her p.c. What nice kids! I wish I had a son."

Shortly after this letter was written, Ford and a brother officer, Mr. Claude P. Lewis, had the pleasant experience of being transferred to Menton, for a period of convalescence on the Côte d'Azur. Mr. Lewis has kindly shown me an inscribed presentation copy of *Entre St. Dennis et St. Georges*, (Payot et Cie, frcs. 3.50. Troisième mille), which bears the date of 11th January, 1917, and commemorates the occasion. Although nearly thirty years had elapsed since they were in hospital together, Mr. Lewis remembered Ford very clearly as an agreeable companion, in spite of the disparity between their ages, and was greatly impressed by the respect in which he was held by the Provençal people with whom, on various expeditions, they came in contact. This may be the place to mention the affection with which "Old Hoof" was regarded not only by some of the more intelligent officers of his own age but also by the subalterns whom, in a letter quoted above, he referred to as "the little boys", and in particular by the Welsh privates in his immediate care. He spared himself no trouble to help his men in their domestic difficulties, learnt some Welsh in order the better to understand them, and generally looked after them "like a father". Mr. Thomas A. Lloyd, who was with him at the depot of the Welch Regiment at Kinmel Park, Rhyl, has sent me the following impression of Ford. "He was Hueffer, then, to me and although he was a 'writer of sorts' as I was informed, I had no idea that the dear fellow, a brother subaltern but twice my age, was the literary genius that he has proved to be. This may have been through lack of self-advertisement on his part!.

"I recollect well our first introduction, and the day shortly afterwards when as a very junior officer in a mess where the dominant figures were the present Marquis of Bath, Capt. Hon. Wellesley Somerset, now Lord Raglan, I believe, and of course Hueffer himself, he sponsored me in my duties as Orderly Officer. I had then the same feeling as you experienced when 'Ford aroused in me all the emotions which a schoolboy can feel for a House Master who befriends him'. Just that! . . . I was at the depot in September (or was it August?). I also met him at the Base in France afterwards and later heard that he was employed interrogating German prisoners."

In a letter to his younger daughter written on 10th December, 1916 (enclosing a cheque for £5 "which I hope may be useful in carrying you over Xmas") Ford makes a vague reference to the experience in the front line which caused his breakdown in health and also mentions that his brother Oliver was badly wounded about a fortnight after he was evacuated. He himself "wasn't so much wounded", he says, "as blown up by a 4.2 and shaken into a nervous breakdown which has made me unbearable to myself and my kind". He says he is better but may go up the line again at any moment "tho' I shd prefer to remain out of it for a bit". Two days later, he writes to say that a Medical Board has sat on him and found that he cannot go up the line again till the summer "as the gas of the Huns has pretty well done for my lungs—wh make a noise like a machine gun". As recorded above, the Board later ordered him into hospital.

Ford tells his daughter that of the fourteen officers who came out with him he is the only one left at the Base, and "I am pretty well a shattered wreck—tho' they say my lungs will get better in time. And I sit in the hut here wh is full of Welch officers all going up—and all my best friends—and think that very likely not one of them will be alive in a fortnight. I tell you, my dear, it is rather awful." On 7th January, 1917, when in hospital, he wrote the moving poem "One Day's List", in an agony of compassion for "the little boys".

It has not been possible for the writer to discover the details of Ford's movements immediately after his return from Menton but by the 19th July he was back with the 3rd Battalion at Redcar, in Yorkshire. In a note of that date to Mrs. Masterman, he refers to some articles which Violet Hunt had sent to Massingham, editor of *The Nation*, "who turned them, naturally, down. I think she then sent them to Rendall with the idea, I suppose, that they might do for 'propaganda'—but nobody will print me nowadays".

On 8th September he writes to Mrs. Masterman, again from Redcar, asking for a copy of "that poem about M.Gs. that I sent you from Dieppe". He says he is "trying to get together, languidly, a small volume—that no one, probably, will want to publish". He adds that he is pretty hard worked "but not yet passed fit—wh is vexing as I suppose I shall get shoved out in December again and I rather dread the bad weather out there". An enlightening comment is that the local population "swim amazingly in money". A few weeks later, owing to some change of mood, he has lost interest in the project of issuing a volume of war poems and writes to tell Mrs. Masterman that he has decided to suppress it. "Publication means very little to me—and the publication of poems, less than any other form." He says he is personally pretty fit, "fit enough not to bother about how I am and generally rather prosperous in a military sense, tho' certainly not in any other".

On 13th January, 1918, he is able to announce the good news that John Lane is to issue a volume of his war poems. A mercurial change, typical of Ford but common also to many, perhaps the majority, of writers has evidently taken place, now that publication is assured. He says that the forthcoming book has "got some pretty good stuff in it. I have just finished a patriotic poem that I fancy is rather beautiful—with nothing about Britannia and the lion and so on, in it". As regards his future movements, he tells Mrs. Masterman that as the doctors won't pass him for General Service, "confound them", he has just put in an application to be attached to a Labour Battalion in France. "I have a desire to be out there which is almost nostalgia." He is annoyed about the doctors' decision, "because a Labour Bn is just as dangerous and uncomfortable as a Service one, yet the credit is less. However, I don't mind that". He says he intends to apply for a week's leave and asks Mrs. Masterman if she knows of any cheap lodgings he could take in her neighbourhood. "South Lodge does not seem to be available. I wd not worry you, but you are the only people I care to see in London now, so does the world of men of goodwill shrink and shrink!"

Instead of being sent out to France to join a Labour Battalion, Ford seems at last to have secured some sort of Staff job, which no doubt to some extent relieved his always acute financial difficulties. In a letter to his younger daughter, headed "H.Q. Northern Command 13.4.18." he encloses a cheque for ten guineas which he hopes will reach her on her birthday and mentions that he is telling Cox & Co. to send her £2 at the beginning of each month and has put a little money into the War Loan for her, in case she wants £4 or £5 for any special purpose, at any time. He tells her that he is at present, and has been for about a month, attached to the Staff and goes all over the North of

England inspecting, training and lecturing. "It is in many ways lucky for me as I was passed fit and should have gone out to my Bn again just the day after I got the order to join the Staff—and my Bn has been pretty well wiped out since then and I suppose I shd have gone West with it. However I shall be going as soon as I have got my job here done in about a fortnight or three weeks." He mentions that he has just received an advance copy of his volume of poems, "the first book I shall have published for three years or so", and that most of the poems were written in Albert and just in front of Bailleul "where the Germans now are again. It is rather an eerie feeling, because, having had to pay so much attention to the nature of the ground, I seem to know say Armentières and Plugstreet better than any other place in the world—and now it is all gone again, or worse than gone, for itself, poor dear". He offers to send her a copy of the book which he says is "pretty good"—as indeed it was.

There are several indications in the *On Heaven* volume that Ford found some congenial friends among his brother officers in the Welch Regiment. The book, for example, is dedicated to "Lt.-Col. G. R. Powell some time commanding a Battalion of the Welch Regiment this with affection". At the end of it, added as an appendix, are some verses "written to *bouts rhimés* supplied to me by my friend and old O.C. Coy. H. C. James. When in a minute or two I had filled in the lines in English, in a few seconds he would supply the Latin version". Even if we allow for some exaggeration, the result is impressive as a combined operation in the field of elegant scholarship.

I have been unable to trace Ford's movements in the remaining months of the war though it is evident from what Stella Bowen tells us in *Drawn from the Life* that, towards the end of 1918, he managed to spend a good deal of his time in London, renewed contacts with such old friends as Ezra Pound and went to studio parties in Chelsea.

A curious glimpse of him, in March 1918, is given in Mr. Ferris Greenslet's autobiography, *Under the Bridge* (Collins, 1944). Mr. Greenslet says he tried to board a train at Euston which was already full and overflowing. After many failures to effect an entrance his porter "laid his hand on the door of a first-class compartment labelled Reserved, occupied only by a single large British officer exuding an incredible hauteur, and said, 'Let's try this, sir'." Mr. Greenslet was doubtful of his chances of admission, but the officer looked up and suddenly recognized him. "By God, it's F. G.!" It was his old friend Ford. The door was locked after Mr. Greenslet's entry and the two travelled together in great comfort as far as Liverpool. Mr. Greenslet relates that in the intervals of an animated conversation Ford applied himself to two pieces of literary work he had in hand. "He read proofs of an erotic novel he had written in French for publication in Paris to eke out his Captain's pay, and he prepared an elaborate report for his regimental adjutant concerning four blankets missing from his company's quota." They parted at Liverpool and Mr. Greenslet relates that "three weeks later, Ford, with his company of Canadians, was among the first over Vimy Ridge".

Mr. Greenslet does not give the source of his information about Vimy Ridge, but though I am unable to confirm it there is no reason to regard it as inaccurate. Ford had, in every sense, a hard war, did his full share of service in France and Flanders, never shirked a job or exploited his age and ill-health to avoid unpleasant duties. As an officer, his record was unblemished, undistinguished, but none the less highly honourable.

Some doubts must be expressed, however, about the "erotic novel in French" to which Mr. Greenslet refers. Mr. Greenslet is an eminently respectable Bostonian, with all that that implies, and Ford could never resist the temptation to play up to him by making remarks of this kind, such remarks being afterwards quoted—the writer recalls several instances—with irresistible humour.

Ford's small volume of poems "written on active service", though too authentic and too moving to pass unrecognized by the discerning few, never had anything like the *réclame* accorded to the fashionable "war poets". That he was shabbily treated by those influential personages who, by their control of space in the leading journals are able, temporarily, to make or mar reputations, can scarcely be denied at the present day. Whether this neglect was an indirect result of ill-natured gossip based on Violet's self-pity, or of vague disapproval of Ford on "moral" grounds, remains a matter for conjecture. In view of the *New Witness* attack, of which mention has been made, it is impossible to dismiss as nonsense Ford's own conviction that there was a sort of conspiracy to discredit him and to deny his work the recognition it deserved, although probably, being human, he exaggerated its extent. There were two ways of achieving fame as a war poet; one of these was to be killed, like Wilfred Owen and Edward Thomas, the other was to meet and be liked by the right people at the right moment. To Ford neither of these aids to success was available. His literary intimates, being for the most part young *avantgardistes*, were not in a position to advance his claims with the Establishment.

What, we may ask ourselves, was the effect of Ford's war experiences on what Wells described as his "system of assumed personas and dramatized selves"? It is a question which even his most intimate friends would be chary of attempting to answer with any degree of assurance. In the light of the Tietjens novels, on which he embarked five years after his demobilization, we may at least hazard a guess that his war service compensated him for many of the humiliations to which he had been subjected since his wife abandoned her divorce proceedings. It restored his pride, his belief in himself, while, at the same time, increasing his view that society owed him as a reward for his services, as it owed to all his comrades-in-arms, the right to live his own life, immune from civilian criticism. The sense of guilt which as he told his daughters in the dedicatory letter to *Ancient Lights*, had dogged him from his childhood, was replaced by something like moral self-confidence. He had been through hell, stuck it out, made good, done his bit and in consequence was armoured against all reproaches, whether from Violet or from any other source. There is no doubt that he derived an enormous satisfaction from having held the King's Commission in an historic regiment. As we have seen, he was much liked by the men under his command and by most of his brother officers. The experience of belonging to a distinguished corporate body must have made up, in large measure, for his lack of an old school tie and an English University degree, to the particular "persona" which occasionally felt the need of such social supports. As for Ford's attitude towards the opposite sex, we can only guess that he felt that women owed him something and that, on various grounds, including his position as retired warrior, he was entitled to take what he wanted from them when he could get it. He had, whether rightly or wrongly is immaterial, a grievance against his wife, and a grievance against Violet, while there is no doubt that he was deeply disappointed in his daughters, though no one will suggest that they were to blame for it. In a word, Ford left the Army tougher in character, though impaired in health, and emotionally deepened, if the word "emotion" can be used to cover the passions of the mind. He also left it very much advanced in his political thinking. His "ivory tower" period was definitely ended. All humanity was now his preoccupation. He was spiritually prepared for the advance from being a good novelist to becoming a great one.

CHAPTER XV

Sussex "Small Producer"

IN HER honest and courageous autobiography, *Drawn from the Life*, Stella Bowen describes her early experiences in London, during the Four Years' War. She was a young Australian, with a little money of her own, who, after her mother's death, had persuaded her trustees to let her come to London for a year to continue her artistic education. She arrived in the spring of 1914 and, by a series of fortunate coincidences, found her way into Chelsea, was taken by friends to such "haunts of vice" as the Café Royal and the Crabtree Club and soon got to know a number of advanced young people. These included Ezra Pound, John Rodker, Margaret Cole, Mary Butts, and Phyllis Reid, who later became Mrs. Vallance. With the latter girl friend she shared, for three years, a studio in Kensington which belonged to an artist who had gone to the front. Here she quickly collected a circle of acquaintants, many of whom were Socialist-pacifists, joined the Westminster School of Art and came under the inspiring influence of Sickert. At their first studio party, held to say good-bye to some artist who was leaving for France, Ezra Pound appeared. With his characteristic friendliness he induced his two girl-hostesses to join his dinner club at Bellotti's in Soho, where, in course of time, Stella Bowen met "a whole heap of people", all of whom knew Ford. Among them were T. S. Eliot, Arthur Waley, May Sinclair, Violet Hunt, the painter Edward Wadsworth, G. B. Stern, Wyndham Lewis and W. B. Yeats. Those, as she recalls, were the days of the American *Little Review*, when the "reverberations of *Blast* were still shaking the air". "There were," she says, "lovely things for us to admire—Eliot's 'Prufrock', Ezra's 'Lustra', or Gaudier-Brjeska's stone carvings and drawings of animals and Wyndham Lewis's drawings. . . . There was also James Joyce's 'Portrait of the

Artist'. Joyce and Lewis were Ezra's twin gods, before whom we were bidden to bend the knees most deeply." A third god was the absent Ford, for this, as she was later to discover, was Ford's own particular "world". Ford, she tells us, was one of the few writers whom Ezra allowed them to admire. "*Ladies Whose Bright Eyes* and *The Good Soldier* were two of the best-thumbed books on our shelves, and Ford's war poems, *Footsloggers* and *Old Houses in Flanders*, were much discussed and admired at Harold Monro's Poetry Bookshop, whose weekly poetry readings we frequented." Ford first appeared among them, she records, in the spring of 1918. He was, she tells us, "the only intellectual I had met to whom army discipline provided a conscious release from the torments and indecisions of a super-sensitive brain. To obey orders was, for him, a positive holiday, and the pleasure he took in recounting the rather bucolic anecdotes of the Army was the measure of his need to escape from the intrigues and frustrations of literary London". He was older than the rest of her friends, but much more impressive. "He was very large, with a pink face, yellow hair, and drooping, bright blue eyes. His movements were gentle and deliberate and his quiet and mellow voice spoke, to an Australian ear, with ineffable authority." At first Stella Bowen reacted violently against him on the ground that he was a "militarist", but she soon discovered that "every known human quality could be found flourishing in Ford's make-up, except a respect for logic". His attitude to science was very simple: he did not believe a word of it. On the other hand, what he did not know about the depths and weaknesses of human nature was not worth knowing. "The hidden places of the heart," she adds, "were his especial domain, and when he chose he could put the screw upon your sense of pity or of fear with devastating sureness." There follows a passage of analysis the truth of which anyone who knew Ford at all well would be bound to acknowledge. "The stiff, rather alarming exterior, and the conventional, omniscient manner, concealed a highly complicated emotional machinery." She adds, with rare insight, "it produced an effect of tragic vulnerability; tragic because the scope of his understanding and the breadth of his imagination had produced a great edifice which was plainly in need of more support than was inherent in the structure itself. A walking temptation to any woman, had I but known it!"

The particular "persona" on which Ford relied for his wooing of Stella Bowen was that of the wearied Titan who after a career of literary achievement, inadequately appreciated, harassed by domestic griefs and shaken by the trials and horrors of war, longed for the perfect tranquillity of love-in-a-cottage. He "wanted to dig potatoes and raise pigs and never write another book. Wanted to start a new home. Wanted a child".

That Ford was perfectly sincere in all these protestations is no more in doubt than was the certainty that Stella Bowen, in her youth and inexperience, would accept this strange proposal. She did not realize "to what extent he would be putting the clock back, whilst I put mine forward", and still believed that happiness was a kind of gift that one person could bestow upon another. She was passionately eager to bestow it on Ford since he evidently wanted it so badly. And when Ford wanted anything, she says, "he filled the sky with an immense ache that had the awful simplicity of a child's grief, and appeared to hold the same possibilities of assuagement". Looking back on a union that was to last only ten years, she has the magnanimity to admit that it was an excellent bargain on both sides. Ford got what he was then hungry for; his cottage, his domestic peace and eventually his baby daughter. What Stella Bowen got was, she tells us, "a remarkable and liberal education, administered in ideal circumstances". With an intelligence and generosity which command respect she adds that "to have the run of a mind of that calibre, with all its inconsistencies, its generosity, its blind spots, its spaciousness and vision, and its great sense of form and style, was a privilege for which I am still trying to say 'thank you'."

Ford's escape to his cottage was not accomplished without many painful scenes and much correspondence with Violet, which must have tried his nerves to breaking point. Edgar Jepson, as the friend of both parties, was the recipient of Violet's confidences. No good purpose would be served by recording the almost frenzied outpourings of an ageing woman thwarted in her possessive instinct and painfully lacking in dignity and self-control. To Jepson, who regarded the whole episode with sympathetic detachment as a clash of temperaments for which neither party could be blamed, Ford least of all, the receipt of her letters must have been a painful experience. Although her reproaches, which Ford regarded as "insults", would have driven him out of South Lodge even if Stella Bowen had never entered his life, Violet was incapable of accepting the breach as final or of surrendering what she regarded as her "rights" over Ford and making the best of the situation. Having made it impossible for him to stay, she was nevertheless unwilling to let him go. On one occasion she even persuaded May Sinclair to accompany her on a visit to inspect Ford's cottage, and the two women peered at him over a gate while he was feeding his pigs. To anyone of Ford's nervously sensitive disposition this sort of perse-cution was maddening and unendurable and it is charitable to suppose that, in subjecting him to it, Violet was temporarily out of her mind. One of her troubles, which she greatly exaggerated, was what "people would think", and she appealed to Ford's chivalry to save her face, in the eyes of their circle of friends, by making regular reappearances at South Lodge, in order to prove that she had not been cast off completely. Her plea was that she must see him, if only occasionally. She evidently persuaded Ford to go over to her cottage at Selsey, while his mother was staying there, for she wrote a full account of the interview, which lasted three hours, to Jepson. She says that she told Ford that she was very conscious of having been "rather horrid to him in the last year . . . and wanted to see him to say so, to get it off my chest. Then he walked about and said you can see yourself we never can live together. . . . You don't realise how you hurt me. How you drove me out of the house by insults—saying I only lived with you for the sake of your money. I will not, I will not sleep in the house again. . . ." The wrangle continued and Violet says that he was "panting and pouring all the time —walking about. He said he couldn't sit still, he was so nervous, that the doctor had said that he could not *live* a fortnight in

London and he meant to live in the country all his life". After that Violet admits that she "let out" and called him various names which may have induced Jepson to describe her behaviour, rather brutally, as "middle-class". Either before or after this interview, her letters are invariably undated, she sent Jepson a draft of a letter she proposed to send to Ford saying that she wanted to see him "pretty often". "I just do want this, and I have lived with you as your supposed wife for eight years counting from the fifth of September 1911 till the twenty-ninth of March 1919, so you will (can surely) give me say an hour once a fortnight if I ask for it." Jepson's reply was wise but crushing. "Dear Violet," he wrote on 5th August, 1920, "That letter is a truly hopeless production—the kind of thing that —— must have written frequently. It sounds as if you just wanted to see him to have an unpleasant row with him; and human intercourse is not really conducted on those beastly lines." He appends a draft of a letter which is "much more the kind of thing to get you what you want" and tells her not to add anything to it.

Ford had made a more or less formal announcement of his departure from South Lodge in a long letter to C. F. G. Masterman, written from the Authors' Club on 28th June, 1919. It begins with an interesting expression of his political sympathies and an offer to put his voice and his pen as wholeheartedly at the service of the Liberal Party as they were at the disposal of the country during the war. "I should like to say one thing, for what I am worth and that is that I believe after long consideration and some knowledge of the war that the greatest credit of all is due to the Asquithian Liberals; that the winning of the war was altogether due to your people and that the behaviour of the country at the last election was a piece of dastardly ingratitude." Turning "to other matters", he says that he has left South Lodge for good and set up a home of his own in the country. "At the time I did this, in April, I was fairly penniless and lived for some months as a jobbing gardener, but lately I have made a good deal—indeed, a great deal—of money, quite unexpectedly, by the sale of various cinema rights in the U.S.A.

and in other ways." He says that at the beginning of the year he gave Violet the choice between his leaving South Lodge and her giving up the acquaintanceship of certain people whom he regarded as his enemies. Violet's course, he says, "seemed to me to be so radical a disloyalty to any sort of joint life that I saw no other way open than to retire from the scene".

He goes on to tell Masterman that he has taken a labourer's cottage in the country and adds that "to-day I have changed my name by deed poll to 'Ford'. I would not do this, out of obstinacy, while the war was still on but I see now no longer any reason to continue to put up with the inconvenience that a Teutonic patronymic causes in the rather humble sphere of life that I now adorn". He says he has made a rather beautiful garden with the work of his own unaided hands and subsists rather largely on its products, and adds that he is also writing some "rather pretty stuff. So *me voilà planté* and so I hope to continue".

No mention is made of Stella but he tells Masterman that he won't appear again in London "except that, in order to spare Violet the mortification of the appearance of an official abandonment, I shall figure at her larger parties from time to time—as for instance on Monday next. I don't like doing it but I take it to be a duty". The letter concludes with expressions of gratitude to Masterman and messages of affection to his wife and children. "As you may have observed," he writes, "I dislike talking about my feelings or affairs and I only do so to you because I am really grateful to you for all your backing in the past four years so that I think I owe it to you to keep you posted as to my motives and movements."

Regarding the party referred to in Ford's letter I have received some interesting comments from Mr. Alec Waugh who was present at it. "Has any one told you," he writes, "about a curious party Violet gave in July 1919? I only realised later the dramatic undertones. (I had dined with them at South Lodge in Jan. '19 where I met W. L. George for the first time, and knew nothing of their having parted.) I heard later that by July 1919 they were apart but that Violet wanted there to be a public occasion when they could appear together. It was one of the biggest parties I have ever been to—champagne, white ties, etc. I got there a little early and Violet kept saying 'I wonder what's keeping Ford. I wish he'd hurry'. When eventually he did arrive it was to moon around looking very lost. He did not seem to know if he was a guest or host. He appeared surprised when I went up to say 'good-bye' and 'thank you'. I suppose it was their last public bow. It certainly was a party.

"They were by the way entertaining briskly in Jan. 1919. They had a *bouts rimés* party—I think in Clifford Bax's studio."

The cottage, in a wild and lovely part of West Sussex, in which Ford and Stella first set up housekeeping in May 1919, was picturesque, built of old red brick and old red tiles, charmingly situated, and, as it had a big hole in its roof, extremely damp. Its name, or that of the remote village to which it belonged, was Red Ford and they paid the farmer who owned it a rent of five shillings a week. They were very poor to start with, the "great deal of money" of which Ford boasted in his letter to Masterman seems to have been about £400, which came to him as a half share of the film rights of *Romance*.[1] Ford distempered the living-room and white-washed the kitchen of the cottage, collected an assortment of second-hand junk as furniture and also attempted some not very successful carpentering operations of which he was, no doubt, inordinately proud. But, as Stella says, if he was "inexpert in the use of tools, he was extraordinarily skilful with his hands when it was a question of making things grow, or concocting some of his famous dishes. Then his movements were easy and sure, and everything he touched succeeded and came right".

When, at Stella's instigation, he started another book, she deputized for him in the kitchen, but nothing could induce him to break off work to eat the dinner she had cooked until his inspiration flagged. Thus a meal timed for eight would often not be eaten till two hours later. And yet, in spite of the acute discomforts of their rural hovel and the, to orderly people, exasperating nature of Ford's habits, they enjoyed themselves. Indeed, whenever the "persona" of the small-producer gained

[1] I learn from an American source that he also received £250 for the film rights of *Mr. Fleight*.

o

the ascendancy in Ford's complex make-up, as it did at recurrent intervals throughout his life, he passed his happiest and most contented hours. He had a passion for gardening and derived real satisfaction from growing his own food and cooking it. Another passion, almost as strong, was sociability. This was difficult to combine with the primitive conditions at Red Ford and it is with amusement, mingled with acute sympathy for the "woman of the house" that we learn that there were frequent week-end visitors. "Herbert Read and his wife came, and Francis Meynell, and Roy and Daisy Postgate, and Phyllis, of course, and Mary Butts, now married to the young poet, John Rodker."

What with a normal host would have seemed like a revolting *mélange* of mess, muddle and squalor, was transformed, for his visitors, by the impact of Ford's personality and the adaptability of Stella, into an enjoyable experience. "The simplicity of his heart," says Stella Bowen, "which made small things seem important, like the earliest salad, or the purchase of an old bit of brass or an effective arrangement of our meagre possessions made Ford a delightful companion. He was never bored." There was, indeed, about Ford no "mediocrity". His mere presence, in a tumbledown labourer's cottage, urban garret or "bourgeois" flat, so permeated his surroundings as to lend them a curious distinction. This seems to be a quality which all men of genius possess in common.

After nearly a year of discomfort and short commons at Red Ford, Ford's windfall from the sale of film rights, combined with some capital which Stella Bowen withdrew from Australia, enabled the couple to buy the cottage of their dreams. It was situated on a "great wooded hill" in the village of Bedham, about ten miles from their original home, commanded one of those "immense views" which meant so much to Ford, and had behind it an orchard full of wild daffodils. Below it was a wood full of bluebells and, lower down still, a rough ten-acre field. The cottage, called Coopers, was about three centuries old, "with plaster and oak beams with a steep tiled roof", and they took possession in the summer of 1920, after some necessary alterations had been completed. By this time they owned a "high, ill-sprung dogcart and a big, lively old mare" which Stella had learnt to drive. She was now an expectant mother, so that the amenities of her new home, though not remarkable by ordinary standards of comfort, must have been welcome. Driving the mare along the steep, narrow and winding lanes around the house was, however, something of a problem as the animal was obstinately hard of hearing and had a hard mouth. On one occasion, however, Stella records that they had the "pleasure of passing, without a flicker of recognition, a whole car-load of uninvited London busybodies coming to peep at Ford in his new retreat, gently rolling backwards down the hill!"

The baby, Esther Julia, afterwards known as Julie or Juliette, was born in a London nursing home on 29th November, 1920. She was not only a "lovely child", but had also an excellent digestion and almost never cried. Ford, it goes without saying, adored her. He called her *"ma petite princesse"* and, as soon as she grew old enough to enjoy them, invented for her more of his enchanting fairy stories.

We see him now at one of the happiest moments of his varied and restless career. The "persona" of the small-producer had received its fullest gratification. He had his typical smallholder's cottage, his child, his companion, his animals—"two litters of pigs, thirty hens, twenty ducks, three goats and the old mare, not to mention a cat and a dog"—and ten acres to play with. As the big field could not be cultivated without the expenditure of large sums in clearing it, Ford decided to use it for breeding black pigs on the open air system, and to start operations, purchased two expensive pedigree sows. Unfortunately Ford was only an amateur, rather inefficient and hopelessly unbusinesslike pig-breeder, whereas, despite his frequent "farewells" to literature, he was, by talent and long training, an expert professional writer. He could live by the pen, but not by the pigs: and the more his literary work was appreciated the more it absorbed him. On Stella Bowen's shoulders fell the task of seeing that he had somewhere to write and unmolested quiet while he was doing it. This meant that, in addition to looking after the baby and attending to the needs of a constant succession of guests, she had to do the major part of the farm work, as well as supplying all the "household management". How she did it is described with equal modesty and good humour in her book, but remains in the nature of the miraculous. Ford, as all who knew him agree, was completely unmercenary and just as completely unable to plan or manage what money he had. "His whole system," Stella says, "rejected any knowledge of money matters, and if forced to contemplate them at a bad moment, he would collapse into such a misery of despair that our entire lives became paralysed." On the other hand, if he received the smallest unexpected cheque he immediately "felt like a million dollars". In an undated letter to Edgar Jepson, probably written in the early summer of 1921, he invites either Jepson and his wife, or his wife and one of their daughters, to occupy his spare bedroom. "We are," he says, "but for the drought which is ruinous for my agricultural pursuits, remarkably flourishing, for us, in our humble scale—at least. I am enjoying a mild boom-kin in the U.S.A. and thus the New World redresses . . ."

He tells Jepson that if he would come it would be delightful and "I could give you plenty of poker of which I have been playing a good deal with U.S.A. pilgrims to this shrine. They come in small shoals to talk highbrow; and we set them to feed the pigs—of which I have a number—or to carry the hay of which we have successfully harvested a nice little stack. And in the evenings I take their money at poker—and we have sweet corn and pumpkins growing, so they feel homesick". He adds that picquet is the better game, "the only game, really". The letter ends with an interesting reference to Stella Bowen's work as a portrait painter. How she managed to practise her art, amid all her other occupations, is a mystery, but Ford mentions that "this spring she did a portrait of the Mayoress of Edgbaston so successfully that the Mayor fainted".

Ford retained throughout his life a great liking for cards and other parlour games. His nephew, Oliver Soskice, remembers spending a summer holiday with Ford at Coopers "and passing the evenings playing chess at which he was not very good and composing sonnets to '*bouts rhimés*' at which he had a truly amazing skill. There were numerous visitors there, mostly writers and poets . . ."

Edgar Jepson and his wife accepted Ford's invitation and spent a week at Bedham at the end of August. In a letter dated 15th September, 1921, Ford thanks Jepson, presumably for getting him commissions for articles, and promises "to do something for Dark". Mr. Sidney Dark was then editing *John O'London's Weekly* and it appears from the context that he had expressed a desire for an article on Conrad. Ford remarks: "I sort of feel that I have written enough about Conrad in the course of a toilsome life: and to tell the truth his later work appeals to me so relatively little that I don't want to write any more about it. I mean it's difficult to do so without appearing and, for all I know, being ungenerous." A reference follows to Ezra Pound who wants Ford to place for him "some stuff he is writing about one of his God-given Czechoslovak sculptors of the Metrovitch-Brjeska type". At Christmas time Ford sent Jepson a present of a boar's head. In the note announcing its despatch, he says: "*Caput apri accipe.* That is to say that we are despatching the head of a small boar pig to you per passenger train at the same time as this letter. (The brains should be taken out at once and put in salt and water.) We like them brained: but I believe you prefer chaps and things."

On the 12th February in the following year, Ford wrote to thank Jepson for sending his novel *The Whiskered Footman*. "I have glanced at it and find it to be obviously a play; but Stella has torn it away from me so I have gathered no more." After thanking him for inviting Stella and "Esther Julia" to stay, an invitation temporarily declined because "at the moment E. J. is going through such a peevish stage with her teeth", he refers to his literary affairs. "I am worried out of my mind myself by the death of Pinker which happened in New York without any warning at all just as he was—or was supposed to be—fixing up my contract with Macmillan's that was to have kept me in clover for the rest of my life." There follows a request for advice from the businesslike Jepson because, Ford says, "I have just caught a publisher out, doing me in the eye flagrantly over concealed

profits and don't just know how to deal with this". In writing
to a fellow-author like Jepson, Ford was commendably circum-
spect and I have been unable to discover, from other sources, any
details about this dispute. Certainly, in the course of his career,
Ford had more than a fair share of financial bad luck. For example,
like other English authors, he lost some money through the
bankruptcy of a progressive and well-intentioned New York
publisher. Such accidents must be regarded as normal occupational hazards, and, in the case of secure and prosperous authors,
are quickly forgotten and written-off. It was in the nature of
Ford's mercurial temperament to be cast into an abyss of gloom
by a mishap and extravagantly elated whenever things went
reasonably well.

On the 10th May, 1922, he wrote to Jepson informing him
that "I shall be reading at the Poetry Bookshop tomorrow at six
and we shall be lunching at the Mont Blanc at one-thirty or so;
in case you or any of yours are in either vicinity do look or let
them look in". As he says that "we shall be sleeping at the
Grosvenor Hotel, Victoria", he was presumably enjoying a
period of comparative prosperity. In a later letter, written on
the 1st July, he says he is forwarding a copy of *The Yale Review*,
containing an article for which he had received Jepson's help and
mentioning other American activities which suggest that he was
already beginning to establish the New York connections which
were, later, to prove of so much importance to him.

On the 15th August, he wrote a long letter to Jepson concerning his literary affairs, beginning with a comment on "Ulysses",
about which he and Jepson appear to have argued. "Ulysses,"
he says, "we shall no doubt differ about till the end of the
chapter; personally I'm quite content to leave Joyce the leading
novelist-ship of this country, think he deserves the position and
hope it will profit him."

Referring to his own prospects in Great Britain he states it
as his firm resolution to have nothing to do with any publisher
who will not take up his work for good. He says that America
seems ready to provide that, Great Britain does not, so he sees
no prospect of publishing any more in Great Britain since "there

is not in these islands any periodical at all that would publish me or in which I could contemplate with equanimity being published". In America, he says, there are ten or a dozen. He admits that one does not stick "to one's even firmest resolutions" and that if any English publisher approached him on bended knee and asked for the privilege of publishing the novel which he had in his drawer "beneath this machine" and offered a lump sum down for that privilege, he would probably succumb to the temptation. The reason for the reluctance of London publishers to offer Ford attractive terms was due to the painful fact that his earlier books had not proved commercially profitable. Shortly after the London publication of *Some Do Not*, the writer encountered Mr. Gerald Duckworth, the most faithful of Ford's London publishers, who had recently issued it. Mr. Duckworth expressed himself full of admiration for Ford's works, but added that "the trouble is, we can't sell the old boy".

In further explanation of his resolve, Ford tells Jepson: "You see, I have written four or three—I am not sure which—books that ought to be 'classics' and from which I ought to draw a comfortable if small provision for my approaching old age. They are all out of print and unlikely to be re-published. I *want* to force the hand of some publisher to the extent of getting him to republish those books and to keep them on the market and to go on publishing whatever I write, on equitable terms which are not difficult of working out."

Ford was not the first, nor will he be the last, neglected English novelist to indulge in such not unreasonable aspirations. He does not expect to succeed in realising them and says that if he can't he seems to be able "to make just enough out of America to scrape along".

Jepson, in the letter to which this is a reply, had evidently made some references to South Lodge and had perhaps passed on a renewed request from Violet Hunt that he should visit her there. "I am afraid that what you suggest" [about South Lodge] "is impossible. If you will look at the last—not the current—*Saturday Review*, you will see one quite sufficient reason why you should not even have suggested it. For it is really too much to expect the very mildest of men to aid in sharpening a pen whose sole occupation is the describing of himself as, let us say, a maquereau. There is such a thing as trying a horse too high." The reference is presumably to an article which Violet had published and which Ford regarded as a reflection on his honour. He adds that there are now many other reasons against his following a course in regard to Violet which Jepson had apparently proposed, and "those I leave to your perspicacity to divine, for I am firmly determined—and from *this* determination I don't think I shall draw back—never to speak a word on these subjects. One's friends must accept one's actions and divine the justifications for those actions—or one must do without friends!"

The letter ends with various family messages. "Esther Julia flourishes, the centre of a perfect cloud of other babies whom she flaxenly dominates, like a monstrous Germania among the nations. At the moment the sun shines."

The next letter in the Jepson series, dated 8th October, is written by Stella on Ford's behalf and mentions that he is struggling with a Great Poem. Other items of news are that he is going to London to stay with Mr. Dyneley Hussey, at 21 Old Buildings, Lincoln's Inn "on Thursday morning" and that "we are going abroad about the middle of next month, and are engaged in trying to squeeze our fares out of the pigs—which is to say that the whole eleven are going to market".

Stella Bowen's account of their life at Bedham provides the complete picture of the domestic scene of which the Jepson correspondence only gives glimpses. Although to the town-dweller the "fatigues", what with the pigs, the goats, the baby and the visitors, which fell to Stella Bowen's lot during the four summers and three winters she spent in the wilds of Sussex seem calculated to wear out the strongest constitution, the compensations, as she is the first to acknowledge, more than made up for the hardships. Even the long, pitch black winter evenings, with gales of rain raging outdoors, had their unforgettable charm. "It is then," says Stella, "that the big log fire, the soft lamplight, and the fragrant, simmering stew-pot have an allurement that no amount of central heat, electric light, and well-served dinners in London can touch, and they exercise an irresistible invitation to the opening of conversational bosoms. The people round the fire have come from a long way off, and being isolated in space together, they soon begin to feel the urge to tell all! If there is some beer as well, that helps . . . ."

Visitors were, of course, fewer during the winter than in the summer months, but even in the winter young poets and writers made their way to the Master's humble abode to show him their efforts and listen eagerly to his patient and discerning criticism and his brilliant exposition of the technique of good writing. Although, to those who shared his life, Ford was, as Stella says, "a great user-up of other people's nervous energy", to the young literary aspirant who sought his advice he grudged neither his time nor the free and generous application of his knowledge, experience and skill to the task of showing them how to make the most of their talents. In return for what he gave them, he received what he valued more than gratitude, the assurance that they regarded him as a master of his craft. For, in spite of the pigs and the poultry, the vegetable garden and the "farewells to literature", it cannot be too often repeated that Ford was an artist, first, last and all the time. "Poor Ford!" says Stella. "There was something about the sight of his large patient fingers tapping at the keys that I always found infinitely touching. He was a writer—a complete writer—and nothing but a writer. And he never even felt sure of his gift!" Even his moments of assertiveness, when he permitted himself to display a sense of his own value and claimed, with perfect justice, to have written books which should be considered "classics", were often prompted by a profound uncertainty. The reason why he "never read reviews" was not because he was indifferent to what the reviewers said of him, but because unkind or imperceptive criticism agitated him more than he could bear. He spent himself in giving encouragement to his juniors because, subconsciously, he was constantly in need of it himself.

The frequent arrival at Bedham of transatlantic admirers, though he treated them with the Olympian geniality becoming in a literary *roi en exil*, must have given him a good deal of secret satisfaction. Ezra Pound, always the most generous of fuglemen for those literary innovators whose works he approved, must have been largely responsible for the influx of American "pilgrims". Monroe Wheeler arrived with his friend Glenway Westcott, now a leading American novelist, also Professor Lawrence Marsden Price of the University of Berkeley, California, who, as Stella records, was surprised and amused to be set to hay-making on a very hot July afternoon. Among the English visitors, mentioned by Stella Bowen, are Anthony Bertram and Dyneley Hussey, Clough Williams Ellis and his wife, Alec Waugh, David Garnett, Edward Shanks and the faithful Edgar Jepson.

Mr. Waugh tells me that it was in mid-February 1922 that he went to stay for a week-end at Bedham. "I never knew him (Ford) well," he writes, "but I got him on to Chapman & Hall's list. We published *Thus to Revisit*—a title he had used for a series of articles in the shortlived *Piccadilly Review*." He adds that he has no very clear recollection of what the house looked like but thinks it was comfortable and spacious. "If I hadn't been comfortable," he says, "I should have remembered *that*." No neighbours called and there were no signs of a communal life. Ford had a chalet in which he worked. "He told me," Mr. Waugh continues, "that he was an expert gardener and had recently grown a potato that he had sold for £400. He wore a dilapidated dinner jacket in the evening. There was a certain feudal air about it all. He was himself called 'Captain Ford'— and he kept describing me to his staff as Captain Waugh. I forget how big his staff was; I think just two. I was met at the station by a pony and trap. The atmosphere of the house was very friendly. Stella was affectionate, teasing and maternal towards Ford. I had never met her before but we had a good deal of common ground over Clifford Bax and Phyllis Reid (now Mrs. Phyllis Vallance). . . . I never saw Ford again— except for a half minute in New York in '37. Violet, by the way, was furious with me for going down."

In spite of the rain and mud of the Sussex winters, the remoteness of the cottage—it was five miles from the nearest town,

Petworth, and the only means of transport was the high, open dog-cart—Ford and Stella might have continued at Bedham had it not been for Harold Monro, the poet-director of the Poetry Bookshop. Monro came down to Bedham for a week-end and mentioned the little villa he had recently bought, situated on the top of a rock at Cap Ferrat. He described, as one poet to another, the sunshine, the incomparable view and all the charm of the Mediterranean in winter. Winter in Sussex, their fourth, was approaching. Stella says that Ford was "filled with nostalgia for his beloved Provence", and she also, she admits, felt a sharp longing to escape. Monro pointed out that his "villa" was really only a peasant's cottage, very inaccessible, tiny, and with no conveniences, but he added that it was going to be empty and they could have it for a nominal rent. Tiny, inaccessible cottages had no terrors for either of them, after their experiences at Red Ford. The sunshine of the south, the wide view of the Mediterranean, Provence, the magical holy land which appealed so deeply to Ford's heart, irresistibly called them. In a few weeks the whole matter was arranged and their plans were laid for wintering on the Riviera.

The only problem which remained was how to raise the money for the journey and how to disentangle themselves from their commitments at Bedham. The animals, the pedigree pigs! The question of clothes! For years they had dressed the part of small-holders and neither of them had anything to wear which would pass muster even in Montparnasse, where they intended to spend a month before going south. Ford's principal financial asset was the completed MS. of his novel, *The Marsden Case*. Duckworth had expressed his willingness to take up Ford's work, more or less on the lines sketched out in the letter to Jepson previously quoted, but he had not read or formally approved the book which was to inaugurate the proposed agreement. However, without waiting for his decision, Ford and Stella went ahead with their preparations, disposed of the animals including the famous pigs, which "had to go at bacon prices", and made all their arrangements for departure. They had decided to take with them their little maid, Lucy, to look after Julie, who was then just two. At the moment when they were setting off from Coopers there occurred one of those incidents, so frequent in the insecure lives of authors, the poignancy of which only those who have experienced them can perhaps realise. How often it happens, in a writer's career, that on the acceptance or rejection of a completed work, hangs the difference between temporary disaster and the successful carrying out of some important domestic project! To the publisher, on whom the author's existence so largely depends, such decisions are matters of routine. The "human story" in the background is no affair of theirs. They are business men, not philanthropists.

"The luggage was packed, the passports obtained," Stella relates, "and we were actually piling into the dog-cart to drive to Fittleworth station, when the postman delivered the manuscript—returned! This caught us hard in the pit of the stomach." As the party stood on the windy station platform, Stella, "feeling that it was the height of folly to have burned our boats and to be leaving our blessed home", contrived to undo a corner of the parcel to see if there was a letter inside. Ford himself always shrank from opening anything that might be disagreeable. There was a letter. It said that Duckworth would like to publish the book if Ford would make certain minor alterations, for which purpose he was returning the manuscript! The sky cleared and the journey was a happy one.

CHAPTER XVI

" *Transatlantic Review* "

THE LETTERS preserved by Edgar Jepson supply some dates and details that lend precision to the general picture of Ford's post-war life in France which Stella Bowen's personal narrative so attractively provides. About a week after his arrival in Paris, on 25th November, 1922, Ford wrote from the "Hotel de Blois, 50 rue Vavin, Paris vi", telling Jepson that they are staying there till the middle of December and then going to the Riviera, near Nice, till mid-spring. "The lowness of the franc makes this just possible even to persons of our exiguous means." He reports that he signed "yesterday" a contract with Duckworth to take over all his work, future, present and past as the copyrights revert to him. "This is what I have been waiting for all these years, so I am rather pleased—and you will see my next book in an English frock. I have also just finished an immense Poem—3,000 lines or more!—wh is to be serialized in Monro's *Chapbook* and afterwards to be republished, with illustrations by Paul Nash. It will, I fancy, annoy quite a number of people." (The reference is to *Mr. Bosphorus and the Muses*, issued by Duckworth in 1923, with decorations by Paul Nash.)

After asking Jepson to propose to Sidney Dark "a lightish article or two about French literary life", because, as he says, "I suffer from a constitutional disability to write letters to Editors suggesting articles or I wouldn't even think of bothering you", he remarks that he, personally, finds Paris rather fatiguing although the rest of his small caravan "trots round the museums, parks, parties and so on with great enthusiasm and vigour; Esther Julia having developed such a passion for motor cars that, if one draws up on the sidewalk near her she bolts into it before the occupants can get out". He says that Ezra Pound is in Paris "going very strong", Joyce "going rather weak" and his brother

Oliver "enormously fat and prosperous". He adds that there is very little French stuff of much value coming out, and that Proust's death has cast an extraordinary gloom on literary parties, "tho' he was pretty generally disliked personally. I just missed seeing him and had to content myself with solemnly attending his funeral, which was a tremendous affair: Stella being the only person in the church who did not shake hands with the next of kin. But her shyness made her bolt out of a back door, whereat the venerable *Suisse* nearly wept". Stella Bowen, in her book, gives an amusing account of this incident.

In mid-December, when the Riviera trains were crowded to capacity with English tourists hurrying south, Ford and Stella resumed their journey to Harold Monro's villa at Cap Ferrat. For Stella, who was making this "classic" pilgrimage for the first time, seeing the dawn break in Provence provided a thrill of rapture. Provence, like Venice, though the track to it has been beaten by generations of tourists, is one of those "objectives" which surpass all expectations and let no one down who has an eye for beauty or a spark of imagination. Although Ford was nearly fifty and had visited Provence many times before, it is probable that he was scarcely less excited than Stella.

Stella says that she wishes she could describe how magical Harold Monro's quite ordinary little villa seemed to them when they got there. The approach was by a rough mule-track, or alternatively by long flights of stone steps "of a giddy and exhausting steepness". All their luggage and all their provisions had to be carried up by hand as no wheeled vehicle could reach the place. The villa had three "microscopic" rooms in front and two behind and all the cooking had to be done on the usual peasant's "charcoal contraption". But there was electricity and the water was laid on and, above all, the whole place and its surroundings were *dry*. After the mud and rain and heavy darkness of Bedham the contrast must have seemed miraculous. As for "views", always an essential to Ford's happiness, there were two of them. Behind the villa, the ground sloped gently downwards allowing a vista of Beaulieu, Monte Carlo and the spectacular stretch of coast-line between Monaco and Bordighera.

The front windows "opened wide on a great luminous sky with a Saracen fortress on the skyline opposite, and the translucent blue-green waters of Villefranche harbour below. Down through the filmy tops of our own olive trees we could see a British man-o'-war, floating like a child's toy above the sunny depths, and to our right the little dome of coloured tiles on the church belfry poked itself up amid the flat, huddled roofs of the harbour".

In a brief note to Edgar Jepson, written on 28th January, 1923, Ford asks permission to dedicate *The Marsden Case* to him, in the following terms: "To Edgar Jepson. Very Gratefully. Coopers Bedham, September 1921. St.-Jean-Cap-Ferrat, January 1923." The address at the head of the letter is "Villa des Oliviers, Chemin des Moulins, St. Jean Cap Ferrat. A.M. France". In a revealing postscript, he adds: "I have just come across this To-day's Great Thought in Jules Renard:

" '*Oui. Homme de lettres! Je le serai jusquà ma mort. . . . Et, si par hasard, je suis éternel, je ferai, durant l'éternité, de la littérature. Et jamais je ne me fatigue d'en faire, et toujours j'en fais, et je me f . . . du reste, comme le vigneron qui trépigne dans ma conte 'Le Vigneron'.*" These words may be said to have expressed Ford's own point of view with exactness. They stayed at the Villa des Oliviers till Easter, enjoying every moment of the Riviera spring and when, reluctantly, they had to move on, Ford said that he wanted to show Stella the real Provence of the Rhône valley, and picked on Tarascon as being a town of just the right size and sufficiently free from tourists to make a good base for excursions. So they put up at a small commercial hotel there, in which they were kindly treated and well fed, and went for frequent picnics in what, for Ford, were "the most beloved spots on earth".

Writing to Jepson from the Hotel Terminus, Tarascon, on 8th May, 1923, Ford says he is sending him a copy of *The Marsden Case*, which had just been published. "I believe that, as a 'treatment', it is the best thing I've done—but the subject is not a very good one, though it's one that has haunted me ever since I was eighteen, on and off. It's the story of Ralston, the first translator of Turgenev—a man I liked very much. At any rate, that suggested it to me."

He remarks that it is too tropically hot to stay in Tarascon, that he is not quite sure where they are going next, that Stella is in Paris having some lessons and seeing the Salons for a day or two, and that they will probably meet on one of the foothills of the Alps where he has heard of a cheapish pension. "Living is really so relatively cheap in France and I find I can work so well—and Stella too—that I shouldn't wonder if we settled down here for good. Besides, the French make much of me—which at my age is inspiring."

Even during their stay at Cap Ferrat, they had made a few French acquaintances who treated Ford with the respect the French always accord to distinguished writers. Stella says that she remembers his receiving, at the Villa des Oliviers, a note which began, "*Cher et illustre Maître*" and filled Ford's heart with simple pleasure. Café contacts at Tarascon, such as the local *avoué* and *avocat*, were equally gracious. With the latter Ford "would discuss at length the proper use of the subjunctive, in elaborate French prose". The former, who was a bachelor, got them seats for a bull-fight at Nîmes. He also, when the noise of the fair at Beaucaire began to get on Ford's nerves—he had just begun to write *Some Do Not*—recommended them, as an escape from the torrid heat of Tarascon, to go up to St. Agrève, a little mountain resort in the Ardèche, not far from Le Puy. Although it looked fairly near on the map, it took them a day to get there and when they arrived they found the place icily cold and the hotel empty of guests and unwarmed. The summer season, for excellent climatic reasons, had not begun. Ford promptly went down with an attack of bronchitis. Summer, however, came "with a rush" in July and was, while it lasted, "incredible", the meadows being filled with amazing flowers and the whole mountainy landscape presenting "a great extravagance of natural beauty". *Some Do Not* had now got well into its stride, and by moving into an annexe of the rather austere "Grand Hotel Poste", Ford was able to have a place in which he could write undisturbed.

On the 14th June Ford wrote from St. Agrève to give Jepson his new address, where he says he will be for some time. "After being grilled—not to mention dusted and torn to pieces by the mistral—in the plains, we are now being cold-stored in the mountains, thousands of feet up. . . . A queer place—seven hours from anything resembling a tavern, yet apparently with a tremendous summer season—tho' that hasn't yet begun. However, I hope to get some work done, and it is cheap."

In September, when the autumn chills were already beginning to descend on St. Agrève, Ford and Stella found the excitements of Paris irresistibly calling them. Ford's four years of rural retirement, including ten months in provincial France, had done much both to restore his health and nerves and to re-invigorate his creative capacity. He had put an immense amount of hard work into the writing of *Some Do Not*, the first of the Tietjens series, and craved for amusement, gaiety and the stimulus of social contacts. Paris was rapidly filling up with young poets, painters and novelists, both British and American, and Ford no doubt felt the urge to take his place among them as an acknowledged Great Figure. As Stella puts it, "the Paris of the gay and glamorous twenties was waiting to engulf us". To Stella, who was to have three of her pictures in the Salon d'Automne, Paris meant pictures and painting. To Ford it meant recognition, reassurance and plenty of young people to whom, with advantage no less to himself than to them, he could pontificate about literary technique. As they had managed to let their Bedham cottage, furnished, for a year, there was no question of their returning to England.

In Paris, one of the first people they encountered was Ford's brother Oliver, whom he had not seen for many years. "On one of our first days in Paris," says Stella, "we bumped into another large, pink-faced, blue-eyed gentleman on an island in the Place des Médicis, and Ford said, 'do you know who this is?'" As the physical resemblance between the two brothers was striking, Stella had no difficulty in guessing his identity.

Oliver Hueffer, a placid genial figure, outwardly, but with an astonishing background of picaresque adventure, took them back with him to his cottage, behind a dilapidated block of studios in the Boulevard Arago, and introduced them to his wife, "a keen-faced writer, with a twinkling smile and thick, wavy white hair".

P

She was just on the point of departing for America and offered to let them her *rez-de-chaussée* for the nominal rent of two hundred francs a month. This, in view of the *"crise de logement"* in Paris, was a godsend to Stella, on whom the problem of ways and means, usually disregarded by Ford, fell most heavily. The maid Lucy, who was now homesick, had to be sent back to England so that, in addition to the economy in rent, it seemed possible to economise on domestic help as well. In addition to providing them with accommodation of a sort—the cottage was damp, shabby and without electricity or gas, but full of "character"—Oliver was, accidentally, the means of starting off Ford on the adventure of editing the *transatlantic review*. Some Paris financiers had asked him to edit a periodical in English having, no doubt, some ulterior motive in view, and Oliver seems to have told them that his brother, the founder and editor of the famous *English Review*, was really the man they wanted. Ford has told the whole story, inimitably, in his book *It Was the Nightingale*, and in so far as it has been possible for me to check the facts, his version seems to be reasonably accurate. Naturally, when Ford discovered that there were "strings attached" to the proposal he would have nothing to do with it. But by this time the rumour had got around that the launching of a new literary review, with the great Ford as editor, was under discussion and Montparnasse, then chock-a-block with young American geniuses, mostly from the Middle West, and with liberated English *avant-gardistes*, mostly from Bloomsbury, was thrown into a frenzy of excitement at the prospect. Ezra Pound, who had not yet deserted Paris for Rapallo, was particularly enthusiastic about the project. As he had been one of Ford's *English Review* discoveries he had special reasons for praising Ford's unique genius as an editor, to his younger compatriots. "With his passion for promoting the sort of writing he approved of," says Stella, "he had a whole line-up of young writers waiting for Ford, with Hemingway at the top. Between them all, it would have been hard to announce that there would be no review, after all." When Oliver Hueffer's friends proved insubstantial as backers, we may take it for granted that Pound exerted himself to find a substitute. The *deus ex machina* proved to be Mr. John Quinn of New York, an admirer of Ezra's poetry and a generous patron of advanced art. Mr. Quinn offered a sum of money if Ford would double it. Unfortunately for Stella, they had recently sold their cottage at Bedham, with its contents, for a price which just about covered what it had cost them. This money was earmarked, in her own mind, for the purchase of a house outside Paris which would set them free from the extortions of the Paris landlords, but the rival claims of Ford's new plaything proved insuperable and the insurance which could have been provided by a roof of their own had to be abandoned. Ford seems to have convinced himself that, apart from taking up shares in the company which was to be formed to acquire and run the new review, he would have no financial responsibility in regard to it. But as his own experience with the *English Review*, and that of his former sub-editor, who also started a magazine for which he had "no financial responsibility", ought to have shown him, the editor cannot avoid being involved, at least in the eyes of his contributors, with the fortunes of the periodical of which he is in ostensible control. On 14th October Ford sent Jepson a copy of a circular letter inviting him, as one of the regular contributors to the old *English Review*, to write for his new venture. To this he appended a postscript saying that he is "at it again—but thank Goodness with no financial responsibility of my own. If you'd send me something rude about literary London I'd love it". He adds that for once in a way he is flourishing as he has fixed up a contract in U.S.A. for all his work, as in England, "and though I shan't make a penny out of this thing and work myself to death on top of it—it pleases me". Stella, he says, "has three pictures in the Salon d'Automne and plenty of commissions for portraits and that pleases me more than anything else".

In a letter written on the following day, to myself, Ford again stresses his freedom from financial responsibility in the new venture. "Alas, the *transatlantic review* will be the old *English Review* all over again except that it will be published in London and New York and except also that, thank goodness, I have no financial responsibility at all. But the editorial offices are much the same ramshackle sort of place that Holland Park Avenue used to be and, although I can't go to the Shepherd's Bush Empire—you infernal scoundrel—I do still as I used to do, do most of my editing in between violent games of tennis, as we've got a court just next door."

Ford's editorship of the *transatlantic review*, like his editorship of the *English Review*, lasted only for a year. Before the end of 1924 it was sufficiently obvious that it could never be turned into a going concern and Ford and Stella, in spite of Ford's alleged freedom from financial responsibility, were left to bury the remains by sending face-saving cheques to unpaid and exigent contributors. How much of Stella's money, as well as Ford's, was absorbed by the enterprise in one way or another has not been recorded, though probably what Stella felt most was the sacrifice of the "nest-egg" which might have enabled them to buy a permanent home.

After spending three months in Oliver Hueffer's cottage, they moved up into one of the big studios in the Boulevard Arago, which was temporarily vacant. Meanwhile Stella's efforts to find a country home, to rent not to buy, led her in ever-widening circles round Paris until, at Gertrude Stein's suggestion, they happened on the village of Guermantes, near Lagny, about an hour from Paris on the Chemin de Fer de l'Est. Here they discovered the inevitable farm labourer's cottage, built of stone, with four rooms and a small orchard, to let at five hundred francs a year. They got the cottage cleaned up and the walls papered, collected some furniture and installed Julie in charge of a French nurse, Madame Annie, who had now taken the place of the departed English maid. They retained this country retreat for nearly three years and used it at week-ends and in the summer. When their tenancy of the studio in the Boulevard Arago expired, they moved into a poky little furnished apartment in the rue Denfert-Rochereau, where they stayed until the summer, which they spent at Guermantes. Towards the end of the year, Nina Hamnett, the best-known of all the English "Montparnos", told them of a vacant studio at 84 rue Notre Dame des Champs. The studio was enormous, having until lately formed part of Dele-

cluse's Academy of Art, but was, as usual, without conveniences
or any kind of living accommodation. There were, however,
a water-tap, electric light and some heavy, movable screens.
With a skill in this kind of work perfected by much practice,
Stella set herself to the task of transforming the barn-like studio
into some kind of habitation. How well she succeeded the
innumerable visitors who attended her parties in succeeding years
can bear witness. But by the end of this remarkable year, one
of the most crowded and productive in Ford's career, they were
both tired out. "I had installed the family in three furnished
and two unfurnished domiciles within a twelvemonth, none of
them with *confort moderne*, and Ford was worn out by the fluctuat-
ing fortunes of the *Review*", Stella records. So they decided to
go south for the winter, leaving the final shaping of the studio
until the spring. The recent devaluation of the franc made this
just possible.

While all these domestic difficulties, which fell to Stella's lot
to cope with, were going on as it were behind the scenes, Ford's
social and literary activities, his "public life", would require a
volume as large as this to describe in detail. As in 1909, his
period of rural retirement as a "small producer" was now compensated for by an incredible expenditure of nervous energy,
creative exuberance, and indulgence in his passion for parties.
Unlike 1909, however, in 1924 he was, largely thanks to Stella
and Julie, blissfully, almost childishly happy. If his temperament
required long periods of solitude *à deux*, of austerity and recupera-
tion in a peasant's cottage in some remote and inaccessible village,
it required also, at stated intervals, periods of existence among
crowds, particularly crowds of admirers, the younger the better.
Paris, in 1924, supplied him with everything he wanted. The
success of the French translation of *Entre St. Denis et St. Georges*,
if it did not have anything like the "million sale" he afterwards
claimed for it, assured him a warm welcome from his French
colleagues, who were masters of the art of flattery. Soon after
his arrival in Paris he was invited to a *lunch d'honneur* by the Paris
branch of the PEN Club, his sponsors—according to his own
account—being M. Edmond Jaloux and M. Benjamin Crémieux,

and was soon receiving the respectful homages of a whole collection of "*les jeunes*", including Philippe Soupault, Jean Casson and a bevy of dadaists. Through Ezra Pound he increased, also, his connections with the large colony of American writers and artists established in Montparnasse, the social leaders of which were Gertrude Stein, the earliest and most influential of Picasso's admirers, and Miss Nathalie Barney, the protectress of Rémy de Gourmont. Ford's relations with James Joyce, the chief constellation in the Anglo-American literary group, were already cordial and intimate and they were soon able to share disciples without a trace of rivalry.

The early days of the *transatlantic review* were, as Stella admits, "great fun". Ford, as an editor, had an extraordinary talent for purposeful confusion. Whomsoever God sent him by way of an assistant he used, with child-like faith that the Almighty would ultimately see him through. To start with, "everything that could possibly go wrong with regard to the printing, paper, packing, forwarding and distribution did go wrong", says Stella. "An elegant White Russian colonel offered his services for a pittance, and was sent to make all sorts of arrangements with printers, bookshops, and forwarding agents. All his arrangements fell through." After that God produced a young poet called Basil Bunting, who offered his services in exchange for his keep. "He slept in a damp little store-room beyond our kitchen and was kept on the run by Ford for eighteen hours a day. He endured much in the cause of Literature, and indeed", Stella adds, "everybody seemed ready to be overworked and underpaid in the good cause."

What Miss Thomas accomplished for the *English Review* was done for its successor by "a real American secretary, called Margery", who had the good sense to demand a proper salary. "She got her salary, and she had the whole thing under control in no time," Stella records. "She became, in fact, the backbone of the concern." In spite of Margery's efficiency, it may be doubted if the review would have got itself launched had it not been for the hospitality and technical experience provided by William Bird who ran the Three Mountains Press on the Ile St.

Louis. Mr. Bird was introduced by Ezra Pound and quickly became an intimate friend of Ford and Stella. In proof of Ford's regard is the fact that he dedicated to him the second of the Tietjens novels, *No More Parades*, which appeared in 1925. Mr. Bird's valuable contribution to the *transatlantic review* was the provision of an editorial address and a tiny office in a gallery over his printing press at 29 Quai d'Anjou. As the press did not operate on Thursdays, Ford and Stella were able to use the downstairs space for their crowded receptions. When Stella had made the tea, Ford descended, Jove-like, from his aerial balcony and moved impressively among the guests. As Stella says, "he really enjoyed himself superbly. He survived all the troubles and set-backs, which ordinarily would have bowled him over, with an amazing buoyancy, so deep was his pleasure in the enterprise". As has already been indicated, the review absorbed all the money which Ford and Stella could raise, but, at least, as far as Ford and the literary public of England and America were concerned, it was by no means wasted. It gave Ford the glow of confidence and the psychological stimulus he required for the production of his finest work. And it provided the first outlet for the talent of a young writer who has since become one of America's foremost novelists. Ernest Hemingway was the most promising of Ezra's stable of cowboy geniuses and Ford, with his unerring *flair*, immediately appreciated his gifts. After Bunting's departure Hemingway became assistant-editor of the review, and during Ford's occasional absences was responsible, not always with the happiest results, for several issues. Although Ford got an enormous amount of pleasure from resuming the role of editor, he did not give the whole, or even the best part of, his mind to the work. The books on which he was engaged, very properly, absorbed the major part of his attention. As a result, the *transatlantic review* was a very uneven production and though it printed good work by various eminent writers, in French and English, it included also a great deal of coterie nonsense by Anglo-American "Montparnos" and other café "types". Among those of other eccentrics, it printed the complete—and shattering—poetical works of a lady named Baroness Elsa von Freytag-

Loringhofen. Ford records, in *It Was the Nightingale*, that the British Embassy rang up one day to ask him what he meant by sending them a Prussian lady, the before-mentioned poetess, "simply dressed in a brassière of milk-tins, connected by dog-chains, and wearing on her head a plum cake!" Her poems, and others like them, at least suffused the review with local colour. For the now elderly folk who can remember Montparnasse in the 'twenties, it thus evokes amusing memories of the past. Much of the contents, however, it has to be admitted, is as dead as dada.

So much of Ford's time in Paris was ostensibly devoted to café-life, to parties, wild at first but later more selective, and various forms of social activity, including a weekly *bal musette*, that to those who remember seeing him "everywhere", on their visits to Paris, it is surprising to realise how much first-rate work he was able to accomplish. There must, actually, have been a certain rhythm, a certain amount of order in Ford's apparently ramshackle and Bohemian way of life. His first parties, held in the large, lofty studio in the Boulevard Arago, were often filled to overflowing with the high-spirited crowd of good-time-seekers, who hurried to Montparnasse to obtain relief, for war-time nerves in the case of the British and from the Volstead Act, in the case of American citizens. As "Jimmy the Barman", a noted Montparnasse character, once observed to the writer, "a year or two of free living does everybody good—provided they don't make a habit of it". Ford, who was still suffering both physically and mentally from his war experiences, had plenty of sympathy and understanding for the explosions and excesses of his juniors. But the pace became too much for him, especially as both he and Stella were serious and extremely hard-working artists while many of the "good-timers", though amusingly frank and uninhibited, were merely sowing wild oats in preparation for a life-time of prosperous respectability in their home towns. Montparnasse in the 'twenties was not only "the nerve-centre of the arts" as Stella Bowen rightly describes it, but also a flourishing business concern, cashing-in on the legend of such famous Bohemians as the ill-fated painter, Modigliani. As a centre of adolescent "tourism", it had no rivals or equals, for the drawing-power of Modigliani's habits proved an even stronger magnet than appreciation of his pictures.

After their departure from the studio in the Boulevard Arago, Ford and Stella never resumed "party throwing" on so large and indiscriminative a scale, but formed the regular café-and-restaurant habits of other "serious" residents of the Quarter. Ford had, moreover, several friends, long-resident in Paris, at whose houses French and English and American guests were successfully blended. Among these, we hear of William Aspenwell Bradley, an American who had known Ford long ago and was now established in Paris as a literary agent, with a French wife of the *haute bourgeoisie*. With the Bradleys they explored a number of unfamiliar *bistrots* and restaurants, such as the "Mariniers" on the Quai d'Orléans and the Maison Paul in the Place Dauphine on the Ile de la Cité. For everyday eating, however, they became "regulars" of the Nègre de Toulouse, in the Boulevard Montparnasse. Here there was a back room containing two tables, which M. Lavigne, the amiable proprietor, reserved for Ford and Stella and their friends. The tables held about a dozen people and were usually fully occupied, as it was, naturally, considered a privilege to eat in Ford's company.

The before luncheon apéritif, the most enjoyable moment in the day for Frenchmen and ex-patriates alike, was usually consumed on the terrace of the Closerie des Lilas, facing the now demolished Bal Bullier and the trees surrounding the statue of Maréchal Ney and within a stone's throw of the chestnut avenues of the Petit Luxembourg. This delightful café, once a *guinguette* which served as the first relay for coaches between Paris and Fontainebleau, had been for generations a favourite meeting place for poets and painters. Celebrities known to have frequented it include Chateaubriand, Baudelaire, Manet, Jongkind, Gauguin, Whistler, Cézanne, Strindberg, Degas, Rodin, Romain Rolland—and hundreds more. In an upper room at the Lilas, prior to 1914, were held the famous "Tuesday Evenings", gatherings of young poets presided over first by Charles Maurras and later by Paul Fort. In the 'twenties, its clientèle was tending to become rather too serious and "bourgeois" for the boisterous younger generation, but no doubt Ford's presence helped to keep alive its literary traditions. The writer recalls hearing him addressed there as "cher maître", by a young transatlantic admirer, which gave him evident satisfaction.

Dancing in the 'twenties was as much the rage in Paris as in other capitals. Ford, in spite of his breathing difficulties, liked dancing, and in order to indulge in this pastime in the company of friends, without incurring the expense of entertaining them, he made an arrangement with a *bal musette*, in the rue du Cardinal Lemoine, by which the hall was more or less reserved for his guests one evening a week. The *bal musette*, a charming feature of Paris life in those days—perhaps it has even survived the Nazi occupation—is a small café with a dance floor, where an accordion player, sitting on a raised seat or gallery, tirelessly churns out music for the local working-class couples who frequent it. The custom used to be for the dancers to put two sous into the proprietor's cap, each time they took the floor. The Bal du Printemps was, as a rule, closed on Friday evenings, but Ford prevailed on the proprietor, by means of a weekly tip, to open it at ten o'clock on Fridays for the benefit of those of his circle who liked to turn up. The word quickly went round the cafés and a number of young painters, among them Lett Haines and Cedric Morris, together with any "transients" of their acquaintance, availed themselves of the invitation to join the informal party. As it was a public place, not a *bal privé*, no one who chose to present himself could be excluded. Like all the genuinely "Bohemian" social life of Montparnasse in the 'twenties it soon became over-publicized, particularly by thrusting journalists, some of whom took ladies there in evening dress, on sight-seeing expeditions, to see how artists amused themselves. Respectable American citizens, who went there because they admired Ford, were distressed at seeing the Master surrounded by persons whom they regarded with distaste, as decadent riff-raff, and wanted to organise the Friday gatherings as a club, with a fixed subscription. As the attraction of these evenings lay largely in their informality, the proposals struck a jarring note and Ford's "fridays" at the Bal du Printemps came to an end. Nothing did more to spoil Montparnasse in the 'twenties than the impossibility of making British and American tourists realise that "Bohemia" is not a place but a state of mind. Over and over again cafés acquired a vogue from the fact that well-known artists and writers were in the habit of frequenting them. The tourists would arrive in hordes, to listen and gape, and when they did so the artists fled, carrying their elusive "Bohemia" with them. Thus nothing gay and amusing ever lasted very long. The "serious" artists, Ford and Stella among them, were eventually forced to save themselves from invasion by erecting barricades.

In retrospect, Ford seems to have crowded as much action and movement into the year 1924 as most people achieve in a decade. Early in January, the illness of his mother made it necessary for him to spend a few days in London, where he stayed with his friend Mr. Dyneley Hussey and wrote to ask Edgar Jepson to call on him. His mother's death occurred shortly afterwards and he was again in London for her funeral. Much of the summer, as already recorded, he spent at the cottage at Guermantes. Joseph Conrad died on 3rd August, and Ford's book *Joseph Conrad: a Personal Remembrance*, was completed at Bruges on 5th October and published by Duckworth before the end of the year. There is some evidence that he paid a flying visit to New York, perhaps in connection with the winding-up of the *transatlantic review*. But we have his word for it, at the end of his introductory letter to William Bird, that *No More Parades* was begun in Paris on 31st October, 1924, and finished at Guermantes on 25th May, 1925. What was he doing at Bruges? When did he go to New York? In his character as "international" artist, equally at home in four great countries and several smaller ones, Ford flitted from capital to capital, from hotel to hotel, from village to village, from cottage to cottage. His personal attachments, whether for men or women, cities or landscapes, were in few cases of permanent duration. He had but two passions which burned steadily throughout his life. One was for the art of writing: the other was for Provence. To these separate but associated loves his fidelity was absolute, until the day of his death.

In the winter of 1924, Ford and Stella made their way south to Toulon.

CHAPTER XVII

"No More Parades"

IN ENGLAND, if an author dies in poverty, without his work having received the approval of Professors of Literature and other leading critics, it is customary to write him off as a failure, to regard him as an unhappy, "disgruntled" person and throw on his grave, in the form of obituary notices, only a wreath of patronising pity. Like most ultra-sensitive men, Ford had his full share of emotional turmoil, worry, and distress. He went through long periods of mental agony, he endured numerous humiliations, financial crises, disappointments and the other incidental ills which come under the heading of occupational hazards, peculiar to the artist. On the other hand he enjoyed compensations of a kind only permitted to the ultra-sensitive and only possible to the artist, who can alone appreciate them to the full. Ford's capacity for pleasure was, in short, as great, and at least as often and as fully gratified, as his capacity for pain. On the whole, he lived the sort of life he chose to live. He went wherever an inclination or mood beckoned, and even the poorest and meanest of his numerous habitations had its own kind of beauty. No one can say that Ford was ever, in the long run, frustrated. He followed his gleam and obeyed, as faithfully as D. H. Lawrence, his daimon. Thus, from the standpoint of those who accept the Standard of Values to which he undeviatingly adhered, the over-all picture is that of a man who had his full measure of success. Whatever may be found in his career, for praise or blame, at least there was no mediocrity. Few wealthy and much-publicised figures have contrived to wear their opulence with as much distinction as that with which Ford, obeying the Christian injunction to take no heed for the morrow, contrived to surround his long periods of poverty. Like the good priest, the artist has spiritual riches of which nothing can deprive him.

These observations are prompted by a consideration of the months of contentment which Ford and Stella spent at Toulon in the winter and spring of 1925. To put the picture in perspective we must remember that a hundred miles further east, at Cannes, Nice and Monte Carlo, tens of thousands of excessively rich, socially prominent and much-publicised English and American pleasure-seekers were enjoying the Riviera season, together with an attendant crowd of fashionable novelists, film-stars, pimps, confidence men, sneak-thieves, press photographers, fashion experts and beauty specialists. The wealthy poured out their money in pursuit of conventional pleasure, for the enormous profit of a crowd of rapacious parasites, in the full glare of a limelight manipulated by gossip-columnists. The object of these publicity experts was to impress on the world that everybody who was anybody stayed in the palatial hotels which line the Côte d'Azur. Associated with them were a number of popular novelists and technically efficient short story writers who exploited the Riviera scene and found a highly profitable market for their wares in the shiny Anglo-American magazines. In this great concourse of foreign invaders it was rare to find a man or woman who spoke French, had any contacts with "the natives" or any appreciation of the art, literature or history of the country surrounding their strictly delimited playgrounds.

In sharp, almost spectacular contrast to the Riviera of the Anglo-American *hivernants* was the ultra-French naval port of Toulon, which, on the advice of the Spanish painter Juan Gris and his wife Josette, Ford and Stella made their headquarters. They took with them a nine-months-old Alsatian puppy, the gift of M. Lavigne of the Nègre de Toulouse, to which Ford was devoted, put up at a cheap and easy-going hotel—probably the Hotel du Port et des Négotiants, a temperamental establishment on the Quai Cronstadt, to which Ford subsequently recommended the writer—and fell in love with the town at first sight. It is sad to think that the Quai Cronstadt with its line of sun-bathed cafés, and the old town behind it with its labyrinthine streets, its little *places*, shaded by plane trees and adorned with Puget's fountains, has now been partially devastated. In spite of the excellence of its winter climate, which compares favourably with that of any of the tourist resorts further east, Toulon made no effort to attract foreign visitors and relied for its social life on the officers of the Navy and their wives "whose slender purses and civilised requirements", as Stella Bowen observes, "kept amenities high and prices low". It had five cinemas and two "dancings", for the amusement of the transient and indigenous population, but no casino, and no fashionable cocktail bars. For painters like Juan Gris, who, although appreciated by a few discerning amateurs, was still desperately poor by English standards, Toulon had everything to recommend it. At the café of their choice, the friends who collected at their table were mostly painters, so that Stella, who in Paris had listened to Ford talking endlessly about literature and "*le mot juste*", now had the satisfaction of hearing painters talk endlessly about painting. Among their circle, apart from Juan and Josette Gris, were Latapie, Madame Georges Duthuit, the daughter of Matisse, and Othon Friez. Friez lived in an old provençal *mas* at Cap Brun, but had also a studio in a warehouse on the Quai Cronstadt. He told Stella of a similar room, below his own, which could be hired for about £10 a year. She took it at once and used it as a studio during the two winters she and Ford spent at Toulon. When she was forced to give it up, she handed it over to Mr. William Seabrook, who there wrote his well-known book *Jungle Ways*.

An amusing companion for Ford was Francis Carco, who stayed with Friez for a while at Cap Brun, and no doubt swapped yarns with his English confrère about the celebrities of Montmartre and Montparnasse. The charm of Toulon and the magic spell of Provence so permeated Ford and Stella that the cottage at Guermantes "appeared by contrast no better than a makeshift and the studio in the rue N.D. des Champs just a *pied à terre*". So once again they began looking about for a little place in the countryside near Toulon, and got as far as making an offer for an old five-roomed house on a hill. Fortunately for their finances, temporarily exhausted by the cost of winding up the *transatlantic review*, the offer was refused.

Meanwhile Ezra and Dorothy Pound, who had also decided

that climate was one of the most important things in life, had
given up their studio in the rue N.D. des Champs, left Paris for
good and established themselves permanently in a sixth-floor
flat at Rapallo. Ford and Stella went to visit them there. Ford,
we may well imagine, was delighted to see his old friend of
the *English Review* days and to plunge into a prolonged discussion
of the world of letters in general and their own careers and
prospects in particular. Ford had for some years past been looking
to America, if not as a future home, at all events as the only
important source of his future income. He was convinced that
Ezra ought to return to his native land and show himself to his
growing circle of admirers, if only for prestige purposes. By this
time, however, Pound had already made contact with Mussolini,
whom he admired and in whose system of domestic finance he
saw a close resemblance to the Douglas Credit System, in which
he fanatically believed. As Stella Bowen tells us, "he looked to
Italy to provide him with all the future he wanted". How right
Ford was, subsequent events in Ezra Pound's career have most
painfully proved.

What completed Ford's happiness during his first winter at
Toulon was the fact that the second and, as many think, the most
powerful of his Tietjens novels was "going well". It was with
the MS. of *No More Parades* almost completed that, on their way
back to Paris, they broke their journey at Tarascon and, leaving
Julie with Madame Annie at the little hotel, went off on a jaunt
to Carcassonne, the Montaignes Noires and Castelnaudary. At
the Hotel de la Reine Jeanne at Castelnaudary, "where the
cassoulet has sat on the fire without a break for the last three
hundred years", Stella records that they "partook of one of
the most stupendous meals of our whole gastronomic experience". Encouraged by it, Stella bought sundry pieces of old
furniture at an antique shop, which subsequently adorned the
Paris studio.

It is improbable that while he was at Toulon, concentrating
on his work, Ford had any knowledge of the unfriendly reception
accorded in London, by the *Times Literary Supplement* and other
papers, to his book on Conrad. If Stella heard any rumours, or

saw any unfavourable reviews, we may be certain that she kept
Ford in ignorance of them. In Paris, however, such concealment
was impossible and that Ford was fully aware of the attacks made
upon him is revealed in his book *Return to Yesterday* (1931) in
which, in a chapter called "Working with Conrad", he makes
a temperate, dignified and conclusive reply. As the writer, in
South Lodge, has dealt at length with the "Conrad Controversy",
which broke out in 1925, it is unnecessary to discuss it here in
detail. Some impetus to the personal attacks on Ford, which
appeared in London and were followed up in New York by
Mr. H. L. Mencken in *The American Mercury* of April, 1925,
and by the *New York Times,* was given by what Mencken
describes as "an indignant manifesto in far from impeccable
English" published by Conrad's widow. Mrs. Conrad's motives
for denouncing Ford "as a cuckoo, shamelessly laying eggs in
her late husband's nest", as Mencken puts it, are not difficult to
understand. She was a loyal and devoted wife to her "lord and
master", had always disliked Ford whom, as a result of his matrimonial complications, she no doubt considered socially undesirable, regarded him as being, from the literary standpoint, a person
of no account in comparison with her husband, and bitterly
resented what she considered an impudent attempt on Ford's
part to "cash-in" on Conrad's fame and glory. "During the
years," she wrote, "that Mr. Hueffer was most intimate with
Joseph Conrad, between 1898 and 1909, Ford Madox Hueffer
never spent more than three consecutive weeks under our roof,
and when we returned the visit, we always, with few exceptions,
had rooms in a cottage close at hand. After 1909, the meetings
between the two were very rare and not *once* of my husband's
seeking." These observations, though possibly accurate as far as
they go, are calculated to show Conrad as a far from loyal friend
to a man from whom he had received so many benefits, and
whose unfailing generosity and profound admiration of his genius,
at a time when both were needed, had contributed so much to
his success. Mrs. Conrad was in no position to understand or
to appreciate the nature of their intimacy, or the links which
bound together two artists who shared a common ideal. From

Q

their intellectual life she was perforce excluded. On the other
hand she was anxious that nothing should be allowed to detract
from Conrad's prestige after his death, and resented the claim
to equality, as a literary figure, of a man who, from her standpoint, was not even respectable. This attitude on the part of
literary widows is not unusual in England or, for that matter,
in America, and must be ascribed, in part at least, to our indigenous Anglo-Saxon snobbery. No sooner does an eminent
poet, novelist, painter or composer sink into his honoured grave
than the friends or acquaintances he made during his lifetime are
arbitrarily divided, by his heirs, successors or assigns, into two
categories: those who might, by their social importance, be held
to contribute to his posthumous fame and those who, by their
obscurity, poverty and lack of publicity-value, might be held to
detract from it. In the latter category are usually found the dead
man's boon companions and his most loyal and affectionate
comrades.

Although Mr. Mencken was far too perceptive and acute a
critic either to be misled by Mrs. Conrad's manifesto, or to
question the validity of Ford's own account of his relations with
Conrad, he permits himself a tone of personal contempt for Ford
borrowed, perhaps, from his London confrères, which is an
astonishing mixture of arrogance, American "toughness" and
sheer bad manners. "This Ford, or Hueffer," Mencken snorts,
"has been a promising young man in England for thirty years.
He got launched early through the fact that his grandfather, Ford
Madox Brown, was much talked of in the 'nineties; he has made
gallant efforts, since then, to realise the high hopes of his sponsors
and rooters, of which last group he has always been an ardent
member himself. Once, with Douglas Goldring, he started the
English Review." The absurdity of the last statement could not
be appreciated by anyone more fully than myself. He might
as truthfully have alleged that "with Basil Bunting" Ford started
the *transatlantic review*. We were, both of us, no more than
cub apprentices, just out of our teens, who as literary aspirants
were glad of a chance of serving Ford as "boys-of-all-work".
After saying that "another time he took to writing history and

biography. Yet another time he consecrated himself to novels. Lately, apparently despairing of making a go of it in London, he moved to Paris and started a *tendenz* magazine called the *Transatlantic Review"*, Mencken adds that luck is not with him and that even his change of name has not got him anywhere. "Half German and half English, he is a sort of walking civil war —too much engrossed by the bombs going off in his own ego to make much of an impression upon the rest of the human race. The high, purple spot of his life came when he collaborated with Conrad, and upon the fact, I daresay, his footnote in the Literature books will depend."

Mencken's last remark serves to illustrate the harm to Ford's literary career which his association with Conrad actually caused him. A few shrewd observers, like H. G. Wells, early appreciated this fact. To-day when, among informed critics, Ford's stock is steadily rising, it scarcely needs to be stressed. The best and most conclusive reply which Ford could possibly have made to his detractors in London and New York was the publication of *No More Parades*. Both in Britain and in the United States there is, compared with France, only a small minority of the population which can appreciate good writing. It was Ford's misfortune, after losing the *English Review*, a misfortune to which a number of hearty enemies contributed as much as his own temperamental weaknesses, that he failed to make lasting contact with the English minority which might have given him the encouragement he required. With the American minority, on the other hand, helped by a number of enthusiastic friends and aided rather than hindered by his capacity for self-dramatisation, his success, while it lasted, was everything that he could have desired. The literary minority in the United States was much larger numerically (though not so in proportion to the population) than that of Great Britain. It was also much richer, so that the intelligent American bought what his equivalent in England only borrowed. Moreover the United States, as Ford pointed out to Edgar Jepson, supported at least ten literary magazines and reviews, in which an author of his standing had every hope of finding a profitable market. There was no periodical in England, in the 'twenties and 'thirties, which allowed a creative writer comparable freedom of expression. In England, the conditions under which he might hope to earn an addition to his income from our highly commercialised periodicals exacted rigid conformity with restrictions arbitrarily imposed. The non-conformist, excluded from the financial rewards of, and the publicity resulting from, free-lance journalism, was forced to rely on pot-boilers and hackwork for his means of subsistence. Ford, like Edward Thomas and other writers in a similar category, had been reduced, before America welcomed him, to grinding out numerous volumes which, while adding to the list of titles standing to his credit in the catalogue of the British Museum, tended to diminish the prestige of his spaced-out masterpieces.

In spite of the outbursts of spleen and venom which the publication of *Joseph Conrad: A Remembrance* had occasioned, the reviews of the Tietjens series by the more intelligent and independent of the English critics were highly complimentary. The *Manchester Guardian* justly observed that "there is no need to worry about the state of the English novel while books like this are being produced". Mr. Gerald Gould said of *No More Parades*, in the *Observer*, that it was "the best thing that Mr. Ford has ever done—and that is saying a lot, for Mr. Ford can be superbly good". Mr. Ralph Straus, an experienced and reliable judge of fiction, said: "Here is something big and startling and new . . ." Unfortunately, in England, such encomiums, unless they happen to catch the eye and endorse the personal opinions of the buyers for the big circulating libraries, have very little effect on sales. Numbers of novels which were praised to the skies never succeeded in selling as many as a thousand copies.

In the course of a reply to welcome "fan-mail" from an English admirer, Mr. Percival Hinton, written on 13th February, 1928, Ford provides some interesting confirmation of this statement. He says that returning from New York "on Saturday" with the not disagreeable knowledge that in the United States 50,000 people had bought *Last Post* within a fortnight of its appearance, he found his English publisher's statement and Mr.

Hinton's letter side by side, awaiting him. Duckworth's statement informed him that just under 1,000 people had bought the English edition of *No More Parades* and just over 1,000 *A Man Could Stand Up*. He adds that "when you consider that 400 copies of each were ordered before publication by New York purchasers of first editions, and at least 100 by Americans in Paris—well, you perceive what feet of clay the image has in our ? country". He says that it is curious that 100 people can be found in one country to buy what only one will in another. He tells his correspondent that his letter was the first English comment that had reached him for many years now—"I don't get press cuttings"—about his work, and that he is "proportionately touched". Of his output in general he remarks that: "I suppose I arrived at a relative robustness somewhat late in life —partly I suppose because of a complete lack of ambition", and partly for other reasons which he says will be found adumbrated in the dedicatory letter to the Avignon edition of *The Good Soldier*. He adds that there will be no more Tietjens. "I am setting about a straight narrative novel about the execution of Ney—to stretch my arms a little!" In a letter written to the same correspondent three years later, he makes a further reference to *The Good Soldier* which may be regarded as his considered view, expressed with complete detachment. "I think *The Good Soldier* is my best book technically," he writes, "unless you read the Tietjens books as one novel, in which case the whole design appears. But I think the Tietjens books will probably 'date' a good deal, whereas the other may—and indeed need—not."

Ford had every reason to be satisfied with the treatment accorded him by the American literary world. On his various visits to New York between 1926 and 1930 he received a warm welcome, was flattered and lionized by hostesses, accepted at his own valuation—as he deserved to be—by the leading critics, and overwhelmed by the open-handed hospitality for which America is famous. Publishers, at least before the Wall Street crash, treated him with marked respect and the editors of literary periodicals were pleased to accept his contributions and to pay for them at what, by European standards, were very liberal rates.

It is scarcely surprising that when Ford returned to Paris in 1926 his success in America and his encouraging future prospects had some effect on his way of life and his general attitude. He and Stella began to meet rich people and Ford, being as much at home in Ritz-Carlton surroundings as he was in labourers' cottages, found no difficulty in adapting himself to the jargon of transatlantic prosperity. As Stella puts it, "he presented a wonderful appearance of a bland, successful gentleman whose shabbiness was mere eccentricity and who regarded a preoccupation with the relative merits of Foyot and Larue, Vionnet and Poiret, the Ritz and the Hotel George V, as very natural and necessary". As he could never tolerate any hint of patronage, and no doubt regarded a certain amount of "window-dressing" as legitimate, he spent far more than he could afford in building up his new "persona" of the flourishing, successful and "arrived" man of letters, who knew everyone and went everywhere. Standing millionaires and their wives a round of drinks in a fashionable cocktail bar, however, empties a pocket-book far more rapidly than standing a few apéritifs to needy friends in a local *bistrot*. On the other hand, to a man of Ford's temperament, it would have been humiliating to have to reject invitations and forgo "the experiences which the world of pleasure has to offer" merely out of consideration for the family budget. "Experiences" were of use to him as a writer, so from that standpoint it is not for his readers to criticise Ford's pursuit of them.

Throughout the 'twenties in Paris, life in the large colony of "ex-patriates", from England, the United States, Norway, Sweden, Denmark and other countries, was a continuous round of excitement, working up to a crescendo of gaiety which had reached its climax at the moment of the Wall Street collapse. Those who took part in it, if only for brief intervals, must agree with Stella Bowen that there will never again be anything like it in our lifetime. The cheapness of the franc made anyone possessed of "hard" currency much richer than he would have been at home, while in France, unlike Britain and the United States, the pleasures and amenities of life have always been available to people of all classes, including those existing on the lowest income levels.

It was, of course, a period of uninhibited freedom degenerating often into licence. Too much drink, too much sex, too much of everything except high spirits, gaiety, energy, and creative excitement. From the point of view of the human community, of, shall we say, "civilisation" as a whole, it has to be judged by what it produced in the way of literature and art. From this standpoint the prolonged Parisian "kermesse" must, I think, be held to have justified itself. It provided liberation, compensation for over-tired nervous systems and, for those strong enough to stay the course, a valuable measure of catharsis. For Ford, whatever may have been its effects, thanks to his impressionable nature, on his personal conduct, it provided the necessary stimulus and the conducive atmosphere which he required for the production of his most enduring work. In the brief interval before the Wall Street slump hit Europe like a blizzard, before the rise of Hitler in aggressive partnership first with Mussolini, then with Franco, threatened vast populations with massacre and menaced with hangings, concentration camps and subtler forms of persecution the intellectual life of a whole continent, Ford and many other artists enjoyed their halcyon days. No one, particularly in Ford's case, can suggest that the "good time" was not deserved, had not been earned. "It is difficult now to remember," writes Stella Bowen, "how completely we were without political preoccupations, but such was the world we lived in, and from England in 1940 it looks like a remote and unbelievable Heaven." From England in 1947 it looks still more remote, still more heavenly.

It can never be said of Ford, at any period of his life, that he was lazy or idle. He was, indeed, a tireless and indefatigable worker, and even in Paris, in spite of his inveterate sociability, his constant parties, he worked regularly for long hours and with intense concentration. This fact is sometimes overlooked by readers of the innumerable books of Montparnasse memoirs in which Ford appears always as a dominant figure in social gatherings. Of the crowds of people who enjoyed his hospitality or knew him as a café acquaintance, few saw him at his desk patiently, tirelessly, engaged on work in progress.

Among those who have recorded impressions of Ford in Paris are Nina Hamnett, who says of him in her book *Laughing Torso* that "he talked a great deal and so well that nobody else wanted · to, or felt they could say anything interesting. He told stories very well indeed. He had most amusing stories about the time he was in the Welch Regiment. He learnt Welsh, as many of the soldiers could not speak English. He and Stella bought some of my drawings and were very kind to me. I met Gertrude Stein at his house". Later, she describes one of Ford's Christmas parties which the writer also attended, with a small, French-speaking son. "We had Christmas lunch in the Boulevard Mont-parnasse, at a restaurant called 'Le Nègre de Toulouse'. Ford had a small daughter, and in the afternoon there was a children's tea-party, with a Christmas tree and a real Father Christmas. Ford dressed up as le Père Noël. He looked magnificent as he was very tall. He wore a red cloak with cotton wool repre-senting fur, and a red hood and a large white beard. He appeared with a large sack and spoke French, as nearly all the children spoke French better than they spoke English, and Ford's child did not speak English at all." Nina Hamnett's present on this occasion was an inscribed copy of Ford's novel *Some Do Not*. Of Stella Bowen, Nina writes that she "painted very well in a very precise and accomplished manner. She did an excellent portrait of Ford asleep. Ford was not too pleased, because she caught him when he had fallen asleep and was snoring with his mouth open. She said that he posed much better when he was asleep".

Another English "Montparno" of the 'twenties, George Slo-combe, refers to Ford, in his volume of memoirs, *The Tumult and the Shouting*, as having "cut a considerable figure" in Paris in these years. "His *transatlantic review* (typography his own) was a brave attempt to re-create the *English Review* in a form com-patible with the newer, younger, and stranger world in which he, a bulky, middle-aged, gentle, courteous and incurably romantic survival from the more sensitive Edwardian epoch, found him-self, to his own never-failing astonishment, amusement and delight. Ford's studio in the rue Notre Dame des Champs was the scene of a weekly party in his prosperous years. All English-speaking Montparnasse crowded into it, drank his hospitably offered libations, and paraded its secret inhibitions in much con-fused talk, much strenuous dancing, much hearty alcoholic laughter, horseplay and petting. Later Ford transported his goods, his enthusiasms and his generous illusions to an attic in the rue Vaugirard."

In an article called "Souvenirs de Ford Madox Ford", by Florence Llona, which appeared in a Paris newspaper after Ford's death, the author also refers to Ford's receptions which she says were always adorned by young American poets whose admira-tion for Ford kept them dumb. From 1924 to 1929, she says, Ford lived chiefly in Montparnasse and for the greater part of the American writers who abounded in Paris during that period, for many young English painters and intellectuals, and for a certain number of French people, it will always be '*L'époque Ford Madox Ford*'. After referring to the mixed crowds who gathered in the big studio in the Boulevard Arago, Florence Llona says that in the studio at 84 rue Notre Dame des Champs, Ford made a careful and rigorous selection of people to be invited, choosing only "*gens sérieux*" who either had a work at the back of them or were genuinely engaged in completing one. All the same, there was a gramophone and people danced, but in a corner one could overhear Ford and Gertrude Stein discussing the case of Marcel Proust. At these gatherings, Ford's smile became more and more Olympian! "*Cher, cher* Ford," her article concludes, "*un des derniers écrivains à savoir ce que c'est que le métier d'écrire, à aimer son métier d'un profond amour d'artisan—le sérieux, le fini, et le poids de votre oeuvre, joints à la fraîche fantaisie de votre vie, nous font terriblement sentir quel maître et quel ami nous venons de perdre.*"

Sometime in 1927, Ford and Stella were fortunate enough to discover an attic flat at 31 rue de Vaugirard, which actually possessed a bath tub and a gas cooker. This apartment was large enough to accommodate Julie and her nurse Madame Annie, as well as themselves, and left the studio free for painting and parties. The cottage at Guermantes was generously handed over, with a nucleus of furniture, to the brilliant but then impecunious Russian painter, Pavlick Tchelitcheff.

The circumstances which led, by gradual stages, to the dissolution of Ford and Stella's ménage have been described with conspicuous honesty and generosity of mind in her book *Drawn from the Life*. As she herself is the only one who can possibly know exactly what took place, the curious reader can safely be referred to her account of the final parting and what preceded it. The atmosphere of "ex-patriate" Paris in the 'twenties, largely influenced by the transatlantic colony, was, in any case, not conducive to permanency in human relations. With Ford, as with other artists, the real "wife of his bosom" was the art he practised and his most romantic and glamorous mistress the land of Provence. In spite of his natural sociability, his kindness, his benevolence, his interest in young people, his large circle of friends and acquaintances, we must accept Stella Bowen's view that personal relationships were not really important to him at all. "In order to keep his machinery running," says Stella Bowen, speaking of the artist in general terms, "he requires to exercise his sentimental talents from time to time upon a new object. It keeps him young. It refreshes his ego. It restores his belief in his powers." When Ford needed someone to give him a new lease of life, after the war, Stella was the "new object" and, for the nine years of their association, they lived on the whole very happily and contentedly together. They were never bored; they did not quarrel and even when they were on the brink of separating they could dine out together and have agreeable arguments on abstract themes.

It was in 1928, after returning from New York, that Ford announced that he had formed a sentimental attachment to an American lady whom he proposed to visit every year. He saw no reason why the Paris ménage could not go on just the same, in between whiles. But Stella was an artist in her own right and, as she puts it, wanted to belong to herself, to "slip from under the weightiness of Ford's personality" and regain her own shape. And as by this time she had fallen out of love with Ford, though without any accompaniment of repining, lasting bitterness, or lack of appreciation of his finer qualities, she preferred to resign him to his latest "object", to take charge of Julie, to rely on her own courage and steadfastness of character, and live her own life. One of the factors which, possibly, conduced to her decision was the tiring effect, on a person naturally truthful, of Ford's salient eccentricity. Ford insisted, as a writer, on the necessity of precision in order to create an effect of authenticity, "in the same way as the precision of a brush-stroke gives authenticity to an image on canvas". He regarded words, as a painter regards paints, purely as the raw material of his art and without the slightest reference to the facts conveyed by them in normal social intercourse. This by no means indicates that Ford was not, like all authentic artists, a seeker after Truth, or that he was lacking either in wisdom or understanding. Few men, indeed, had a deeper instinctive insight into the secret places of the heart, a warmer humanity, a quicker sympathy with suffering or a more paternal interest in the young. But the sort of Truth he was concerned with could be revealed by the artist only by the creation of precise and striking images and the modern equivalent of parables. For the mere "factual truth" of everyday life he had no use at all, so that the more prosaic of his acquaintances were apt to write him off merely as a pathological liar. Most of the stories he told to delighted audiences were as much "fairy stories" as those he related to his daughters at bed-time in their childhood years. His various volumes of memoirs and reminiscences are largely, from the factual standpoint, works of fiction which create "an effect" of authenticity, and, as a rule, convey a just "impression". All this was confusing, and indeed irritating, to many who had not known him long enough to regard his peculiarities with the affectionate tolerance one should accord to the oddities of the Great.

I happened to call on Ford at his flat in the rue Vaugirard shortly before he sailed for New York, in the summer of 1927. He at once embarked upon a story of how he came to be living in that particular flat. "You see," he began, "*after I left Eton* I came to study at the Sorbonne and I was greatly attached to an old Professor who used to live here . . ." The reflection that

Ford was, as they say, "slipping", was true in the superficial sense that his eccentricity was growing upon him, under the influence, perhaps, of his impending visit to a country where it could be indulged with impunity and to the full. But, as the books written in the last decade of his life reveal, the breadth and clarity of his intelligence, the hard, almost ice-cold central core of his mind, functioned unimpaired until the end.

CHAPTER XVIII

American "Best-Seller"

THE YEARS which remained to Ford, after the break-up of his Paris ménage, were among the most productive of his career. In the course of this final decade he delivered his Message, added his voice to those of other European writers who foresaw the impending cataclysm, and summed up a lifetime of continuous and unfaltering devotion to the art he practised in his monumental survey of *The March of Literature from Confucius to Modern Times*. The more we consider Ford's career in perspective the more the reader must be struck by its unswerving fidelity to certain causes, principles and Standards of Value and by the success with which, notwithstanding periods of poverty, abuse, flattery, ill-luck, good luck and domestic entanglements, he did what he set out to do. Ford himself realised that his personal and private life was of no importance compared with the life of his mind, the development of which can be studied only by reading his books. Like all great artists, he put the best of himself into his work, and the residuum that was left over when the gold had been extracted laboriously from the quartz did not always conform to approved, conventional standards. As a human personality he was, no doubt, a mass of contradictions, but his prevailing characteristics were his essential kindness, his boundless generosity, a quality frequently imposed upon by the selfish and unscrupulous, his breadth of mind and freedom from petty jealousy. He had, no doubt, many childish faults, among them a distressing tendency to "show off", which grew upon him in the conducive American atmosphere, and these made him vulnerable to the malicious attacks of people who, at one time or another, had benefited from his help. One such, in a notice of Stella Bowen's book, stated that she and Ford "started housekeeping together at her expense", described him as "the Liar as

Artist", and referred to him as a "humbug-hero". Ford's favourite proverb was that "It would be hypocrisy to seek for the person of the Sacred Emperor in a Low Tea House". Unfortunately for himself he not infrequently drifted by accident into very low tea houses and was pelted with a good deal of dirt in consequence by their frequenters.

Ford's personal life, with the companion of his closing years —a young Jewish artist who signed her work Biala and made the illustrations for two of his books, *Provence* and *Great Trade Route*—could only be described in any detail by the lady who shared it. We know that, in spite of increasing financial difficulties, he was happy and contented in his domestic surroundings, because there is internal evidence of this in the work he was able to accomplish. The financial blizzard hit Ford hard, as it did other writers, both in America and Europe. Moreover, as a result of one of those quick changes of mood which are so characteristic of the United States, the ex-patriates, or rather the literary movement they represented, suddenly went out of fashion and was replaced by "isolationist" fiction, which made a bid for large circulations by depicting the American scene in purely American terms.

Mr. Van Wyck Brooks, in his brilliant and penetrating book, *Opinions of Oliver Allston*, puts the case against the ex-patriates, whom he calls "coterie writers", in admittedly convincing terms. Literary content, he maintains, is the result of responsible living, in a world with which one has real connections. In his view Gertrude Stein, like many other writers who have spent their lives in countries not their own, was "infantile". These ex-patriates were, he says, mostly out of touch with the primary realities, because they had no real connection with the world they lived in, and "their only responsibility was to their art, which thus, by the nature of things, became a game". Mr. Brooks adds that the coterie writers were the "victims of their own personalities, which were floating in a void; and hence the air of the mystagogue that enveloped them all . . . they were international mystagogues, concerned, above everything else, for their own prestige; for, as maladjusted persons, they were insecure, and, being insecure, they developed a morbid will to power". Mr. Brooks's searching analysis does not even spare the towering, almost monumental figure of Henry James. After telling us a fact which will come as a surprise to many English readers, that Henry James, in the middle of the World War (1915) insisted on getting the Prime Minister to sponsor his naturalisation, he adds that "any other Englishman would have served as well. But no, James would have the Prime Minister, if he had to stop the battle of Flanders to get him. Modesty is a virtue these persons can seldom afford. Their self-assertion requires corroboration".

It will be seen, from the above, that there was a powerful school of criticism in New York which offered reasoned opposition, from the "native" American standpoint, to many of the ideas and influences which Ford was supposed to represent. Of Ford himself, Mr. Brooks writes that "in 1925, when Ford was in New York, he called me on the telephone and asked me to have lunch with him. I was most flattered and grateful and Ford was such a kind and good-natured man that no one could have helped liking him . . . no writer was too young or too raw to attract his fatherly interest, his truly astonishing flair for the art of writing". He goes on to observe that "his mind was like a Roquefort cheese, so ripe that it was palpably falling to pieces", and that he did not think it formed a good mental diet for the young western boys, fresh from the prairie, who came under his influence in Paris. Ford he regarded as an "uprooted creature" who, as a half-German, was half an alien in his own country. Mr. Brooks says that he propagated a notion of literature to which the prairie boys were already too much disposed. "Ford and Gertrude Stein," he concludes, "playing into the hands of Joyce, Eliot and Pound, provided a diet of nightingales' tongues for boys who knew nothing of beef and potatoes; and the maternal Miss Stein and the fatherly Ford appealed to their filial instincts also—which made the authority of these writers all the more compelling". This line of argument, which had its supporters also in London, cannot be dismissed lightly, and it will seem to some that Ford's long association with Ezra Pound and his troupe of "cowboys" did almost as much damage to his literary reputation as did his connection with Conrad. Like his grandfather before him, Ford had an engrained propensity for mistaking geese for swans, as well as an incorrigible habit of spending as much time and energy on boosting the work of others as he did on boosting his own. What alone saved him from the fate of being first "overlaid" by Conrad's public fame, and later dismissed, with a shrug, as a patron of the Pound gang and a "coterie writer" like Gertrude Stein, was the indisputable creative genius displayed in his Tietjens novels. Confronted with these masterpieces, malicious tongues, of which there were some in New York, though not so many as there were in London, were silenced. To sneer at a writer who could give such a moving, authentic and unforgettable picture of our Army in France as that contained in *No More Parades*, merely because he had a weakness for telling New Yorkers that he was educated at Eton and served as a captain in the Guards, was rated by sensible people as mean and unintelligent. If civilization is to be enriched by great works of art—and if it ceases to be so enriched it will cease to be civilization—then the human race must learn to be tolerant of the eccentricities of their creators. That is all there is to it. While London reviewers, many of whom over a long period had treated Ford with every sign of rancour and contempt, were forced by an over-riding critical integrity to describe *No More Parades* as "a work of genius", to claim for its author "a larger measure of genius than most men now writing", to hail Christopher Tietjens as "one of the few truly original characters which have appeared in modern English fiction", and Ford's portrait of him as "a marvellous piece of analysis of the mind", American critics, who were, if anything, prejudiced in Ford's favour, were even more lavish in their praise. With the difference, fortunate for Ford, that their enthusiasm, as has already been noted, had an immediate effect upon his sales. It was in New York that Ford, for the first and only time in his life, became a "best-seller". It is interesting also to observe that the novels with which Ford secured his greatest American success were uncompromisingly *English*. They were the work of a man who

had not only fought in the British Army but had absolutely
identified himself with the spirit of the British people, their
traditions, their background, their ideals, their follies, their
oddities, their feelings, their confused aspirations. There is no
trace in them, apart from their actual machinery, their "technique", of anything not native to the British soil. They are not
the work of an international, rootless man, a "half-German",
an alien in his own country. Nor is there any trace of a desire,
so distressingly apparent in *Return to Yesterday*, *It was the Nightingale*, and *Great Trade Route*, to show off before American intimates and to address himself to an American audience. Ford
could, when he wished to do so, make himself feel like a Frenchman, like a German or like an American, but in the Tietjens
series he wrote like an Englishman of the privileged classes, felt
like one and, thanks to his intimate instinctive knowledge of
English character, was able to make his plots progress through
the thoughts of the contrasted individuals who appear in them.
If Mr. Brooks was anxious for middle-western novelists to devote
themselves to representing what they knew and understood—the
American scene and the American way of life—he might have
pointed to the Tietjens series, by reason of their essential English-
ness, as a model for them to imitate. Ford took for his subject,
to use his own phrase, "the public events of a decade", making
the figure of Christopher Tietjens the personification of that
Standard of Values by which all the other characters, as well as
the surge, thunder and moral disintegration of the times they
lived in, are judged. The English ideal type, the "Christian
Gentleman", the disinterested man of the ruling class who lived,
by inherited instinct, in accordance with the Rotarian motto
"service before self", though stemming from far back in our
national life, was only codified and adopted as a model in early
Victorian days, under the inspiring guidance of Arnold of Rugby.
One of his first appearances in fiction is in *Tom Brown's Schooldays*. Squire Brown, though a modest country gentleman by
comparison with the vast wealth of the owners of Groby, would
very well have understood Tietjens, though he might not have
understood why, in years to come, young Englishmen who had

R

inherited Tietjens' moral attitude, dismayed by Chamberlain Conservatism, Fascism, Liberalism, Labour, Social Democracy and what not, should find themselves attracted by an ideal form of Communism. To Ford, who had watched his grand-father developing in this direction, for similar reasons, and who —before the end of his life—developed in the same way him-self, this result of fidelity to a moral code would have seemed logical. For although Ford asserted that Tietjens was a "pro-jection" of the personality of his friend and partner Arthur Marwood, the beloved figure of Ford Madox Brown was always deeply present in his conscious, and still more in his sub-conscious, mind.

The immediate acclaim accorded in New York both to the Tietjens novels and to their author, combined to make the years from 1925 to the end of the decade the most prosperous, expan-sive and resplendent period in Ford's career. In addition to the Tietjens books, Ford re-issued (through the firm of Albert and Charles Boni) *The Good Soldier*, refurbished his historical novel, *Ladies Whose Bright Eyes*, for Lippincott, and published a volume of *New York Essays* through W. E. Rudge, in 1927 and a volume of *New Poems*, in a limited edition, for the same publisher. He had also an assured market, in the literary magazines, for anything he wanted to write. In 1930, when the proposal was made to him to issue an omnibus volume of the Tietjens novels under the general title *The Tietjens Saga*, he wrote to a correspondent, in a letter quoted in the *Saturday Review of Literature*, 2nd August, 1941, deprecating the use of this title. "I do not like the title *Tietjens Saga*," he says, "because in the first place Tietjens is a name difficult to pronounce and book-sellers would almost inevitably persuade readers that they mean *The Forsyte Saga* with great damage to my sales." For a general title he suggested *Parade's End*, with the *Tietjens Saga* for a sub-title. In the same letter he makes the interesting observation that "I strongly wish to omit *Last Post* from the edition. I do not like the book and have never liked it and always intended to end up with *A Man Could Stand Up*." *Last Post* was dedicated to an influential New York critic, Miss Isabel Patterson, of whom Ford writes in his introduction: "I have for some years now had to consider you as being my fairy godmother in the United States. . . . For, but for you, this book would only nebularly have existed—in space, in my brain, where you will, so it be not on paper and between boards. Save, that is to say, for your stern, contemptuous and almost virulent insistence on knowing 'what became of Tietjens', I never should have conducted this chronicle to the stage it has now reached." The MS. of *Last Post* was completed on 12th November, 1927, a year in Ford's life that was crowded with activity, both social and literary.

I happened by chance to be visiting New York in November 1927, and have described in detail, in *South Lodge*, the impression which Ford made upon me, at that time. So far as it was possible for a stranger in New York to judge from his demeanour, he was feeling exuberantly cheerful and self-confident. In periods of adversity Ford had always managed to maintain, where the outside world was concerned, a mask of Olympian calm. He kept his troubles to himself and his immediate circle, and his personal worries never prevented him from taking the liveliest interest in the concerns of his juniors. In New York, the mask seemed to have slipped, for though he was kinder and more considerate than ever to the young, he made no effort to conceal his own contentment. Ford presented himself to his nervous compatriot as the complete New Yorker, on terms of easy intimacy with the town itself and with everyone in it, connected with literature or the arts, who was of the slightest interest or importance. The electric atmosphere, the surge, clamour and nervous, almost hysterical excitement of the vast cosmopolitan city, then under the combined influences of a boom which seemed certain to last for ever and of Prohibition Laws which made the consumption of hard liquor almost a point of honour, seemed to have acted on him only as an agreeable tonic. In spite of the variety of his impersonations as a "quick-change" artist, the number of nationalisms which, at different times he was able, internationally, to personify and represent, it is remarkable how in certain basic and essential qualities he remained, throughout his life, himself. I might never have discovered that New York possessed the equivalent of a slum had he not shepherded me, on the night of my departure, to a party of penniless young writers who received him as the beloved Professor and listened attentively to his patient exposition of the technique of the timeshift and kindred topics. This was the same old Ford of the *English Review* days and of the Paris cafés, faithful to his job and maintaining, unchanged, his Standard of Values.

The little gathering I chanced to attend on the night I sailed from New York showed Ford in a rôle which he subsequently sustained, professionally, with much success, and, let us hope, some profit. It was, he tells us—in the preface to a collection of lectures on *The English Novel*, published in England by Constable in 1930—Sir Hugh Walpole who was indirectly the means of securing him an invitation to give a series of lectures to the English classes of certain American universities. In his introductory letter to Walpole Ford says the book was written solely for the consumption of students in the United States at a time when he had arrived at a decision to publish nothing more in the country of his birth. A set of circumstances, all happening on the same day, made him change his mind. First he received in the morning Constable's offer to publish the book. (He says he thought the publisher must be mad for he must be "as aware as I that a good average of English readers of my works has for many years been about four hundred".) Secondly some kindly person gave him a copy of the *New York Herald's* literary supplement containing Walpole's "far too eulogistic" references to himself, and thirdly a Rhodes scholar told him that mimeographed copies of the lectures were being used by certain students at Oxford as a text-book in their English classes. His expressions of gratitude to Walpole for praising him in a New York literary paper are almost fulsome and show how deeply sensitive he was to the opinions about himself of his English colleagues. "I have never," he writes, "in that city which for long now has been my spiritual home, heard of any other English novelist going out of his way to speak a kind word for any other one, and, that city being the immense whispering gallery that it is, I have heard of many unkind sayings as to my works and much unkinder ones as to my person, uttered there in public and private by visiting English novelists." In a review of *The March of Literature* which appeared in an English weekly periodical after Ford's death, the critic observed that it is "the kind of book which will enable a young man in a hurry to mug up the subject, with a view to pass a degree". Ford, however, says of his lectures on *The English Novel*, which was a similar "kind of book", that "the young, earnest student of literature for professional purposes should, if he desires good marks, write in his thesis for examination pretty well the opposite of what I have here set down". On this point it must be presumed that the author knew better than the reviewer. We can be certain that it was the originality and mentally stimulating quality of Ford's lectures which held the attention of the students who attended them and, knowing Ford, it goes without saying that he spent endless time and trouble in encouraging budding talent wherever he detected it. Details of Ford's lecturing activities during the last decade of his life are not available in England, but it is reasonable to suppose that in the course of them he was invited to visit Olivet College, Michigan, with whose President and "Dean of Men" he evidently established very cordial relations. In consequence he not only accepted at their hands one of those honorary "doctorates" which such institutions are accustomed to distribute rather liberally, but also dedicated to them his last and most monumental work, *The March of Literature from Confucius to Modern Times*.

The fact that Ford seems to have derived satisfaction from his degree of "D.Litt." and allowed himself to be photographed in a gown and mortar board as part of a publicity "build-up" for his lecture tours, indicates that he himself, like other notable scholars and writers had a high respect for Olivet College, although an American correspondent informs me that it is doubtful if one person in one hundred in his country ever heard of it. According to the *Encyclopædia Americana* it was founded in 1844 by one John J. Shipherd, and was first known as Olivet Institute. It was chartered as a college in 1859 and is under the management of the Congregationalists. It confers an A.B. degree (bachelor of arts), has a library of more than 40,000 volumes and a fifteen acre campus. Olivet

Congregational Church is the College chapel and in 1930 there
were 286 students and a faculty of 25. All honour must be accorded
to this progressive seat of learning for having had the good sense to
honour Ford.

To return to Ford in New York in the autumn of 1927 there
was evidence that in exalted social circles and often in the most
opulent surroundings, Ford was dramatising his ego and sub-
mitting with a certain satisfaction to the process of being lionised.
As he puts it, in his book *Ancient Lights*, the artist *must* live with
enjoyment if his work is to be sound and good. "He ought, if
he is to be able to know life, to be able to knock at all doors;
to be able to squander freely on occasions; he ought to be able
to riot now and then." New York, in the final years of the boom,
provided Ford with his last and fullest opportunities of putting
this precept into practice. A portrait of him, by George Hart-
mann, reproduced in the *New York Times Book Review* of 24th
January, 1932, is, on this point, revealing, for it shows him
marvellously apparelled in the top hat and evening clothes of
what he once, in an unfortunate phrase, described as a "Piccadilly
dude". No doubt, by his own previous standards, Ford made a
great deal of money in New York before the Wall Street crisis,
but in that fabulously expensive city it must have required every
dollar he earned to enable him to sustain, for however brief a
period, the role of fashionable man about town. Like Arnold
Bennett, he never acquired any real "clothes sense" and the more
he spent on his apparel, the less distinguished he looked. On the
other hand, no matter what clothes he chose to wear, his agreeable manners and flow of amusing talk made him a success in
any kind of society. The real Ford, however, was not the elderly
"playboy" which momentarily he appeared to be in New York
and Paris, but the hard-working conscientious artist which he
always was and the far-seeing and detached observer of the world's
ills which he ultimately became. For these, his life's interests and
aims, a garret in a capital city or a lonely peasant's cottage in
Provence formed the most congenial and appropriate setting.
The general pattern of Ford's life is thus one of almost monastic
simplicity, for which his occasional outbreaks of extravagant

living and crowded social intercourse provided a change, a renewal of energy and a mental tonic.

After the boom collapsed we soon find Ford back again, living his usual austere life, in his beloved France. As usual, he was constantly on the move and it is only possible to trace his where-abouts from the addresses at the head of his letters. His sales began to fall off pretty steadily, but publishers were still glad, if only for prestige reasons, to have his books in their lists while the cheapness of living in France enabled him to keep his head above water on his diminished earnings. By 26th June, 1930, he was back at St. Agrève in Ardèche, for we find him writing to his old friend Edgar Jepson on that date. "I suppose it's no good trying to coax any of you here?" he asks. "It's very high—1,500 feet in the Cevennes and quite cheap." He says that people keep preferring him to Morand, which is "gratifying, but bitter! For if I'd written in French I'd have had all this ——[word illegible] and more, even in England. For anyhow M. is only following the dear old Dad".

Ford's mind was soon to lead him into very different paths from those in which the literary diplomat was disposed to follow. All his intuitions and perceptions, as he neared his sixtieth birthday, were forcing upon him the conviction that the civilisation to the defence of which he had devoted his whole life, and risked it on the battlefield, was rapidly heading for a crash, very possibly for complete destruction. Far in advance of most of the French writers of the Resistance, he seems to have been forced, reluctantly, to the realisation that the artist cannot remain silent. In his book *European Witness*, Mr. Stephen Spender quotes a passage from the essays of Jean-Paul Sartre which embodies conclusions which, judging from certain passages in his *Great Trade Route*, Ford seems to have anticipated. "The writer," says Sartre, "is situated in his time: each word has its reverberations, each silence too. I hold Flaubert and Goncourt responsible for the repressions which followed the Commune, because they wrote not a single line to prevent them. It may be said that it was none of their business: but was the case of Calas the business of Voltaire?; the sentence on Dreyfus the business of Zola?; the administration of the Congo the business of Gide? Each one of these writers, in some particular circumstance of his life, weighed up his responsibility as a writer. The Occupation has taught us ours." As Britain was fortunately saved from Occupation, Sartre's views, even to-day, find little response among the English literary fraternity who, with a shudder, still dismiss any alternative to silence as "propaganda". Ford had more excuse than most writers for adopting this escapist attitude, but as he had more conscience and more intellectual integrity than most of them, it was impossible for him to take this way out. Any sort of injustice or oppression, whether of nations, races or individuals, aroused Ford's indignation in much the same way as it had aroused his mother's and his grandfather's. In this characteristic the Madox Brown strain in his complex personality proved predominant. Ford had championed the cause of the suffragettes because of his hatred of injustice, and for the same reason he had championed the Irish Sinn Feiners and protested against the brutality of the Black-and-Tans. In the early thirties, while he was living with Janice Biala at Cap Brun, near Toulon, the persecution of the Jews aroused his generous indignation. Passages in the dedicatory letter to his autobiographical novel *It Was the Nightingale*, begun in Paris in January 1933, and completed at Cap Brun six months later, indicate his growing awareness of the world situation and his immediate grasp of the significance of Hitler. In this he was several years in advance of many of even the most politically intelligent of his contemporaries. That *It Was the Nightingale* is to be regarded as a novel, based on two adventures of a "poor man who was once young", Ford explicitly states in his introduction to the book. "In rendering them" (the adventures), he says, "I have employed every wile known to me as novelist—the timeshift, the *progression d'effet,* the adaptation of rhythms to the pace of the action." We must not, therefore, complain if "facts", following Ford's habit, are sometimes invented or distorted to suit the novelist's purpose. The story of the *transatlantic review,* told in Ford's happiest vein, can, however, be accepted as substantially accurate. More important, for the reader to-day, are occasional passages which illustrate Ford's remarkable prescience. For example, after paying tributes, in his introduction, to various American literary friends, he observes: "the layman hates the artist as the atrocious Mr. Hitler hates learning. Indeed the layman regards the artist as a sort of Jew. But, to the measure of the light vouchsafed, my late comrades shine in their places and may be content. The *pogroms* will come but, even as Heine, the greatest of German poets, they have lit beacons that posterity shall not willingly let die." When this was written, Hitler had only just emerged as ruler of Germany. The book opens with a moving account of Ford's experiences after demobilisation which appear even more credible to-day, when all of us have, at one time or other, come in contact with official persons, than they did when the book was published. As with his other autobiographical volumes, Ford gives us vivid impressions of sundry eminent figures—George Moore, Galsworthy, Gosse, Arnold Bennett and several more—but he also reveals the nature of his personal emotions and the development of his thought, in his sixtieth year. There is one particularly enlightening passage in which he tells us that while he had worn His Majesty's uniform he had been not merely politically, but to the mental backbone "as English as it was possible to be". He says that his most glorious memory of England had been that in the 'nineties he had seen hundreds of Jewish refugees from the pogroms in Russia land at Tilbury dock. "And as each unit of these hundreds stepped on the dock he or she fell on their knees and kissed the ground—the sacred soil of Liberty. It was not, of course, because they were Jews or martyrs. And I daresay it was not merely because England was my country. It was pride in humanity." Ford felt that if a body of men confined in one island could evolve that tradition that for centuries had given glory to England, then there had been hope for mankind. Now it seemed, to his bitter and disillusioned eyes, as if England was heading for disaster. "No political fugitives, no martyrs for whatever faith were ever more to land on those shores—because of an Order in Council—an Order in Council evolved by some unknown member of the most suspect Government the realm had ever suffered from!" The treatment of the demobilised soldiers by the *embusqués* officials "born to detest them" aroused in Ford much the same indignation as to-day is aroused in generous natures by the treatment accorded to the partisans in Greece and other liberated countries, by the governments of Britain and America. England, as Ford lamented, had lost its finest sons. The most vigorous and alert of the young men had been killed or mangled—physically and mentally. Those who survived, "the poor flotsam of its best blood, its best sinews and best, normal brains" were denied access to the public service, harassed, insulted, treated like "rats", reduced to beggary. As Ford observes, this treatment "engendered in its victims a cynicism of the betrayed and in the others a still more fatal cynicism of the traitor that were alike of almost infinite detriment to the poor old ship of the British State". He saw England "drifting towards a weir. In pre-war days, the country had been distinguished in her intellectual as in her material harvests by the dead hand of vested interests. Questioning and innovation had been very difficult. But there had been at least some youth, some intellectual clarity, some carelessness, some iconoclasts. And her laws had been made for men relatively free." Ford saw that most of this was to go and that for a generation England was to sink back into a slough "in which despondency and vested interests, however changed in incidence, must strangle all initiative. You cannot kill off a million of your most characteristic young men, cram your workhouses and jails with all that they will hold of the rest and for ever disillusionise those that remained outside those institutions—you could not do all that without at least modifying your national aspect". In writing this, in the summer of 1933, Ford was quoting from an article which, at the time when it was written, no English newspaper could be found to print, and it is interesting—or perhaps melancholy—to note that the machinery for suppressing the utterances of independent minds at the moment when they might have some salutary effect on public opinion has been perfected with the passage of years. The growth of a gramophone press has now effectively stifled warning voices.

In *It Was the Nightingale* Ford not only gives us vivid glimpses of his post-war years in Paris and Provence, but also makes a confession in regard to the Tietjens novels which indicates the influence of public events on his own theories of a novelist's function. He wanted the novelist to appear "in his really proud position as historian of his own time. Proust being dead I could see no one who was doing that . . ." But, in the Tietjens series, he went further than this. "I have always had the greatest contempt for novels written with a purpose," he says. "Fiction should render, not draw morals. But when I sat down to write that series of volumes, I sinned against my gods to the extent of saying that I was going—to the level of the light vouchsafed to me—to write a work that should have for its purpose the obviating of all future wars."

CHAPTER XIX

The Last Phase

FROM 1933, until the end of his life, Ford, like other humanists concerned with the fate of civilisation, became increasingly obsessed by the world catastrophe which he saw was impending. He had always, consciously, written for the Future, and been in advance of his time both as a thinker and as an artist. And now the Future seemed fraught with tragedy for mankind, because mankind was leaderless, because it could not or would not make the necessary effort, combining thought with action, to save itself from the frustration imposed by professional politicians. In preparation for his book, *Great Trade Route*, first published by the Oxford University Press of New York in 1937, he and Janice Biala, who made the illustrations for the volume, travelled extensively in the Deep South of the United States, in Spain, in Germany, in Switzerland, in France, even in England. In the spring of 1932, before the appearance of *It Was the Nightingale*, Ford, with Janice, had paid a brief visit to London, the circumstances of which could hardly have inspired him with any great desire to re-establish himself in his native city. Early in February, the writer had received a letter from him, written from 32 rue de Vaugirard, Paris, in which, after saying "I see you log-rolling me, as per usual, in the *E.R.* If you didn't so persistently—and kindly—do it for me, I'd do it for you", he remarks that he vaguely wants "to go to London for a month or two—mostly to see pictures" and suggests an exchange of apartments. This was not possible for us as the financial blizzard had hit writers and artists in London no less severely than those of Paris and New York. Ford and Janice eventually found a garret flat in Southampton Street, Euston Road, a stone's throw from Ford Madox Brown's old home in Fitzroy Square. Little notice was taken of their arrival by any of the now eminent figures who had been glad enough of Ford's hospitality in his more resplendent days. Most of the loyal friends who were eager to welcome him were as hard up as he was himself. The English ex-patriates, who had known him in Montparnasse, were for the most part a sorry and dispirited crowd, either haunting the dingy bars of Fitzrovia or endeavouring, without great success, to earn their livings by any form of drudgery they found available. Ford was, in fact, a forgotten man. The important and the influential figures in the literary world of the 'thirties knew him only by name and were too much concerned with the rivalry of their own cliques and coteries to hail his return in cordial paragraphs. The cleavage between the literary worlds of London and New York, which is to-day so complete, had by then already begun. If British writers, having lost their American market, were no longer interested in New York's literary celebrities still less so were they in the work of promising young American painters. It must be presumed therefore that Ford and Biala were not sorry to see the last of England in 1932. A few years later when, through the sound judgment of Sir Stanley Unwin, Ford's last four important books, *Great Trade Route, Mightier than the Sword, Provence,* and *The March of Literature,* were successfully launched in this country, the situation was altering. Something like a Ford "revival" was in progress at the time of his death, and even the interruption of six years of war has not entirely arrested it. Although in England the prophet in his lifetime has often even less honour in his own country than is usually the case, post-humous justice is perhaps more generously accorded by the British than by the Americans. It may be that our memories are longer, our loyalties more tenacious, our traditional sense of values more deeply rooted and securely based.

The scope of this book, for reasons explained in the preface, does not include a critical examination of Ford's writings, a task which awaits some eminent critic of the future, but it may be noted that the pre-atomic warnings, with which his *Great Trade Route* abounds, have even more actuality to-day than when they first appeared. Again it must be repeated that Ford wrote for a Future which is rapidly becoming the Present. He was both an upholder of tradition and a pioneer. It may well be that if the United States starts dropping the atomic bombs which she has continuously manufactured during the period of peace-making, any survivors of the resulting holocaust will be forced to adopt Ford's recipe for a peaceful, happy and self-sufficing existence. One of the "mad professors" who has been engaged at the highest level on the task of "making the world safe for Americans" has admitted in a moment of sanity, that any future wars—after "the Third"—will have to be fought with bows and arrows. If Ford's "message" could be disseminated among the young, they would not have to be fought at all. The theme of his book is that "if you could get rid of wars, national barriers, patriotisms, politicians, and written constitutions, you might, at the hands of the Small Producer, experience a return to a real Golden Age."

To the consistent pattern of Ford's life—writing, gardening, travelling and lecturing to literary aspirants on matters of technique—was added, in his concluding years, by the pressure of world events, an inescapable progression of political thought. No doubt his happiest hours were spent attending to his early vegetables in the garden of his Provençal home, the Villa Paul, Chemin de la Calade, Cap Brun, Toulon. But his diminishing sales and the difficulty of earning a living by literary journalism, so far away from his market, made frequent journeys to New York essential. In a letter to Mr. Oliver Stonor, written on 24th September, 1934, he says he must "pass this winter in New York —wh I fear won't be cheerful". Writing to the same correspondent on the 17th February, 1937, from 31 rue de Seine, Paris VI, he says: "I have been travelling about without a fixed address, till now." In the course of his constant journeys, he came in contact with young writers and painters of whom by far the greater number were either swinging, or had already swung, towards the political Left. In Paris, about a year after the outbreak of the Civil War in Spain, a questionnaire was addressed "to the writers and poets of England, Scotland, Ireland and Wales", by a Committee among the members of which were Miss Nancy Cunard, Louis Aragon, Tristan Tzara, Jean

Richard Bloch, and Ramon Sender. The replies received were
issued in a pamphlet entitled *Authors Take Sides on the Spanish
War*, and include one from Ford which clearly defines his
position. "I am unhesitatingly for the existing Spanish Government," he wrote, "and against Franco's attempt—on every
ground of feeling and reason. In addition, as the merest com-
monsense, the Government of the Spanish, as of any other
nation, should be settled and defined by the inhabitants of
that nation. Mr. Franco seeks to establish a government resting
on the arms of Moors, Germans, Italians. Its success *must* be
contrary to world conscience." If there is no specific condem-
nation of Fascism, as such, in this statement, there can be little
doubt that Ford's political thinking was following the general
trend.

Ford's *Collected Poems*, published in 1936 by the Oxford
University Press of New York, with an Introduction by William
Rose Benét, but not yet published in Great Britain, contains a
group of poems called "Buckshee: Poems for Haitchka in France"
—the last he ever wrote—which convey a pretty clear idea of what
he thought about the world in general. At the time of his death
he was engaged on a novel, of which about a hundred pages were
completed, which was concerned with the shift from the Right
to the Left of the intelligentsia, due to the world events which began
with the Wall Street slump and culminated in Munich. The
"shift" must have been difficult for a man of Ford's age, since
it meant abandoning both the high Toryism of his *English Review*
days and the Liberalism he espoused under Masterman's influence,
but the development was logical, consistent, and, in view of his
Standard of Values, inevitable. It is with no surprise that we
learn that Ford "was bitterly ashamed of being English when
the Munich pact was signed" and that "for the first time in his
life he was seriously considering a change of nationality". Most
decent Englishmen were bitterly ashamed of their Foreign Office
during that disastrous period, while patriotic Frenchmen were
no less perturbed by their own Government. But the situation
was as Ford himself described it in *Great Trade Route*. "We have
to consider," he wrote, "that we are humanity at almost its

lowest ebb, since we are humanity almost without mastery over its fate. I sit in Geneva and the whole world trembles at the thought that tomorrow our civilization may go down in flames —trembles will-lessly and without so much as making a motion to preserve itself." In such a situation the gesture of "changing one's nationality" could mean no more than exchanging one's share of responsibility for the actions of one set of guilty or inept politicians for an equal share of responsibility for the actions of another set. Had Ford lived another six months, lived to see the collapse of his beloved France and the common people of England standing alone in defence both of their island and of the rich and vulnerable United States—and being stripped by the latter of all its dollar investments to buy munitions on the "cash-and-carry" principle—no one can have the slightest doubt where his sympathies would have lain. Just as his faith in France would have been confirmed by the exploits of the Resistance and the martyrdom of patriots like Gabriel Péri, so his belief in the English tradition, in spite of the shock of Munich and the disgrace of Non-Intervention, would have been restored in full by the Battle of Britain. What he would have felt about American "expediency" in the matter of Admiral Darlan is sufficiently obvious to make us thankful, on his account, that a severe illness, which occurred soon after Munich and was followed by his death eight months later, prevented him from taking a step which he would certainly have regretted. We may be glad, therefore, that in spite of his mixed racial strains and international outlook Ford died, as he was born, an Englishman.

We have few glimpses of Ford in his last days. In the winter of 1939, the need to make enough to live on, a task which he found increasingly difficult, had driven him back to New York, where he retained an office or small apartment at 10 Fifth Avenue. Here he must have been exceedingly gratified to receive a letter from an old friend, E. S. P. Haynes, who had defended him in 1915 when he was insulted by a reviewer in the *New Witness*. The letter, which I have been permitted to reproduce, was dated 10th January, 1939, and ran as follows:

10th Jany 1939.

DEAR FORD,

I have been reading your volume *Provence* with great enjoyment. I thought that I knew most of the Bordeaux wines and I should be glad to know whether Chateau Pavie 1906 is white or red. I have never come across it.

I was particularly interested in your remarks on garlic because I am convinced that the consumption of it protects the lungs and may also be a preventive of Cancer. I have not been much in Provence, but perhaps you can tell me whether there is much pneumonia or cancer in the country.

I never know where you are nowadays; but if you are in London, perhaps we might have a talk.

With best wishes,

Yours sincerely,

E. S. P. Haynes

F. M. Ford, Esq.,
c/o George Allen & Unwin, Ltd.,
40 Museum Street, W.C.1.

There was nothing Ford enjoyed more than to be regarded as an authority on French wines. The reply he dictated answers the queries about Chateau Pavie and contains the characteristic comment that Ford is personally convinced that "without a reasonable amount of garlic in your diet, you cannot be completely whole either mentally or physically". He tells Mr. Haynes that he passes his time as a rule almost equally between Paris, the Côte d'Azur and New York. He refers to having spent four or five months in London a couple of years ago and remarks that he didn't find it very exciting as there didn't seem anybody there to talk to and "those one could talk to didn't much understand what one said". He says also that he went to Canterbury Cricket Week and "had the dissatisfaction of seeing Lancashire beat Kent after a too early declaration on the part of Kent". After this rather pathetic evocation of a long-discarded "persona", he adds that "on the whole little old New York remains good enough for me".

S

All the same, in a country so youth-conscious as the United States, where people other than "tycoons" or professional politicians are regarded as more or less finished at fifty, Ford was reduced to some strange shifts to keep his end up. He had a well-deserved reputation in the United States as a gourmet which secured him some useful publicity. An American correspondent informs me that "his picture appeared in countless magazines in this country as the author of a recipe for Welsh rarebit".

Poor Ford! What a pity it is, as Arnold Bennett pointed out, that the world will not willingly let die those of its famous authors who are not yet dead. An Englishman cannot but regret that Ford had no literary friends in London with sufficient influence or generosity to provide him with the financial security which a weekly column could have afforded. A regular £5 a week for a "literary causerie", which he could have written with so much ease and authority, would have enabled him to live comfortably in his villa at Cap Brun and saved him from having to wear himself out by lecturing to small audiences in remote American cities.

In the spring of 1939, Ford, in spite of failing health and a weakening voice, embarked on a lecture tour which took him as far south as North Carolina. The following account of their meeting has been kindly supplied me by Mr. Gerard Tetley, Editor of the *Danville Register*, who, in his youth, had done secretarial work for Ford but had not seen him since. Mr. Tetley writes:

"A newspaper published in Greensboro N.C., about fifty miles from Danville, announced that Ford Madox Ford would discuss the romantic age of literature in a lecture. I took the day off and drove my car to Greensboro N.C. and there met Mr. Hueffer for the first time in many years. He was not particularly glad to see me, but he was not disposed by nature to show much animation. He was very much heavier than he used to be, but he had a good colour and still had the light moustache. He laboured badly for breath and did not look healthy. We had a few drinks (he preferring beer) and I stayed for his morning lecture but was quite at a loss to understand more than a few words because his voice was very bad and as I learned later, this was some aftermath of his first world war experience.

"Mr. Hueffer did not much want to go over past history. All of my eager questions about what had happened to so and so drew little more than monosyllabic replies. He asked a few polite questions about my work and what I had been doing and made it rather clear that he had some letters to write. In any event we shook hands and left. He alluded at the time to the fact that his wife was with him in Greensboro but I never saw her. At the night lecture, which I did not attend, people told me later that his wife was in the audience and Mr. Hueffer had a way of refreshing his memory by calling out to her in the audience and asking her questions which she answered.[1]

"On April 26 1939, Mr. Hueffer wrote me from New York asking me if I could find him a cottage in this part of the world as he had decided not to go back to Europe but would do some writing in this country. He said he wanted the place from June to September 'for as moderate a price as possible, postulating that we do not care how rough the accommodation is so long as the beds are good and the cottage clean'. In another passage he wrote 'both Janice and I smoke and consume rye' (I have the letter).

"Acting on this request, I found a small house in a village called Stuart in the Blue Ridge Mountains about seventy miles from here, very interesting to me, because of the untrammelled English, Scotch and Irish stock to be found there, and where mothers still sing Tudor lullabys to their babies.

"On May 23 1939, came another letter (I have this also) saying there was a complete change of plans and that 'we are imperatively called to Europe and must leave at the end of this month on the *Normandie*'.

"Then, of course, later, came the cable despatches carried in most American newspapers that he was dead at Deauville."

What were the imperative reasons which caused Ford to change his plans and return hurriedly to France are not known to the writer. Ford was a man of keen intuitions, at moments

---

[1] I am informed that Ford's memory was excellent and that he never needed Janice Biala's aid in lecturing. He called out a question to her once as a joke.

he almost seemed to be clairvoyant, and it may therefore b
conjectured that he had a premonition that he had not long t
live and that he wanted to die on the sacred soil of his "*Secon*
Patrie". His knowledge of the international situation must als
have made it obvious to him that the catastrophe of a secon
invasion might, in a few weeks or months, overwhelm Franc
and it may be conjectured that he felt he ought to receive i
impact side by side with his French literary colleagues.

At Honfleur in June 1939, his heart failed—and with it all h
bodily functions. He was removed in a dying condition to
nursing home at 141 Avenue de la République at Deauvill
where he succumbed at five o'clock in the afternoon on 26t
June, Janice Biala being the only person present. He was burie
in the English cemetery in Deauville and only two of his friend
one from Paris and one from London, had received sufficier
warning to enable them to attend his funeral. As the Deauvil
area was heavily bombed during the war it is not yet know
whether his grave can be identified.

Ford died poor, neglected by his compatriots, without th
homage of his confrères and admirers. We are told that h
"made a good death, as they used to say. He bore his dreadf
agony which lasted for weeks, with stoicism and dignity an
was extremely considerate to the last: he even managed to mak
a joke a few minutes before his death".

The obituary notices in the London papers, particularly *T*
Times, saw fit to represent Ford as a "failure" which, measure
by their yard-stick for "success", no doubt he was. Many, if nc
most, of the great names in our literature, music and painting we
similar "failures" from the social-financial standpoint. Ford's onl
British "decorations" were his war medals, his only academi
honour was the degree of Doctor of Literature bestowed on hi
by Olivet College, Michigan. Much of the work done in h
laborious life was done for nothing and without hope or desir
for any material reward. He was constantly surrounded by youn
and unknown writers on whom he spent endless time and troubl
He worked with them on their MSS. and tried to find ther
publishers. He had about two hundred MSS. in his possessio

t the time of his death and his last energies were spent on
hem.

Ford, as this record shows, suffered all his life from a congenital
nability to manage his personal affairs, whether emotional or
financial, with reasonable common sense. He was constantly involved in difficulties, which astuter men would have avoided
with ease, many of which were due to his own good qualities.
He was broad-minded, humane, perceptive, and without petty
ealousy. His long bouts of neurasthenia made him acutely sensitive, but the more he shrank, as a child shrinks from a dentist,
from any sort of "unpleasantness", the more hopelessly he became
enmeshed in it. And he certainly was not lucky in some of his
closest personal associations. But even when his traducers were
doing their worst, his essential quality as a man did not escape
so shrewd an observer as D. H. Lawrence who, in a letter to
Violet Hunt, pointed out that "his eyes, after all, remain like the
Shulamite's dove's eyes". "A dove-grey kindliness" Lawrence
called it. There was none too much of it left in the world, after
Ford's departure, which is no doubt one of the reasons why
some of us, who knew him, cherish his memory.

Appendix 1

Bibliography—Ford Madox Ford (Hueffer) 1873–1939——

The Brown Owl. The Children's Library No. 1. T. Fisher Unwin. 1892. (Reviewed, *Times*, 7th October, 1891.)

The Feather. Uniform with above. T. Fisher Unwin. 1892.

The Shifting of the Fire. T. Fisher Unwin. 1892. Author's name on cover: Ford H. Hueffer; on title-page: H. Ford Hueffer.

The Questions at the Well. (Poems.) Digby & Co. 1893. (Published under the pseudonym "Fenil Haig".)

The Queen Who Flew. (Signed "Ford Hueffer".) Frontispiece by Burne Jones. Bliss, Sands and Foster. 1894.

Ford Madox Brown. A record of his life. Longmans. 1896.

The Cinque Ports. Illustrated by William Hyde. Blackwood. 1900.

Poems for Pictures. John Macqueen. 1900. Note on reverse of title says three poems previously published in pseudonymous volume "in 1892".

Rossetti. Duckworth. 1902.

The Face of the Night. (Poems) John Macqueen. 1904.

The Soul of London. Alston Rivers. 1905.

The Benefactor. Brown, Langham & Co. 1905.

Hans Holbein the Younger. Duckworth. 1905.

The Fifth Queen. Alston Rivers. 1906.

The Heart of the Country. Alston Rivers. 1906.

Christina's Fairy Book. Pinafore Library. Alston Rivers. 1906.

Privy Seal. Alston Rivers. 1907.

From Inland. Alston Rivers. 1907. ("The Contemporary Poets Series.")

An English Girl. Methuen. 1907.

The Spirit of the People. Alston Rivers. 1907.

England and the English. New York. 1907. Omnibus volume containing *The Soul of London*, *The Heart of the Country*, and *The Spirit of the People.*

The Pre-Raphaelite Brotherhood. Duckworth. 1907.

The Fifth Queen Crowned. Nash. 1908.

Mr. Apollo. Methuen. 1908.

The Half Moon. Nash. 1909.

Songs from London. Elkin Mathews. 1910.

A Call. Chatto & Windus. 1910.

The Portrait. Methuen. 1910.

Ancient Lights. Chapman & Hall. 1910. (Published in U.S.A. as *Memories and Impressions*.)

The Simple Life Limited. (By "Daniel Chaucer".) John Lane. 1911.

Ladies Whose Bright Eyes. Constable. 1911.

The Critical Attitude. Duckworth. 1911.

High Germany. (Poems.) Duckworth. 1912.

The Panel. Constable. 1912. (Published in U.S.A. as *Ring for Nancy*.)

The New Humpty-Dumpty. (By "Daniel Chaucer".) Lane. 1912.

The Monstrous Regiment of Women. (Pamphlet.) Women's Freedom League. 1913.

Mr. Fleight. Howard Latimer. 1913. (Never actually published in Great Britain.)

The Young Lovell. Chatto & Windus. 1913.

Collected Poems. Goschen. 1913.

Henry James. Secker. 1913.

The Good Soldier. Lane. 1915.

When Blood is Their Argument. Hodder & Stoughton. 1915.

Between St. Dennis and St. George. Hodder & Stoughton. 1915. There was a translation in French by M. Butts, with an unsigned biographical foreword on Hueffer, published by Payot et Cie. 1916.

Antwerp. Poetry Bookshop. 1915. Decorations by Wyndham Lewis.

On Heaven and other poems. Lane. 1918.

Thus to Revisit. Chapman & Hall. 1921.

A House. A Modern Morality Play. The Chapbook. No. 21. March, 1921. (The play occupies the whole of the magazine.)

The Marsden Case. Duckworth. 1923.

Mister Bosphorus and The Muses. Duckworth. 1923. Decorated by Paul Nash.

Women and Men. Three Mountains Press, Paris. 1923.

Some Do Not. Duckworth. 1924.

Joseph Conrad, A Personal Remembrance. Duckworth. 1924.

No More Parades. Duckworth. 1925.

A Mirror to France. Duckworth. 1926.

A Man Could Stand Up. Duckworth. 1926.

New York is not America. Duckworth. 1927.

New York Essays. W. E. Rudge, New York. 1927.

New Poems. Rudge, U.S.A. 1927. Limited, signed edition of 325 copies.

Last Post. Duckworth. 1928.

A Little Less than Gods. Duckworth. 1928.

The English Novel. Lippincott. U.S.A. 1929. Constable, England 1930.

No Enemy. Macaulay, U.S.A. 1929.

I Saw Thrones. Limited Edition. Gollancz. 1931.

Return to Yesterday. Gollancz. 1931.

When the Wicked Man. U.S.A. 1931. Cape. 1932.

The Rash Act. Cape. 1933.

It Was the Nightingale. Heinemann. 1934.

Henry for Hugh. Lippincott, U.S.A. 1934. (Not published in England.)

Collected Poems. With Introduction by William Rose Benét. Oxford University Press, U.S.A. 1936. (Not published in England.)

Vive Le Roy. Lippincott, U.S.A. 1936.

Portraits from Life. Houghton, U.S.A. 1937. (Published in England by Allen & Unwin in 1938 as *Mightier than the Sword*.)

Great Trade Route. Allen & Unwin. 1937. Oxford University Press, U.S.A., 1937.

Provence. Allen & Unwin. 1938.

The March of Literature from Confucius to Modern Times. Dial Press, U.S.A. 1938. Allen & Unwin, England. 1939.

COLLABORATIONS

With JOSEPH CONRAD:

The Inheritors. Heinemann. 1901.

Romance. Smith, Elder. 1903.

The Nature of a Crime. Duckworth. 1924. (Reprinted from *The English Review*.)

With VIOLET HUNT:

Zeppelin Nights. John Lane. 1915.

TRANSLATIONS

Loti, Pierre. *The Trail of the Barbarians*. Longmans. 1918.

PREFACES AND CONTRIBUTIONS TO BOOKS BY OTHERS

Stories by De Maupassant. Preface by Hueffer. Duckworth. 1903.

Hutchings, W. W. *London Town Past and Present*. Cassell. 1909. Contains "The Future In London", by Hueffer.

Hunt (Mrs. Alfred and Violet). *The Governess*. Chatto & Windus. 1912. Violet Hunt states in Preface to *Thornicroft's Model*, by Mrs. Alfred Hunt, that Hueffer wrote Preface to this book.

Hunt, Violet. *The Desirable Alien*. Chatto & Windus. 1913. Preface and two additional chapters by Hueffer.

Transatlantic Stories. Duckworth. Preface by Hueffer.

Appendix 2

Books by Ford Madox Ford copyrighted in the U.S.A.[1]

England and the English. Illustrated by Henry Hyde. N.Y., McLure, Phillips & Co. 1907.

London Town Past and Present. N.Y., Cassell. 1909.

The "Half Moon". A Romance of the Old World and the New. N.Y., Doubleday, Page & Co. 1909.

Ladies Whose Bright Eyes. A Romance. N.Y., The Baker & Taylor Co. 1911.

Memories and Impressions: A Study in Atmosphere. N.Y., Harper & Brothers. 1911. (Also published under title *Ancient Lights.*)

The Simple Life Limited. By Daniel Chaucer (pseud.). N.Y., Lane. 1911.

The New Humpty-Dumpty. By Daniel Chaucer (pseud.). N.Y., John Lane. 1912.

Ring for Nancy. A Sheer Comedy. Illustrated by F. Vaux Wilson. Indianapolis, Bobbs-Merrill Co. 1913.

The Good Soldier. N.Y., John Lane. 1915.

When Blood is Their Argument: An Analysis of Prussian Culture. N.Y., Hodder & Stoughton. 1915.

Women and Men. Paris, Three Mountains Press. 1923. Limited edition of 300 copies.

Joseph Conrad, A Personal Remembrance. Boston, Little, Brown & Co. 1924.

Some Do Not. N.Y., Seltzer. 1924.

No More Parades. N.Y., A. & C. Boni. 1925.

A Man Could Stand Up. N.Y., A. & C. Boni. 1926.

New Poems. N.Y., W. E. Rudge. 1927. Limited edition of 325 copies.

New York is not America. N.Y., A. & C. Boni. 1927.

New York Essays. N.Y., W. E. Rudge. 1927. Limited to 750 copies.

A Little Less than Gods. N.Y., The Viking Press. 1928.

The Last Post. N.Y., Literary Guild of America. 1928.

No Enemy. A Tale of Reconstruction. N.Y., The Macaulay Co. 1929.

[1] This list was transcribed from the Library of Congress records at the New York Public Library by Mr. Leon Edel of New York. It is not complete, among the omissions being *The March of Literature* first published in New York by Dial Press in 1938.

The English Novel. Philadelphia & London, Lippincott. 1929.
When the Wicked Man. N.Y., H. Liveright, Inc. 1931.
Return to Yesterday. H. Liveright, Inc. 1932.
It Was the Nightingale. Philadelphia & London, Lippincott. 1933.
The Rash Act. A Novel. N.Y., R. Long & R. Smith Inc. 1933.
Henry for Hugh. Philadelphia & London, Lippincott. 1934.
Provence. Philadelphia & London, Lippincott. 1935.
Collected Poems. With Introduction by William Rose Benét. N.Y., Oxford University Press. 1936.
Great Trade Route. N.Y., Oxford University Press. 1937.
Portraits from Life. Boston & N.Y., Houghton Mifflin. 1937. (Also published as *Mightier than the Sword.*)

With JOSEPH CONRAD:

The Inheritors. N.Y., McLure, Phillips. 1901. Doubleday, Page & Co. 1914. Reprinted. 1925.
Romance. (Illustrated by C. R. Macaulay.) N.Y., McLure, Phillips. 1904. N.Y., Doubleday. 1925.
The Nature of a Crime. Doubleday, Page & Co. 1924.
[1]*The Sister* . N.Y., Crosby Gaige. 1928. Limited to 926 copies.

PREFACES

The Left Bank. By Jean Rhys. N.Y., Harper. 1927.
Robinson Crusoe. Limited Editions Club. N.Y. 1930. 1,500 copies.
The Survivors. By René Behaine. Boston, Houghton Mifflin. 1938.

[1] No information about this book has been obtained by the writer.

Appendix 3

Contributions by Ford Madox Ford to periodicals published in the U.S.A.

"For a Married Couple." Poem. *Living Age*. 18th August, 1900.

"Lullaby." Poem. *Living Age*. 29th September, 1900.

"Gypsy and the Cuckoo." Poem. *Living Age*. 6th October, 1900.

"Mother." Song-drama. *Fortnightly*. April, 1901.

"To a Tudor Tune." *Living Age*. 4th January, 1902.

"At the End of a Phase." Poem. *Living Age*. 12th April, 1902.

"Old Conflict." *Living Age*. 6th February, 1904.

"Individualist." *Living Age*. 20th June, 1905.

"Every Man." Poem. *Living Age*. 1st July, 1905.

"Philosophy of a Lover and a Gentleman." *Living Age*. 9th September, 1905.

"Old Lament." Poem. *Living Age*. 9th June, 1906.

"After All." Poem. *McLures*. February, 1907.

"Midwinter Night." Poem. *Living Age*. 9th March, 1907.

"Fascination of London." *Putnams*. May, 1909.

"Old Circle." *Harpers*. February, 1910.

"Pre-Raphaelite Reminiscences." *Harper*. April, 1910.

"Modern Poetry." *Living Age*. 15th June, 1910.

"Group of Pre-Raphaelite Poets." *Harpers*. October, 1910.

"William Holman Hunt." *Fortnightly*. October. 1910.

"Christina Rossetti." *Fortnightly*. March, 1911.

"Masters and Music." *Harpers*. March, 1911.

"Pace That Kills." *Atlantic Magazine*. May, 1911.

"In High Germany." Poems. *Fortnightly*. December, 1911.

"De Morgan's When Ghost Meets Ghost." *Living Age*. March, 1914.

"Poem." *Living Age*. 4th November, 1916.

"What the Orderly Dog Saw." *Poetry*. March, 1917.

"Sanctuary." *Poetry*. April, 1918.

"Iron Music." Poem. *Literary Digest*. 5th October, 1918.

"Old Houses of Flanders." Poem. *Literary Digest*. 5th October, 1918.

"Ypres Salient." Poem. *Literary Digest*. 5th October, 1918.

"Claire de Lune." Poem. *American Opinion*. November, 1918.

"After the Rain." Poem. *Living Age*. 18th October, 1919.

"Thus to Revisit." *Dial*. July–September, 1920–January, 1921.

"Poem." *Poetry*. March, 1921.

"Haughty and Proud Generation." *Yale Review*. July, 1922.

"Rhymes for a Child." *Living Age*. 4th November, 1922.

"Seven Shepherds." Poem. *Poetry*. June, 1923.

"Mister Bosphorus and the Muses." *Poet Lore*. December, 1923.

"Stevie." *Literary Review*. 12th July, 1924.

"From a Paris Quay." *Literary Review*. 13th December, 1924.

"Young America Abroad." *Saturday Review of Literature*. 20th September, 1924.

"Poeta Nascitur." *Poetry*. March, 1927.

"Traveller's Tales." *Harpers*. April, 1927.

"Lordly Dish." *Harpers*. June, 1927.

"Pax!" *Harpers*. September, 1927.

"Tiger, Tiger." *Bookman*. January, 1928.

"Romantic Detective." Story. *Yale Review*. April, 1928.

"O Hygeia." *Harpers*. May, 1928.

"On Conrad's Vocabulary." *Bookman*. June, 1928.

"Miracle." A Story. *Yale Review*. December, 1928.

"English Novel." *Bookman*. December, 1928 to March, 1929.

"Working With Conrad." *Yale Review*. June, 1929.

"René Behaine." *Saturday Review of Literature*. 12th October, 1929.

"Stage in American Literature." *Bookman*. December, 1931.

"*Chez Nos Amis*." Poem. *Literary Digest*. 6th February, 1932.

"Poems." *Poetry*. February–March, 1932.

"I Revisit the Riviera." *Harpers*. December, 1932.

"For Poorer Travellers." *Harpers*. April, 1933.

"Contrasts." *Atlantic Monthly*. May, 1933.

"Hands off the Arts." *American Mercury*. April, 1935.

"Small Producer." *American Mercury*. August, 1935.

"Master." *American Mercury*. November, 1935.

"W. H. Hudson." *American Mercury*. March, 1936.

"Galsworthy." *American Mercury*. April, 1936.

"H. G. Wells." *American Mercury*. May, 1936.

"D. H. Lawrence." *American Mercury*. June, 1936.

"Conrad and the Sea." *American Mercury*. June, 1936.

"Hardy." *American Mercury*. November, 1936.

"Stephen Crane." *American Mercury*. January, 1937.

"Dreiser." *American Mercury*. April, 1937.

"Flame in Stone." *Poetry*. June, 1937.

"Sad State of Publishing." *Forum*. Aug–Sept., 1937.

"Food." *Forum*. April, 1938.

"Memories of Oscar Wilde." *Saturday Review of Literature*. 27th May, 1939.

"Travel Notes." *Saturday Review of Literature*. 10th June, 1939.

Index